The Fiction of Robert Antoni

The Fiction of Robert Antoni

Writing in the Estuary

Richard F. Patteson

University of the West Indies Press
Jamaica • Barbados • Trinidad and Tobago

University of the West Indies Press
7A Gibraltar Hall Road Mona
Kingston 7 Jamaica
www.uwipress.com

CATALOGUING-IN-PUBLICATION DATA

Patteson, Richard F. (Richard Francis), 1947–
The fiction of Robert Antoni: writing in the estuary / Richard F. Patteson

p. cm.
Includes bibliographical references.

ISBN: 978-976-640-229-7

1. Antoni, Robert – Criticism and interpretation. I. Title.

PR9272.9.A58 Z78 2010 813.19

Cover illustration: Rafael Martinez, *Bodeguera* (oil on canvas, 2000).
Photographed by Troy DeRego.

Set in Centaur MT 13/16 x 24

Cover and book design by Robert Harris.

Printed in the United States of America.

. . . water is the beginning of all things

– Antonio Benítez-Rojo, *The Repeating Island*

CONTENTS

ACKNOWLEDGEMENTS

I am indebted to Robert Antoni for many things, not least for providing me with indispensable information about himself, his family and his ongoing work that would have been otherwise inaccessible. Sincere thanks also to Lynne Rienner, for allowing me to use material from my previous book (*Caribbean Passages: A Critical Perspective on New Fiction from the West Indies*) as the basis for my discussion of *Divina Trace* and the early stories.

Students in my Caribbean literature seminar over the years (Amy Myrick, Brad Campbell, Marian Montgomery, to name a few) have influenced my thinking in innumerable ways. I should cite in particular Dean Karpowicz and Eric Smith, who went on to become Antoni scholars in their own right. The input and support of many colleagues, particularly Brad Vice (*il miglior fabbro*), have also been invaluable.

I began work on this book in late 2000, shortly after purchasing Raphael Martínez's Bodeguera from Bettye Marshall at her gallery in Santo Domingo. From the moment I saw it I associated that face with all the enduring, culture-laden women in Antoni's fiction. The painting's reincarnation as book cover is due to the photographic expertise of Troy DeRego and the talent of the design department at the University of the West Indies Press.

I would certainly not want to forget to mention, with much gratitude, Dr Matthew Little, for facilitating a sabbatical near the beginning of this project, and Dr Rich Raymond, for providing me with extra time off and a research assistant toward the end of it. And speaking of that assistant, I should close with a special note of recognition to Nick White, who went through the entire manuscript twice, helping me get it into the correct format for the Press. His fingerprints are on every page.

1

FRONTIERS OF THE WORD

. . . the Caribbean calls for a Cervantes who has read Joyce
– Patrick Chamoiseau, *Texaco*[1]

Occasionally a brief passage, perhaps one composed even before a writer has formed a distinct conception of himself, can reveal much about his subsequent development as an artist. The opening lines of Robert Antoni's early story "Two-head Fred and Tree-foot Frieda" are a case in point:

> I loved Zoe because she helped raise me, because she let me pinch her breasts when my mother wasn't around, and because she told me she ate Barbados rat for whooping cough. I loved Jook Jook because he helped raise me, because he let me sip from his rum bottle when my father wasn't around, and because he told me he ate Whatlin's Island iguana for grimps.[2]

The symmetry of this sequence of observations forecasts the tendency towards binary structures in Antoni's later, much more complex verbal compositions. But we have here as well, in the counterpointed pairs of the verb phrases *raised me/let me/old me,* a nuanced suggestion of future themes: roots, freedom and the telling of tales. In *Divina Trace* these elements have assumed the shape of a singular creative vision: Antoni's exploration of his Caribbean origins, his forging beyond experiential, cultural and aesthetic frontiers, and the discovery of narrative's transformational powers. The colonial and post-colonial worlds of Trinidad, where Antoni's parents were born, and the Bahamas, where he grew up, are quietly evoked in the beginning of "Two-head Fred" by the tacit reference to laws laid down by the mother and father. *Thou shalt not pinch breasts. Thou shalt not drink rum.* Gently opposing this system of rules and received authority is the liberating influence of Zoe and Jook Jook. The narrator, Addy, loves them because they allow him to grow, removing in their small way some of the restrictions of his childhood, but also because they open up his imagination to a wider world – and thereby extend the boundaries of his identity – through their storytelling.

Four centuries ago Cervantes tapped into a current of fascination with reality and dream that has run through the novel ever since, like the Guadiana River in *Don Quixote,* flowing sometimes above the surface and sometimes just below. The fiction of Robert Antoni – even such an apprentice piece as "Two-head Fred" – exhibits in a myriad of ways the capacity of imagination to alter fact and charts the highly problematic frontier between the known and the narrated. Addy is a boy given to believing in the reality of the imagined worlds conjured up by Zoe and Jook Jook, while his brother Christopher, his Sancho Panza, constantly pulls him in the direction of phenomenal reality, conventional morality and parental rules. Addy talks about Jook Jook's made-up characters Two-head Fred and Tree-foot Frieda as if they were actual people, while Christopher insists that they do not exist. The brothers are spending part of their vacation at the family's summer place on Deep Water Cay in the Bahamas. Zoe has cared for them since they were babies, and Jook Jook, who does "odd jobs" for their father, takes them "fishing, conching, and misbehaving". Jook Jook's name derives from his reputation as "the greatest conch and woman jooker in all the world",[3] and this summer he has set his sights on Zoe.

As the season progresses, a romance develops between Jook Jook and Zoe. At the same time Addy copes with the boredom of island life by imagining ways to make his daily routines more interesting. "I had lots of time on my hands," he recalls; "ideas were already taking shape in my head."[4] Chief among those ideas is a scheme to follow Jook Jook and Zoe around until he sees them "in action".[5] Near the end of his stay on Deep Water Cay he manages to hide himself in a box that Jook Jook uses for a closet. When the lovers come in, Addy knocks over a bottle of rum stowed on the floor but manages to salvage enough of it for several large swallows to calm himself down. What follows is a comic collision of imagination and reality:

> The closet began to spin. I closed my eyes. Two-head Fred snapped at me, *Why you do dis, boy? Why you do dis to me?* I screamed. Zoe screamed. "Tief in de house! Tief!" I tried to shove out of my closet. It flopped over, trapping me inside, rum spilling, Zoe screaming. Tree-foot Frieda kicked me. *How you could do me dis mischief, chil'? How you could neglec' me so?* Commotion filled the house: the sounds of people rushing, crying, yelling.[6]

"Two-head Fred" might well have been titled "A Portrait of the Artist as an Eleven-Year-Old". Its climactic scene enacts the implications of its opening sentences, with Addy's adulthood brought closer by his attraction to rum and sex and his already creative consciousness enriched and expanded (though somewhat confusingly) by "ideas" originating in Zoe's and Jook Jook's stories.

Enrichment and expansion – recuperating origins and breaking through boundaries – can both be seen as fundamental constituents in Édouard Glissant's construction of the Caribbean as "the estuary of the Americas". Throughout the region, Glissant points out, "each island embodies openness. The dialectic between inside and outside is reflected in the relationship of land and sea. . . . A Caribbean imagination liberates us from being smothered."[7] An estuary is the part of a river that is also, in a sense, part of the sea: an area where it flows into the sea and is in turn influenced by oceanic tides, or, to put it another way, an arm of the sea that extends inland to meet and become the mouth of a river. An estuary is by definition a borderland between two different states of being. But where is the border between river and sea? It can never be seen as an exact, unchanging point or line on a map; it is indeterminate, shifting, subject to interpretation and change – an always open frontier.

The Caribbean imagination is profoundly estuarial; its most recognizable characteristic is a preoccupation with its multiple origins combined with an imperative to reach out and mutate, like an estuary merging into the sea, each in a constant state of exchange and translation. The Caribbean writer may well be the harbinger of a new kind of world where, as Roland Littlewood suggests, "syncretism and heteroglossia contest . . . hybrid and parodic, creolised and polyphonic, self-creating, endlessly recursive".[8] Obviously today's "transnational literature"[9] is hardly limited to the West Indies,[10] or even to the "New World". Neither the cultural mixing (often associated with or subsumed by such terms as creolization, *métissage* and *mestizaje*)[11] nor the flowing outwards is unique to the Caribbean, but these elements – along with the region's lengthy oral tradition and widespread acceptance of language as a means of fashioning a culture recuperated, through narrative, from the ruptures of history – are uniquely vital to its historical matrix, its sensibility and its poetics.

Robert Antoni is an estuarial writer if ever there were one, and he is quintessentially Caribbean in terms of both his background and the trajectory of his adult life. Raised in Freeport, Bahamas, where his father practised medicine, he spent many summers and other holidays in Trinidad, where both branches of his family have lived for generations. Today he effectively holds three passports: Trinidadian, American (by virtue of his birth in a Detroit hospital while his father was completing his medical training) and Bahamian.[12] He attended Duke University, Johns Hopkins and finally the University of Iowa. With a Trinidadian background, a Bahamian upbringing, an American education and several years of residency in Spain, Antoni is, like many other writers with roots in the Caribbean, a member of the West Indian expatriate community. The three citizenships are a source of satisfaction to him: he revels in the ambiguous hybridity of his legal status. It is certainly no accident that in *Carnival*, his most nearly autobiographical fiction, all kinds of borders are blurred: racial, sexual and political. But even though Antoni has arguably slipped the bonds of narrow nationalism to a greater extent than most writers from the region, that same liberational impulse is deeply embedded in the Caribbean psyche. Antonio Benítez-Rojo has observed that "Antilleans . . . tend to roam the entire world in search of the centers of their Caribbeanness, constituting one of our century's most notable migratory flows. The Antilleans' insularity does not impel them toward isolation, but on the contrary, toward travel, toward exploration, toward the search for fluvial and marine routes."[13] Fluvial and marine, the river and the sea – the diaspora itself is a manifestation of the estuarial imagination, which is, to take Glissant just a bit out of context, "both rooted and open . . . both settled and migratory".[14] From the expatriation of Claude McKay and Jean Rhys before the Second World War to the emigration of V.S. Naipaul, George Lamming, Sam Selvon and Derek Walcott after the war to the present day's ongoing movement of Caribbean writers to various other countries,[15] the river continues to surge into the sea, enriching and altering it. If Antoni's work can be properly understood only in terms of the Caribbean's disparate and sometimes fragmented cultural origins, it can also be fully appreciated only as part of the diversity of the Caribbean diaspora. In his first novel, *Divina Trace,* his second, *Blessed Is the Fruit,* and his more recent and somewhat more accessible books, *My Grandmother's Erotic Folktales* and *Carnival,* Robert Antoni has both grappled with the complex composite nature of Caribbean identity and origins and charted the movement of a dynamic, evolving and outwardly flowing culture.

☾

The narrative process is the ground of being in Antoni's world. J. Michael Dash characterizes Glissant's *Caribbean Discourse* as "an unflaggingly ambitious attempt to read the Caribbean and the New World experience, not as a response to fixed, univocal meanings imposed by the past, but as an infinitely varied, dauntingly inexhaustible text".[16] This could just as easily be a description of *Divina Trace,* undoubtedly Antoni's most complex work, with its seven voices channelled through the memory of nonagenarian *über*-narrator Johnny Domingo and their enunciation of the myths and histories of European, African, East Indian and Amerindian components of a composite Caribbean identity. *Blessed Is the Fruit* has only two primary narrators (the predominantly white woman Lil, last member of a ruined plantation family, and her black employee Vel), but their discourses intricately reflect, answer and complement each other on virtually every page. Clearly less formally difficult is *My Grandmother's Erotic Folktales.* This book is a near-novel composed of five tales in which expanses of continuous diegesis (the plots of the individual tales) are interrupted by "downward" shifts into embedded stories and "upward" ones to the framing narrative of Granny Myna's own life and personality.[17] And finally there is *Carnival,* Antoni's first fictional foray into contemporary life and his only extended work of fiction with a single narrator unambiguously telling his own story.

Much of Robert Antoni's fiction, like that of Gabriel García Márquez, has its genesis in stories told to him by older people during his early years. Antoni recalls several figures who planted in his fallow imagination tales of the old days in the southern Caribbean. They included, for instance, Velma Clarine Bootman, a maid who raised him from infancy and who was the prototype of Vel in *Blessed Is the Fruit*; a great-uncle who provided him with invaluable information about colonial Trinidad and ultimately became one source for Papee Vince in *Divina Trace* (the other being his maternal grandfather); and most of all, as in the case of García Márquez,[18] a grandmother: "Things that I know now, that I can talk about to students as fictional techniques and narrative strategy, Granny Myna did naturally. She knew all the tricks, all the stunts. How to make absurd things believable by focusing on detail – you know, everything."[19] This grandmother was incalculably influential, providing Antoni not only with a treasure trove of material for his fiction but also with a commanding persona, one that would eventually grow into Barto's long-suffering wife in *Divina Trace* and the protagonist/narrator of *My Grandmother's Erotic Folktales*.[20] With respect to Antoni's literary vocation, there are few facets of his biography more consequential than his growing up among such expert practitioners of West Indian yarn-spinning. The telling of a tale marks the most ancient trace of migration, the pouring forth of an idea, encountering the Other; it is an estuarial transaction that has an expansive effect on the imagination of both teller and listener. In the hands of an artist like Robert Antoni, narrative constitutes a meta-current comprising both the process of *métissage* and the impulse towards diaspora: the flowing into the Caribbean of numerous cultural streams and the endless dispersal of that new and continuously developing culture beyond its sources.

The body of Antoni's work may seem small when measured solely by the number of books, but each of them is so substantial that the fictional territory he has staked out is already quite extensive. If there is any common denominator in terms of technique among these four very different (and each formally unique) works, it is a plainly displayed need for all of his various narrators to get their stories told. And they are always told to an implied listener, as if the narratives were extended prose versions of dramatic monologues. Most obviously in *Divina Trace* (1991), but throughout his other work as well, the object of cognition – what might be called reality – is continuously displaced, or replaced, by its story.

Antoni's reality tends to hover in a mysterious limbo between precognitive conjecture and post-cognitive memory. Johnny Domingo, the primary narrator of *Divina Trace,* rakes through his recollections and dreams on the night of his ninetieth birthday, listening once again to the accounts related to him many years before by Granny Myna and other older members of his strange family. In *Blessed Is the Fruit* (1997), two women lie in bed telling their life stories to the unborn baby Bolom. In the middle of the novel their narratives are recapitulated in the form of dreams that intertwine with one another in the developing consciousness of Vel's fetus. *My Grandmother's Erotic Folktales* (2000) brings back a version of Granny Myna, now telling her grandson Johnny tales of her comic escapades on the island of Corpus Christi[21] during the Second World War, as well as two traditional (though largely invented) Caribbean folk tales. None of Antoni's narrators, with the possible exception of William in *Carnival* (2005), is more patently aware of the storyteller's estuarial role than the Granny Myna of this book. She knows that her stories, which embody her identity and her culture, go out to encounter the imagination of not only her grandson within the text but also all her listeners in the world outside it.[22] And *Carnival*'s narrator/protagonist, William Fletcher, is an aspiring novelist who, as a member of the West Indian diaspora, recognizes that in telling his own story he is also addressing a wider audience among which he, like so many others from the Caribbean, has chosen to live. Though neither he nor Granny Myna would put it this way, their narratives correspond to Benítez-Rojo's explanation of text as "born when it is read by the Other", at which point "text and reader connect with each other like a machine of reciprocal seductions".[23]

One of the most beguiling seductions embedded in the mechanism of Antoni's storytelling is the incorporation of the reader – and the reader's reality outside the text – into a thoroughly Caribbean fictive space. This is accomplished in ways both large and small. In *My Grandmother's Erotic Folktales* Granny Myna not only throws the net of her narrative over such neocolonial icons as General Eisenhower and the Kentucky colonel of fried chicken fame, she also yanks Ernest Hemingway (along with his style of reportage)[24] back to "the old, old-time time"[25] and weaves him into the fabric of West Indian folklore.[26] On a grander scale, Antoni appropriates the framework of an entire novel by Hemingway, *The Sun Also Rises,* to tell a wholly Caribbean story in *Carnival.* In *Divina Trace* Pope Pius XI is reduced to a somewhat ridiculous figure in the accounts given to Johnny Domingo by family members who go to Rome to persuade the Pope to canonize Magdalena, the frogchild's mother, a revered figure back on the island of Corpus Christi.[27] The satirical treatment of the Holy Father and of the Church in general is consonant with the subordination of European power structures to Caribbean storytelling throughout *Divina Trace.* That clever form of "seduction" can be seen even in the book's most startling effect: the mirror page in the middle of it. The mirror makes the reader a participant in the novel's construction,[28] but readers attempting to "master" the text find themselves literally assimilated into it. *Divina Trace* makes West Indians out of all its readers.

That counter-colonizing impulse in Antoni's work is only part of a broader engagement (discernible as early as "Two-head Fred") between a mythic consciousness and a view of everyday life accessible mainly by reason. Benítez-Rojo defines Caribbean literature in general "along Lacanian lines, as a paradoxical literature oscillating between the languages and episteme of Europe (the Name-of-the-Father) and nature and the folk tradition (the Image of the Mother)".[29] Neither of these "sources of legitimation",[30] in Benítez-Rojo's view, is completely attainable. Within Antoni's own vision of the Caribbean "imaginary", myth in its broadest application is an alternative to the linear, rationalist epistemology of the West, most fully embodied in literary realism and in the "rigid, hierarchical discourse" of history, which, as J. Michael Dash points out, "attempts to systematise the world through ethnocultural hierarchy and chronological progression".[31]

The subversion of rationalist, Western "reality" by myth manifests itself most simply in "Two-head Fred and Tree-foot Frieda" and most complexly in *Divina Trace,* where the ceaseless intertwining of myth (European, African, East Indian and Amerindian), history, memory and dream fashions a virtual model of human consciousness that breaks through the frontiers of empirical modes of thought. The very form of *Blessed Is the Fruit,* encoding the voluntary merger of the sensibilities of two damaged women, one black and one white, gives birth to its own myth of a creolizing Caribbean future – a myth that, for better or worse, will necessarily shape the lives of the characters whose stories and dreams engender it. The dialectic can be seen operating in the foreground of *Erotic Folktales,* where Granny Myna exists both in the world of phenomenal reality and in that of myth. As a "real" person she tells her tales to her grandson, transmitting to him the received legends of the Caribbean past; by including three accounts of her own life, she becomes, if not a mythic being, at least a larger than life self-created fictional character. Moreover, the tales she tells often function as reimaginings of the linear "history" imposed on the Caribbean by hegemonic colonial powers.

At first glance *Carnival* might seem to lie altogether in that rational hegemonic realm (Benítez-Rojo's "episteme of Europe"), but appearances in Antoni can be deceptive. The collision between myth and everyday life is almost brutally explicit in this novel. When several sophisticated expatriates return to the Caribbean for Carnival, they join a band (Peter Minshall's) whose mas that year is titled "River". "Mr Minshall's theatrical myth-making," as William Fletcher puts it, "retold the cosmogony of the Earth People."[32] Despised and shunned by the other islanders, these simple folk, who live in a remote redoubt called Hell Valley, practise their own non-Western religion, which eschews the unnatural practices and rationalist culture of the modern Western world. After the period of fête ends, the main characters go up into the mountains; among the Earth People they find themselves in the very world that the carnival band had turned into an artistic construct.

Divina Trace, Antoni's own most prodigious artistic construct to date, began modestly as part of his work for a PhD degree at the University of Iowa. When Reynolds Price, who had earlier been one of his teachers at Duke, read "Granny Myna Tells of the Child", he encouraged Antoni to write a novel, and that piece ultimately became the first chapter. But of course the true genesis of Antoni's fictional world, including that of *Divina Trace,* lies much deeper – in generations of family experience in the Caribbean and particularly, as I have already noted, in stories about that experience told to Antoni when he was young. Many of the most memorable elements of *Divina Trace* come from that body of lore. There were tales of his maternal Grandfather Tucker, an entrepreneur and adventurer: his exploits in South America among head-hunters and giant snakes were the stuff of legend in the Antoni family. Granny Myna told young Bobby stories about her late husband, Bartolome (called Barto in life as well as in the novel), who died when Antoni's father was quite young; he heard about his grandfather's philandering as well.[33] The list of characters and situations that can be traced back to this web of family narratives is long. But Trinidad as a whole – transfigured into Corpus Christi – should not be underestimated as a major source for Antoni. This island, with its exotic history and legends, could almost be regarded as a voice in itself, telling the future novelist its stories of El Dorado, plantation days and especially the Black Madonna of Siparia. Over the years devotion to this little statue, known in Trinidad as La Divina Pastora,[34] spread to Hindus and other non-Catholic groups. The syncretic nature of the cult – its importance to Trinidad's disparate ethnicities – made it an ideal focal point for Antoni's exploration of the relationship between consciousness and community in *Divina Trace.*

Reflecting on that very link, Eva Hoffman observes that "a culture does not exist independently of us but within us. It is inscribed in the psyche, and it gives form and focus to our mental and emotional lives. We could hardly acquire a human identity outside it. . . . In a way, we are nothing more – or less – than an encoded memory of our heritage."[35] Caribbean writers seem particularly attuned to this phenomenon. There are many novels from the West Indies in which the community, more than any single character, is the protagonist. One thinks immediately of Lovelace's *The Dragon Can't Dance,* Lamming's *In the Castle of My Skin* or Mais's *Brother Man,* which Edward Brathwaite describes as "pointing not to the development of the Faustian novel, where individual characteristics triumph and are stressed; but towards the alternative tradition of inter-related perceptions".[36] Frequently too there are narrators or characters whose point of view is clearly that of the community, such as in Olive Senior's "Real Old Time T'ing".

But few Caribbean writers have ventured as far into the forbidding territory of collective identity that Antoni attempts to survey in *Divina Trace.* In one section of the novel, Johnny Domingo is sitting in a church pew behind his great-aunt, Mother Superior Maurina, on the night before his departure for school in America. She hands him "a folded piece of paper" that a few minutes later becomes, as he listens to her story, "the black surface of my collective unconscious", which is "already crowded with words".[37] In a later recollection of the scene, the text is partially spelled out in almost the precise words that Johnny uses to begin the novel: "The boulderstone was big and obzockee. I was having a hard time toting him."[38] And as if to underscore the extent to which *Divina Trace* is a transcription of Johnny's collective unconscious, similar words (this time the exact opening of the novel) come to Johnny again in a dream on the morning of his ninetieth birthday.

As the novel originating on that piece of paper unfolds, the seven voices of Johnny Domingo's family members – recollected, dreamed, perhaps partly imagined – gradually increase in intensity (and in difficulty for the reader), culminating in a declamatory poem. This part of the novel – a Caribbean vernacular version of the *Ramayana* shaped to fit the history of the Domingo family, the story of the frogchild Manuelito and the account of his mother's virtual canonization – is arranged around a brief passage of nearly impenetrable prose corresponding to the most basic pre-linguistic part of Johnny's selfhood. All of the voices, including this one and the second half of Magdalena's poem, recur in reverse order on the other side of the mirror page lying at the novel's dead centre: a place in Johnny's, and the reader's, being where words fail.

The idea, Antoni has explained, is to move "into the unconscious" in order "to get back to something like the 'source' of Johnny's Caribbeanness (identity)".[39] There is a tension here between the individuality that Johnny claims and the cultural and family history that seems at times to possess him. The question of balance between collective consciousness and the degree of individuation needed to articulate it recurs in *Carnival*, with its novelist narrator who somehow needs both to separate from his home island and to return to it. In *Divina Trace* Johnny repeatedly tries to step away from the swamp of his inner being and see it as an individual, from the outside. These brief moments always give way to sinking back again into memories, stories, nightmares that blend into one another in an endless process of revision. The result is a rather difficult (though richly rewarding) reading experience. Antoni himself has admitted, "I put everything I had into it. It has faults because it's reaching too far."[40] In fact, as I will argue in the following chapter, it reaches almost farther than fiction – or even articulate thought – can go.

In *Blessed Is the Fruit* Antoni brings to life a paradigm for a composite and changing Caribbean selfhood by weaving together the memories of his two protagonists. Once again he draws on familiar matrices for both voice and setting. The Corpus Christi of *Blessed* is less a mythic place of the distant past than a historical one, set rather precisely in 1958 (although Vel's and Lil's accounts of their lives go back more than two decades earlier). As in the case of *Divina Trace*, the arrangement of the narrative's constituent parts is starkly visible. Every aspect of the book's structure, as I will demonstrate in chapter 3, is calculated to enact the theme of *métissage* or creolization: the coming together of the two women's "encoded memories" to form the beginning of a confluential identity, which manifests itself in the unborn child's double dream at the centre of the novel.[41] The clear plastic window page in the exact middle serves as both a barrier and, like other windows in the text, an entranceway from one life to the other. Both this scheme and the book's other obvious superstructure – its division into the three chaplets, fifteen decades and 150 beads of the circular rosary – create a textual space in which partitions can be transformed into convergences and in which human selfhood can break out of the boundaries dictated by history. In *Blessed Is the Fruit* this essentially generative (one is tempted to say *gestational*) process takes place within the immense tropical vacancy left by the disintegration of a plantation system that once filled much of the social space of the West Indies. The dynamics of the narrative, the comingling of two streams of cultural discourse, function, like Benítez-Rojo's somewhat romantic characterization of creolization in general, as "a mutual exchange . . . rather than the acculturation of subjugated peoples to the coloniser's culture".[42] It is of the utmost importance in *Blessed Is the Fruit* that neither woman's identity is simply subordinated to (or colonized by) the other's. The novel moves toward an idealized moment of complete, almost transcendental reciprocity.

An early version of the initial story in Antoni's third book, "My Grandmother's Tale of the Buried Treasure and How She Defeated the King of Chacachacari and the Entire American Army with Her Venus-Flytraps", appeared in *Conjunctions* in 1992, a year after the publication of *Divina Trace* in Britain. However, the tale "had been hanging around a long time"[43] and so is certainly one of the earliest manifestations of Corpus Christi in the landscape of the Caribbean word. Eventually Antoni returned to this story, adding four more until Granny Myna, the first and last voice we hear in *Divina Trace*, had a book all her own. The resulting collage of tales, embedded tales and digressions is a testament to the power of storytelling to open up the frontiers of imagination, but the tales she tells (like some of Zoe and Jook Jook's behaviour in "Two-head Fred") could easily be construed by unimaginative guardians of propriety – such as parents – to be a bad influence. Granny's coarse language (and indeed, that of several other Antoni narrators) recalls the often scatological speech of the Earth People, who used obscenities as "demotic and carnivalesque subversions of social power".[44] Granny's linguistic rebelliousness is essential to her more serious purpose as the narrator of a new Caribbean reality: to rewrite history, break rules and unravel patriarchal patterns of thought left over from colonialism.[45]

My Grandmother's Erotic Folktales, though tied together with many subtle threads (not the least of which is the commanding voice of the narrator herself), must be seen as a dramatic departure from the massive symphonic novels that preceded them. Yet the difference lies in a shift of emphasis as much as in a reduction in scale. Antoni is quick to insist that America plays "a large role in *Divina Trace*",[46] but there is so much else going on in that mammoth book that the reader might be forgiven for not paying too much attention to it. This is decidedly not true of *Erotic Folktales*. From Granny's amusing reworking of the island's colonial history in "The Tale of How Iguana Got Her Wrinkles" to the chronicles of her own epic confrontations with outsiders such as the King of Chacachacari and the Kentucky Colonel, the book is filled with comic encounters between the Caribbean (as evoked through Granny's persona) and the outside world. Not the least important of them, particularly in the retrospective light of Antoni's subsequent novel, is an appearance by Ernest Hemingway in "The Tale of How Crab-o Lost His Head". According to Granny Myna, this "Ernesto", a butterfly collector and "famous American author" with a penis like a "little pencil-eraser", eventually goes home and writes down the "real-life newspaper details"[47] of the story – a pedestrian account lacking the power and poetry of Granny's voice.

One might think from the rough treatment accorded to Hemingway in *Erotic Folktales* that Antoni does not think highly of him. Nothing could be further from the truth, as *Carnival* clearly proves. "Ernesto" is slipped into *Erotic Folktales* as a caricature of a journalistic realist whose reportage is at variance with the lush tonalities and frequent mythologizing of Caribbean storytelling. But the actual Hemingway is evoked with great respect (and a good deal of playfulness) in *Carnival*, as a writer who bequeathed the language of everyday speech to his successors and who gave to Robert Antoni in particular a model for exploring human value and identity in the wake of global cultural trauma. On his website Antoni says that *Carnival* is "in some ways a recasting, in other ways a parody" of *The Sun Also Rises*, and this seems to strike just about the right note. Antoni's debt to Faulkner in *Divina Trace* is well documented. He has gone so far as to claim that "[t]he whole structure of *Divina Trace* comes from *Absalom, Absalom*. . . . The idea of situating various narrators at different distances from the story, with different perspectives on it . . . all that comes from Faulkner."[48] In *Carnival* the use of *The Sun Also Rises* as a frame of reference is much more readily apparent. If the result is that Antoni becomes known as both the Faulkner and the Hemingway of the

Caribbean, these two great writers must already be writhing in their graves.[49]

Carnival moves from New York City to an unnamed Caribbean island that is closer to present-day Trinidad than the Corpus Christi of Antoni's other books.[50] Most of the story takes place there (with a brief coda returning William and his cousin Rachel to New York at the end), and this long section is divided between the characters' experiences during Carnival itself and their excursion into the mountains to meet the Earth People, whose belief system was the subject of the mas they played. While *Carnival* is undeniably the most accessible of Antoni's novels, the subtleties of a narrative related in a "realistic" Hemingway fashion – incorporating within its realism both the fictionalization of a myth through mas and the myth itself as lived by the Earth People – should not be underestimated.

To complicate matters further, the novel's overarching plot (with its phantom framework borrowed from *The Sun Also Rises*) is an exhaustive meditation on the diasporal experience: expatriation, the longing for a return to some "hypothetical center or origin"[51] and the lingering, painful effects of wounds inflicted by history. The three main characters, despite their relative education and affluence, all suffer from afflictions of the soul that no amount of revelry during the brief period of Carnival can heal. Their final journey, to an island subculture that is attempting to dial itself back to a pre-colonial, pre-modern condition, is motivated at least in part by their need to recuperate something lost – to be somehow restored. For this critical movement in the novel, Antoni has drawn extensively on his own life as an expatriate writer who has struggled to stay connected with his West Indian roots. Although he "only really started to visit Trinidad" when he was "sixteen or seventeen",[52] he has been back there frequently, often for extended periods. And, like William, he once made a practice of returning for Carnival and twice trekked up into the mountains to visit Hell Valley after the celebrations had played themselves out.

Carnival is more firmly planted in a recognizably contemporary world than any of Antoni's other books, but it was his fascination with the strange mythology of the Earth People that finally, after considerable difficulty, brought this novel into being.[53]

Antoni has commented that "[t]here's no heritage of Caribbean literature",[54] and he is certainly right, if *heritage* implies a tradition extending over a number of generations. The region's indigenous peoples, unlike their Mayan, Zapotec, Mixtec and Aztec neighbours on the mainland of Middle America, had no system of writing. Of course, beginning with Christopher Columbus, many outsiders (including European colonists) have written about the West Indies; some of the more recent of these, such as Peter Matthiessen and Madison Smartt Bell, have done outstanding work, but their perspectives are still extrinsic to the region. The literary heritage is in fact a brief one, going back in any meaningful way only to the early twentieth century.

Claude McKay's *Banana Bottom* (1933) can plausibly lay claim to being the first significant West Indian novel, and certainly the first by a person of colour. McKay's contemporaries in the period before the Second World War include Jean Rhys (who wrote most of her novels years before *Wide Sargasso Sea*) and the writers of the "Trinidad Awakening", a movement that included such figures as C.L.R. James, Eric Roach, Alfred Mendes and Albert Gomes.[55] James and Mendes founded a short-lived magazine called *Trinidad*; two years later, in 1931, Gomes had better luck with *The Beacon*, which can be given much credit for helping to establish the idea of a Trinidadian literature. Such modest beginnings laid the groundwork; after the war a new, astonishing generation of novelists, poets and playwrights emerged, many of them, like V.S. Naipaul, beginning their careers with a British education. In addition to Naipaul and his fellow Nobel laureate Derek Walcott, there were Sam Selvon, George Lamming, Edward Kamau Brathwaite, Earl Lovelace and Wilson Harris, among others. These major figures paved the way for a veritable eruption of gifted artists such as Robert Antoni whose work has appeared in the post-independence era.[56]

The word *eruption* is not inappropriate, and the diversity of these writers' origins is remarkable. They come from Guyana on the South American mainland, from Trinidad and Barbados in the southern Caribbean, from relatively large countries such as Jamaica and tiny ones such as St Kitts, Grenada and Dominica and, of course, from lands that were never under the British flag: Haiti, Cuba, the Dominican Republic, Martinique. Even Gabriel García Márquez, who hails from near the coast of northern Colombia,[57] takes pains to claim the Caribbean as his own. This multiplicity of origins has been matched by the diversity of the writers' destinations. As for the previous generation, the present-day wave has splashed abundantly onto foreign shores, part of the far larger diaspora of ordinary West Indians – millions of them – driven to emigrate for economic or political reasons.

And Caribbean writers, like their compatriots living "in foreign", manage to stay connected. Many of these *écrivains sans frontières* (writers without borders) know one another and read each other's books; the linkages they maintain are carefully documented in Antoni's *Carnival*.[58] Papee Vince in *Divina Trace* tells Johnny Domingo, "[Y]ou can only tell your own story. You can only hear your own story too",[59] but if the self is indivisible from the culture that produces it, that story is never entirely one's own. A kind of cultural *cousinage* (or "affiliation" in Edward Said's sense of the word)[60] can be detected in the work of most of today's Caribbean writers – including those who are scattered around the globe.

One member of the West Indian diaspora whose work most clearly displays affiliations with Antoni's is Lawrence Scott. Born in Trinidad in 1944, Scott has lived in London for many years. His family, like Antoni's, were long-established members of the island's so-called plantocracy, a heritage he explores and reimagines brilliantly in his ambitious, technically innovative first novel, *Witchbroom*. The book's hermaphroditic narrator Lavren[61] – a self-proclaimed "Tiresias"[62] – "levitates between races, a creole in a creole world"[63] as he seeks his own identity by relaying his version of Caribbean history through the story of the Monagas de los Macajuelos family. But Lavren is a disguise. The subsections of *Witchbroom* are called "carnival tales", and true to the spirit of the mas, the narrator adopts the mask because his "actual" persona and style are not sufficient to work his magic. The tale, he says, "I had once started . . . neat, clipped and distanced", but "it seemed impossible for the story to hold . . . in sentences so always balanced like the prose of another land, the one we were taught in schools in order to write good compositions in our royal-blue exercise books with the picture of the king on the front".[64] Much later he comments, "I have the sentences of my colonial education. Secretly I envy him his creole loudness"; and "The clear balanced sentence, the sequential paragraph would not always do, the linear logic would not hold. Lavren would have to take hold."[65] The parallels between *Witchbroom* and *Divina Trace* are fascinating, especially considering that the novels were published only one year apart and, Antoni has told me, their authors were unaware of each other's existence at the time.[66] Both are formally eccentric, capacious attempts to imagine a kind of Caribbean "history" that is neither *sequential* nor *linear* – and certainly not inspired by "colonial education".

Tonally the two books could not be more different. *Witchbroom*'s narrator is arch, witty, scholarly, allusive – and at the same time elegiac – while Johnny Domingo's voice and the elder voices he remembers are filled with fear and wonder. But the Trinidad past folds itself into the texture of both in ways that are often eerily similar. *Witchbroom*, like *Divina Trace*, features a founding family named Monagas,[67] a walking statue, several references to La Divina Pastora, and a near-miraculous birth. Lavren is discovered by the attending physician to have both male and female genitals. While this scene is by no means rendered with the comic bravado of the frogchild's birth in *Divina Trace* (a bit of *comédie rosse* without many parallels in the history of literature), Lavren's physical condition is as thematically significant as Manuelito's, inasmuch as Scott needed a narrator "who levitates between centuries, races, and genders"[68] to tell the story of such a fragmented new world. Scott employs similar techniques in his other books,[69] where, as in Antoni, the complex relationship between Caribbean identity and culture always poses difficult and disturbing questions. Scott's characters tend to be haunted by a sense of alienation that clearly has its origins in the various ruptures brought about by the Caribbean's tortured history. This is an undercurrent in Antoni's work as well, reaching its fullest development only recently, in *Carnival*. But perhaps the strongest bond linking the visions of these writers is revealed near the end of *Witchbroom*, when Lavren admits that "no words here would have been possible without the poetry, prose, history, painting, sculpture, the mobility of mas, the invention of pan, calypso and the spoken voice which had come out of the yard of this archipelago, and which had invaded my ears, sitting on the sill of the Demerara window."[70] *The spoken voice*, the story told to a listener, is the most fundamental estuarial act – a living link between past and present, between the Caribbean and the lands beyond.

A primary force that guides the movement of Robert Antoni's artistic growth even more than Scott's is a desire to break through boundaries. In various interviews and conversations he has spoken of opening up language, freeing himself from racial, national and other "restrictions" and admiring books "that test limits".[71] "The landscape of your word is the world's landscape", Glissant has remarked, addressing Caribbean writers. "But its frontiers are open."[72] This highly implicative metaphor illuminates Antoni's work in several ways.

Most obviously, he participates in the estuarial movement of the Caribbean voice outwards, beyond any delimited island, into the "sea" of the wider world. There is too the urgent and protean articulation of that voice by Antoni's narrators. All of them are obsessive, constantly expanding the territory of their own identities, even in such an early work as "Two-head Fred and Tree-foot Frieda", which does not quite end with Addy's drunken confusion of fact and fiction during his attempt to spy on Jook Jook and Zoe. The next morning the two of them take Addy home on Jook Jook's boat; he is convinced that Zoe will never speak to him again after his mortifying interruption of their tryst the night before. But when his thoughts "find a center", he brushes a leaf along Zoe's bare shoulder and effectively wills her forgiveness – enlarges the borders of his reality – by telling himself a little story: "She allowed me this, and I put the leaf on my tongue and imagined that it could melt slowly in my mouth, could cool my hot insides."[73] From Addy to William Fletcher, Antoni's storytellers seem to understand on some level that narrative is not just decorative but transfigurative, containing within it the power to readjust the world's lines of demarcation.

The narrative that runs throughout Antoni's fiction and contains all others, the postulation of an evolving, pluralistic Caribbean identity, necessitates the violation of certain categories of thought imposed by colonialism. If this extension or erasure of "frontiers" is a political act, it also becomes an aesthetic choice for the Caribbean writer. Commenting on the memoirs of Father Jean-Baptiste Labat, who wrote about the Caribbean in the late seventeenth and early eighteenth centuries, Benítez-Rojo finds that the French priest conceived "the hypothesis of a common Caribbean culture . . . unbounded by the linguistic and political frontiers imposed by the various colonial powers".[74] As many students of postcolonial literatures have doubtless observed,[75] spatial delineations on maps have often been only the outward manifestation of much deeper ones. But those lines are deliberately breached in Antoni's books. The various narrators of *Divina Trace,* for instance – representing European, African, East Indian and Amerindian heritages – combine to produce a collective, boisterous deconstruction of that quintessential novel of filiation, the family chronicle. And in *Blessed Is the Fruit,* a post-plantation narrative space is created by the insistent growing together of two "plots" that the *ancien régime* would have kept apart. Both novels (not to mention *My Grandmother's Erotic Folktales*) unravel the filiative threads of received history and weave them into new, distinctly non-linear forms of discourse. Brian McHale's definition of the "postmodernist historical novel" fairly accurately describes Antoni's project. That genre, he explains, "is revisionist in two senses. First, it revises the content of the historical record . . . often demystifying or debunking the orthodox version of the past. Secondly, it revises, indeed transforms, the conventions and norms of historical fiction itself."[76]

Closely related to Antoni's ideation of a collective Caribbean consciousness liberated from extrinsically imposed boundaries and divisions is his expansion of the formal and technical frontiers of fiction. Like Lawrence Scott, Antoni has often found "the clear balanced sentence, the sequential paragraph" and "the linear logic" insufficient for his purposes. In exploring alternatives he has not hesitated to acknowledge bonds of kinship with writers from "foreign" who have spurred his imagination. Although his work is unquestionably rooted in the oral tradition of the West Indies, he has allowed books that "test limits" – such as *Ulysses, Finnegans Wake* and *Absalom, Absalom!* (not to mention the works of Freud, Lacan, Julia Kristeva and others) – to influence him enormously. It is, I believe, this complex combination of relation to Caribbean culture and an acknowledgement of filiative links[77] with canonical European and American writers that places him in a company that includes Derek Walcott, and few others. Like Walcott he navigates both the headwaters and tributaries of Caribbean folk tale and the limitless oceans of modernist and postmodernist text. Benítez-Rojo has commented that "to reread the Caribbean we have to visit the sources from which the widely various elements that contributed to the formation of its culture flowed",[78] but he has also written eloquently on the Caribbean impulse "toward travel, toward exploration". That exploration leads a writer like Antoni along "fluvial and marine routes"[79] to search for origins, yes, but also to enlarge the landscape of his identity as a human being and an artist, to open up the frontiers of the word so that others may follow.

2

DIVINA TRACE
The Inexhaustible Myth

It was a story to top all others. Even the Biblical one.
– *Divina Trace*[1]

There is no story that is not true.
– Chinua Achebe, *Things Fall Apart*[2]

Like several other capacious, innovative works that have emerged from the region (Derek Walcott's *Omeros,* V.S. Naipaul's *A Way in the World* and Patrick Chamoiseau's *Texaco,* for instance), *Divina Trace* is part of what Antonio Benítez-Rojo calls a movement "toward the creation of an ethnologically promiscuous text that might allow a reading of the varied and dense polyphony of Caribbean society's characteristic codes".[3] A generic cross-dresser with a long mock-epic poem enfolded in its prose, *Divina Trace* conjoins disparate cultural and religious traditions within a multivocal narrative that contests itself at every turn, continually undoing and retelling the story. And at its centre that protean story confronts matters that we scarcely have the vocabulary to describe: the nature of human consciousness, the dialectic of consciousness and culture, and the possible link between consciousness and something indefinable beyond it.

"Break a vase," Derek Walcott said in his Nobel address, "and the love that reassembles the fragments is stronger than the love that took its symmetry for granted when it was whole."[4] If the Caribbean writer's task (as Glissant repeatedly implies) is to plumb the collective memory and reassemble the broken fragments of culture, Antoni certainly rises to the challenge; *Divina Trace* stands at or near the forefront of those recent literary efforts to reclaim a past distorted by the corrosive legacy of colonialism. Precisely because that past has been shattered into so many discrete pieces, its reconceptualization must be, at the very least, collective and composite – an evolving, multifaceted history for a complicated, multifaceted culture. This is the kind of history that Antoni obsessively evokes in *Divina Trace*: a circular, interconnected series of narratives about the past that is both internally coherent and as centrifugal in its expanding waves of signification as Benítez-Rojo's repeating island, "unfolding and bifurcating until it reaches all the seas and lands of the earth".[5] The novel is also characterized by the countercolonizing movement described by Edward Said: an incorporation of non-linear thought structures associated with southern Asia and west Africa into the narrative design of a very Western form of discourse – the fictional family chronicle – transforming it into something truly rich and strange.[6]

Although the repeated interpretation and reinterpretation of family and island past generate the narrative structure of *Divina Trace*, the novel also explores other issues related to the ambiguous interplay between past and present. Like Zee Edgell in *Beka Lamb*, Antoni addresses the question of how personal and cultural identities together evolve and grow after the historical ruptures brought about by colonialism. The novel is, among many other things, an astonishingly complex and ambitious anatomy of the collective composition of human personality. The most emotionally compelling element of the novel is the difficult struggle of the central character, Johnny Domingo, at the age of ninety, to understand who he is by examining particles of island history and legend available to him through memory, imagination and dream. Critical to the island's sense of identity and independence is the figure of Magdalena Divina, whose story is inextricably entwined with that of Johnny's family, and whose role as Caribbean mother assumes – quite literally – mythic proportions. The myth that *Divina Trace* gradually produces for the reader is, fittingly, a highly syncretic one; the statue of Magdalena Divina and the stories surrounding it have sublime meaning for Amerindians, Catholics, Hindus and followers of West African religious traditions such as Shango. Magdalena is the novel's principal embodiment of the creolization process that has become history's answer to its own dismemberment.

It is relatively easy to sketch out the areas in which Antoni's work can be seen as part of the same experiential territory as that of many of his West Indian contemporaries: the search for identity, the role of the mother, the creolization of Caribbean societies, the imagination's engagement with history, and particularly the importance of storytelling in the retrieval and transmission of culture. But in *Divina Trace* these themes are raised to an altogether higher power. The method of storytelling becomes a meditation on the intrinsic attributes of narrative, with all of its attendant retelling, variation and elaboration. This aspect of the novel in turn raises questions about the shifting, variable quality of the truth accessible to human beings. As in Karl Popper's "non-authoritarian theory of knowledge",[7] the "truth" of *Divina Trace* is gathered into a seemingly endless cycle of hypotheses, rejections and new hypotheses. But Antoni goes even further, towards the very frontiers of fiction's possibilities, using the Caribbean's estuarial/diasporal hypostasis to explore the nature of human consciousness itself and its relationship to language and storytelling. The deepest mysteries of *Divina Trace* hauntingly echo that ancient insight encoded in the Indo-European root *gno-*, the common ancestor of both *knowledge* and *narration*. And throughout the novel, the ancestor-plagued Johnny keeps returning to questions raised by those mysteries: What is history?

Does an objective history even exist? What is the connection between history, storytelling and myth? What, in "fact", is the difference between imagination and reality?

A STORIED WORLD

Even a preliminary exploration of *Divina Trace* requires a good bit of circling around, doubling back, overlapping and returning to terrain already trodden, if only because that is the way the book is constructed. The form of *Divina Trace* resembles Benítez-Rojo's evocative description of the whole Caribbean:

> If someone needed a visual explanation, a graphic picture of what the Caribbean is, I would refer him to the spiral chaos of the Milky Way, the unpredictable flux of transformative plasma that spins calmly in our globe's firmament, that sketches in an "other" shape that keeps changing, with some objects born to light while others disappear into the womb of darkness; change, transit, return, fluxes of sidereal matter.[8]

The subjectivity of the seven voices that speak to Johnny Domingo as he pieces together his family's story makes the "spiral chaos" of *Divina Trace* a fluctuating space of shifting events, relationships and dates. Like the Milky Way, Antoni's text is also a pattern, paradoxically in a state of constant change, self-destruction and recreation. Much of this effect can be traced to the book's origins in the oral tradition – in the stories told to Antoni by his own grandmother and other family members. A sense of the spoken word is a dominant feature in all his work, and nowhere more so than here, with such a crowd of voices speaking, all inscribing themselves "on the black surface" of Johnny's "collective unconscious".[9] Indeed, the epistemological signification that Glissant attributes generally to Caribbean folktales seems almost an analysis of the mechanics and implications of *Divina Trace* itself: "The oral techniques of accumulation, repetition, and circularity combine to undo the vision of reality and truth as singular, introducing the multiple, the uncertain, and the relative instead."[10]

Just as useful to an understanding of the novel's mechanics is Benítez-Rojo's notion of the Antilles as a meeting place of "the discourse of myth with the discourse of history".[11] Early and late in *Divina Trace* the two are intertwined, coming together even in the name of the island – Corpus Christi – denoting as it does a union of the temporal and the eternal. History may produce myth, but myth in turn remakes history, as Papee Vince explains:

> Because son, the fact is that Magdalena did not precede, or anticipate, or in any way inspire the creation of this black madonna. She did not give birth to this statue: the statue, or more precisely *history*, gave birth to Magdalena. And history took she life too – long before she was dead – only so that history could give Magdalena a *second* birth, could bring her back to life in this black madonna which preceded her.[12]

Not just here but throughout Antoni's vast structure of recollection (to borrow a phrase from Proust), Benítez-Rojo's two discourses engage in an ongoing dialectic as the family history that Johnny struggles so mightily to make rational is penetrated and transformed by the frightening irrationalities of myth. And, for Johnny Domingo, the deeper wellsprings of that myth are powerful and lifelike enough to fire his narrative with a childhood terror that ninety years of ordinary historical experience, in both the United States and the Caribbean, do little to extinguish.

The arrangement of the voices in *Divina Trace* is concentric, like the winds surrounding the eye of a hurricane. The first five "narrators" – Granny Myna (Johnny Domingo's paternal grandmother), Papee Vince (his maternal grandfather), Evelina (the family's black servant),

Dr Domingo (Johnny's father) and Mother Superior Maurina (Granny Myna's older sister) – all "speak" to Johnny through the medium of his memory, in prose. Near the middle of the book, Magdalena, the focal point of Johnny's ruminations, recites in her southern Caribbean dialect a two-part verse variation on the Indian epic the *Ramayana*, which is simultaneously a variation on the plot of *Divina Trace*, so that in this section the Magdalena of Johnny's imagination relays her version of past events on the island of Corpus Christi. Between the two halves of Magdalena's poem, and at the dead centre of the novel, lies an even more oracular utterance, the narrative of Hanuman the Hindu monkey god. Hanuman, in his "calypso-simian tongue" – an asyntactical, highly associational flow of words and syllables – spins out his own account of the "subplot of the monkey tribes" found in the *Ramayana*. This brief segment, as Antoni describes it, "provides a transition between the two halves of the book, which are constructed as mirror-images, and it stands apart as an encapsulation of the novel as a whole".[13] Following the second half of Magdalena's poem, the novel's five prose narrators finish their accounts in reverse order: Mother Superior Maurina, Dr Domingo, Evelina, Papee Vince and Granny Myna. These voices, having brooded over the birth of the frogchild in the book's first half, now offer up their varying interpretations of the mother's later elevation to island sainthood. And though Johnny's voice is the medium that holds and transmits all these others, his is like Marie-Sophie's in Chamoiseau's *Texaco*: "only part of a chorus, a multi-layered, multi-perspective identity that is revealed as an even more dominant force" than that of any individual.[14]

The middle of the novel – Magdalena's poem and Hanuman's monkey talk – is its most forbidding stretch of territory: a verbal version of the tangled Maraval Swamp at the end of the path called Divina Trace. In the poem Hanuman himself asks playfully, "Where are dere monkeys enough to read it? Where, in truth, are dere monkeys patient to trudge, / Dis mudthick-mudswamp of monkeylanguage?"[15] Hanuman's section suggests a level or source of consciousness beneath or prior to rational thought, and therefore a prelinguistic, perhaps even prehuman, origin of storytelling and myth. Later in *Divina Trace* Johnny Domingo himself recalls thinking, "[T]his story does not belong to this voice. To these voices. *This story belongs to that moon. To that black sky and that black sea. This story belongs to the same foul smell of the swamp when the wind blows.*"[16] Johnny's odyssey through the novel's voices takes him at last into this inner swamp – deep into himself – and what he encounters there is crucial to his understanding of his own identity.[17] When he emerges from it and into the comparative light of the rest of Magdalena's poem, he is ready to retrace his steps back through the other voices that have spoken to him. The poem itself is much more than a witty Caribbeanized retelling of the events in *Divina Trace*. As one of the oldest stories in human history (as well as one of the most widely known), the *Ramayana* serves as a prototype – a particularly apt one in that it arose out of an oral tradition and exists in many different written versions. Philip Lutgendorf characterizes the epic as "a meta-story never exhaustively encompassed by any one text but always inspiring new and variant readings".[18] Finally, the *Ramayana*, like *Divina Trace*, records the birth of a myth out of storytelling and its inscription on the consciousness of a people. As Aamer Hussein put it in one of the most perceptive reviews of the novel, "The voice of a myth, recounting a myth, lies at the heart of this chronicle of the creation of a myth."[19]

The *Ramayana*'s remarkable regenerative capability, its endless retelling of itself, may well be its most consequential link to *Divina Trace*, where a story is conceived not as the opposite of reality (as "fiction" is thought to be the opposite of "fact") but rather as one possible revelation of the real. Two brief sequences somewhat removed from the novel's central events demonstrate the difficulty of ascertaining a truth apart from truth-as-told. Just five pages in, Granny Myna tells Johnny that the scar on his father's forehead derived from her looking at a picture of Saint John with a similar scar during her "moments of passion",[20] including the moment of Dr Domingo's conception. But much later Johnny recalls his father's own explanation of the scar: that he got it jumping out of a tamarind tree. Still another version has Uncle Amadao accidentally hitting him on the head while skipping stones across the duck pond. Within the storied world of *Divina Trace*, all three versions are equally true, just as Magdalena remains, in Papee Vince's words, "a saint, a whore, or both".[21] Moreover, neither Papee Vince's "factual" or "historical" account nor Dr Domingo's "scientific" one is prioritized by the novel's overall deployment of narratives. On the contrary, they are placed on the same level as the emotional, superstitious and hysterical testimonies of Granny Myna, Evelina and Mother Maurina.

Although the plot of *Divina Trace* constantly evolves and mutates as the different voices speak to Johnny Domingo in his recollections and dreams, it does possess a determinate core, and that core is Johnny's *search* for the plot.[22] That the search must be conducted through storytelling is intimated in the subconscious "monkeylanguage" at the centre of the book. Hanuman concludes his monkey speech (effectively beginning the novel's second half) with "*Krick-krack, monkey break he back, all fa piece of pommerac*".[23] This is a traditional Caribbean call-and-response signal to begin a story, and its placement here, within the nucleus of Johnny's consciousness, clearly signals that in the beginning is the word, or even an unnameable pre-word.[24] All of the storytellers whose words are recorded in *Divina Trace*, along with Johnny Domingo's frequent commentaries on them, are recalled in one long night of rumination – the night before Johnny's ninetieth birthday – but they have traced themselves on the slate of his mind over a period of decades. At first he thinks of the process only in general terms, as "a collection of voices merging and separating, and occasionally falling into rhythm with my own quick breathing".[25] Later, reflecting on Mother Superior Maurina's version of the story and how it came to him, he realizes how much more is involved:

> First it was only the isolated words: short phrases, fragments of a language which I knew belonged only to her. And as the years progressed and I continued to listen I began to hear whole passages, coming to me from somewhere out of my childhood – from somewhere out of that vast storehouse of words and images constantly disassembled and reassembled and surfacing again mysterious, new – so that now at the end of ninety years of blind hearing I can sit here and listen to the whole story.[26]

And what is that story? In Papee Vince's words, the facts are these: Long before Johnny Domingo was born, when his father was a young man just back from medical school in London, an adolescent girl named Magdalena emerged from the bush, joined Mother Maurina's convent, and seven months later gave birth to a child said to be half frog and half human, although it may actually have been anencephalic.[27] Magdalena herself died immediately afterwards, under circumstances that are hotly disputed, and the child, christened Manuelito Domingo, lived for just three days.

Of course these "facts" do not go uncontested, and as the tale is fleshed out with detail, revisions and additions multiply. Magdalena first appeared in the town of St Maggy's when she was thirteen (according to Mother Maurina) or fifteen (according to Papee Vince). She was brought up in the bush among Warrahoons[28] (Amerindians), yet she sported a Hindu *tilak* in the middle of her forehead. Johnny's family members regard her as the illegitimate child of Barto, Johnny's paternal grandfather, and Mother Maurina, his sister-in-law (who is herself probably one-quarter Amerindian). The frogchild (or "crapochild",[29] as he is frequently called) Manuelito was apparently the equally illegitimate issue of Barto and his own daughter, Magdalena. Dr Domingo, Johnny's father, swears that Magdalena's hymen was imperforate, yet she was pregnant and gave birth. Dr Domingo also insists that Magdalena committed suicide after seeing the baby, by holding her breath, even though he acknowledges that such a feat is "impossible".[30] Later, Mother Maurina admits to suffocating her daughter with a pillow. Still later, Papee Vince (or, it must be stressed, Johnny's *recollection* of Papee Vince) reveals that Magdalena did not die at all, but was nursed back to health by the Warrahoon bush doctor Brito Salizar, who may have been Granny Myna's grandfather. As Johnny turns these matters over and over in his mind, he is acutely aware that the legend of Magdalena Divina associated with a statue in a nearby chapel "belonged to a time much older than Mother Maurina".[31] How then, he wonders, could the Magdalena known to his father and grandparents have been, as they claim, the woman behind the myth?

Johnny Domingo's effort to find answers to this and many other questions is the novel's constant. The basis of his inquiry is epistemological, and like the search for V. in Pynchon, it is complicated by a seemingly endless proliferation of signs. Johnny's confusion is evident from the novel's first episode, in which he recalls making his way down the ten miles of Divina Trace[32] to the Maraval Swamp, clutching a large glass bottle containing Magdalena's supposedly dead frogchild. It is the night before his thirteenth birthday and, on her deathbed, his Granny Myna has asked him to remove the frogchild's body from the family plot so that she will not be buried next to her late husband's bastard. At the end of this section Johnny remembers opening the bottle, tilting it and watching the creature, miraculously alive after so many years, swim into the dark waters of the mangrove swamp. The incident, whether real or imagined, haunts Johnny Domingo for his entire life; in his mind it is the experiential link that connects his own story to that of Magdalena and, through her, to the entire island. The glass bottle containing the miraculous child (and also containing Johnny's own reflection) is Antoni's version of Eliot's still point of the turning world – in this case the nexus between fact and imagination, history and myth.

As information about the frogchild accumulates, so does Johnny's bewilderment. That his bewilderment might itself be part of the story's dynamic, however, does not become clear to Johnny until very late in *Divina Trace.* Once again the explanatory voice is that of the novel's most nearly impartial narrator, Papee Vince:

> I can only give this story back to you the way life give it to me – the way the story asks itself to be told – with all its many deceptations, and combructions, and confufflations. Because all that is as essential to the telling of this story – as essential to the understanding of it – as any amount of poetry pile up in the po beneath you bed. . . . Because of course, in the end, as with any other tale told of man or monkeys since the beginning of time, you can only tell your own story. You can only hear your own story too.[33]

Papee Vince makes two vital points here: the "deceptations" of story reflect those of reality, and every story is a product of the creative minds of both teller and listener. Furthermore, if Magdalena's story is really Johnny's own, the architecture of the novel, with its overwhelming emphasis on Magdalena and her child, argues that the most important parts of all our stories lie not in the routine events marking our lives but within our imaginations. The linear, rational, conventionally "realistic" elements of Johnny Domingo's biography – his alienation from the Church, his decision to become a doctor, his education in the United States, his marriage and children and his return to Corpus Christi to practise medicine – all emerge, almost as asides, from the interstices between blocks of narrative recounting his family history. It is important that Johnny has come back to the Caribbean, but it is the magic and terror of the Caribbean past, swarming in his thoughts, that has brought him there.

The "combructions" and "confufflations" of *Divina Trace* certainly mirror an uncertain and fluid reality. Even in the first scene, Johnny recalls his footsteps along the trace falling into the rhythm of his grandfather Barto's voice uttering "Na-me-na-na-ha!" Johnny admits that he does not know what the words meant, "or whether they were words at all".[34] Only later does Dr Domingo reveal that the phrase is Warrahoon for "don't understand a *fart*".[35] Appearing in the novel's first paragraph and subsequently spoken by several characters, "na-me-na-na-ha" becomes a minute but important leitmotif acknowledging the difficulty of Johnny's efforts to plot an intelligible trace through his world. Increasingly in the second half of the novel, however, his own imagination appears to play a role in shaping, and even distorting, the events purportedly described by others. At several junctures he confuses memory with dream as scenes from his early childhood intersect in his mind with episodes from his later life. His account of a medical problem experienced by his daughter Evy when she was on the brink of puberty is a case in point. Did both Evy and Magdalena have imperforate hymens, or has Johnny's memory of one bled into and influenced his memory of the other? His recollections are also strewn with anachronisms: K-Marts, VCRs and Kentucky Fried Chicken outlets that can exist only in Johnny's memory, not in the memories of his long-dead relatives. One of those family members, Papee Vince, even refers to his own death when he "says" to Johnny, "[I]f you recall the chronology of this story, you will remember how Evelina sheself wouldn't be dead fa good few years to come, and in fact, I myself would be dead fa good few months before her."[36]

Many of these elements, including the frequent repetition of words, phrases and whole paragraphs, belong to the topography of an old man's past-plagued mind. But not all of the text's problematic features can be explained away so easily. The "chronology of this story", for example, is complex even on the surface, with four main time frames: Johnny at ninety, remembering being told tales by his elders; the occasions on which those tellings took place; the time of the events related in the stories; and interpolated flashbacks (analepses) to various periods in Johnny's adult life. But beneath this modernist scheme – intricate, yet intelligible – temporal determinacy wanes. If Johnny

Domingo is ninety years old in 1999, as he repeatedly claims, he would have been born in 1909; but when he leaves Corpus Christi on his eighteenth birthday, the year is 1938, according to a letter from his father.[37] And although Johnny says that Granny Myna was ninety-six when she asked him at age thirteen to dig up the frogchild and throw it in the swamp, if he was born in 1909, the incident would have taken place in 1922. According to Papee Vince, Barto left Granny Myna "a widow at the age of thirty-six" – in 1899.[38] There are many other such conflicts in the novel. Johnny recalls Mother Maurina stating on the eve of his eighteenth birthday that she is 113 years old. If he was in fact born in 1909, this would fix the year of her birth at 1814. But she also claims to be the mother of Magdalena, who is fourteen or fifteen when she gives birth to the frogchild in 1899. Mother Maurina, therefore, would herself have become a mother at the biblical age of seventy! At another point Evelina supposedly tells Johnny when he is sixteen (presumably in 1925) that his grandfather Barto has been gone "fa longer den forty years."[39] Since Barto disappeared shortly after the frogchild's birth in April 1899, Evelina's words to Johnny cannot have been uttered until at least 1939. Johnny's birthday, moreover, is cited as both April 16[40] and April 17,[41] while the feast of Corpus Christi, which takes place "every year"[42] on April 16, also seems to fall on April 15[43] and April 17.[44]

These dates simply do not add up, but it would be a violation of the novel's integrity if they did. The refusal of the chronology to unfold in a straightforward and consistent pattern contributes to the sense of dimensions beyond the immediate reach of human perception, as in the *Ramayana*. Describing the Hindu epic, R.K. Narayan says, "The time scheme . . . is somewhat puzzling to us who are habituated to a mere horizontal sequence of events. . . . One has to . . . get used to a narrative going backwards and forwards and sideways."[45] Reality is more complicated than our conscious, rational, waking minds let us understand. Perhaps we have developed a rational, linear way of ordering reality for the sake of survival, but our dreams remind us that there is more to it than that. I would argue that even if some of these discrepancies were read as authorial oversights, they still contribute substantially to the book's meaning. While Antoni's conscious intention may have been to impose a fixed chronology on the plot – to enhance the kind of intelligibility that we expect in our daily lives – that effort is subverted by "mistakes" arising from the a-rational, dreaming territory of his imagination. In a novel like this the dates *should* contradict each other, just as the characters should have multiple, self-revising identities and tell stories containing contradictory "facts". If the dissonance of dates within the text arises from "error" – the subconscious refusing to let the conscious mind tell a definitive, univocal version of the story – that only enforces the authenticity of the reality manifested by *Divina Trace*. In the Caribbean, Benítez-Rojo reflects, "time unfolds irregularly and resists being captured by the cycles of clock and calendar".[46] That resistance is quite consistent with the ontological fluidity of Antoni's novel as a whole. A single, determinate truth is impossible to pin down. Papee Vince, the novel's "historian", is fond of saying (as if to convince himself), "The facts are these", and Dr Domingo, the other character who chases after the chimera of objectivity, often employs a similar discourse marker: "Realize." But the facts repeatedly contest one another, and the word *realize* means not only *understand* but also *make real* or *bring into being*. The truth of *Divina Trace* remains in the telling.

THE LAND OF MYTHMYTHILIA

Chronology, then, like the varying and conflicting accounts of the events themselves, constantly dissolves and is reassembled, suggesting an irreducible indeterminacy in the very fabric of human experience. Dr Domingo puts it bluntly: "Is you reality any less real than my own?

All this confusion begins before we open we eyes, before the first stories begin to tell, so how can we *ever* expect to understand it?"[47] Yet the telling of stories, and their transmutation into myths, is the strategy by which human beings and human cultures try to understand and tame the unfamiliar and the uncertain. Mark Kurlansky relates a revealing incident that occurred when he was a passenger on a catamaran off the north coast of Jamaica in 1973. A man who had been singing and playing a banjo on the boat fell overboard and drowned. When the catamaran returned to Montego Bay, "Everyone on the pier seemed to know what had happened, but they still wanted to hear the story. Knowing the story and telling it is the Afro-Caribbean version of immortality." Kurlansky goes on to say, "I never learned his name. It was the story that was important. A man was gone, he left behind his story."[48] When people tell stories about themselves, they participate in the construction of their own cultural identity, both individually and collectively, and this process is particularly important in the Caribbean, where historical disjunctions and ethnic diversity have intensified the "*métissage* without limits"[49] that is the region's most elemental characteristic.

Antoni has long been transfixed by the evolution of storytelling into myth as a response to the "confusion" inherent in human experience. In an unpublished paper comparing "the myth-making process" in *Absalom, Absalom!* and *One Hundred Years of Solitude,* he enumerates several techniques used by both Faulkner and García Márquez to transform their stories into myth.[50] Among them are the use of "primeval, regional settings to achieve a universal context" and the frequent repetition of events "to impart a sense of mythic importance", as well as "the repetition of names and personality traits", the "disruption of temporal continuity to place the stories in the realm of discontinuous, universal or mythic time" and the employment of the devices of "oral narration".[51] Antoni eventually used all of these techniques in his first novel; the list, in fact, serves as quite a useful introduction to much of his work. But it is in another unpublished essay that he most openly identifies the path he follows in *Divina Trace*: "In it I attempt to create the myth of my own origins, of my own family history, and I attempt to create it around the figure of a mother-goddess who has long inspired me: she is La Divina Pastora, the black madonna who features in the Catholic church of Siparia, a small East-Indian village in southern Trinidad."[52] Antoni's myth in *Divina Trace* grows out of a series of stories told by and about members of a single family, but it comes to encompass much of Corpus Christi's history and all of its principal religious traditions: the Catholicism of the European colonists, the Hinduism of indentured workers imported from India and the belief systems brought to the "New World" by African slaves.[53]

The "mother-goddess" around whom the myth gathers in *Divina Trace*, La Divina Pastora, is an object of devotion little known outside of Trinidad. C.L.R. James has described her simply as "a small image of some two feet in height which stands in the Roman Catholic Church at Siparia". She is "nothing more than a symbol of the divine" to many, but to others she "possesses limitless powers".[54] A more recent account, in a travel guide to Trinidad, fills in some detail. The devotion to Mary as Divine Shepherdess was brought to South America and the West Indies by Capuchin monks from Spain. As the years passed, Hindus "and other non-Catholic groups" adopted her as their own, the Hindus even identifying her as the goddess Kali.[55] In the novel Papee Vince expounds upon the significance of the fictional black madonna's appeal across the ethnic and religious spectrum. The statue has appeared "to the Pañyols as Divina Pastora, to the Amerindians as Akambo-Mah,[56] to the Africans as Mamma Latay, to the East Indians as Kali Mai". All that was required, he explains, for her to truly become Corpus Christi's patron saint was for her "to resurrect and reunite she previous four incarnations",[57] and this was accomplished through her association with Magdalena Domingo.[58]

Of the three religious traditions that shape and vitalize the myth of Magdalena Divina in Antoni's novel, Christianity is the most prominent, both because the cult of La Divina Pastora originated with missionary monks and because the Domingos themselves (like the Antonis) are Catholics, and their history on Corpus Christi is intimately, if not always amicably, linked with that of the Church. The name of the island itself has religious significance, and the island's biggest celebration – almost a national day – is the feast of Corpus Christi. In *Divina Trace* the festival honouring Magdalena coincides with that holiday, which is celebrated on Holy Thursday,[59] so several important elements of Christian doctrine and worship – the Mass, the Blessed Virgin, the Passion – come into play.[60] The Carmelite convent and St Maggy's Cathedral are the hubs of Catholic power and influence on the island, but there is a major difference between them. The cathedral is the official seat of a church whose headquarters are in Europe; the convent, which promotes the cult of Magdalena under the direction of Mother Superior Maurina, comes to embody nascent nationalistic feelings among Corpus Christi Catholics. Even from the time of its establishment (by none other than Barto Domingo), the convent has been seen as a kind of rival to ecclesiastical authority centred in Rome. As Mother Maurina recalls, "[T]hey said Barto is going into competition now with Papa God in He cathedral on the other side of the square."[61]

Mother Maurina, according to the voice of Papee Vince, "was the first to tell this story. This story of Magdalena Divina. She was the only one to know it complete, perhaps even better than Magdalena sheself."[62] Her central role in the novel not only reinforces the Catholic core of the syncretic myth that accrues around Magdalena but it also allows Antoni to indulge in some further forays into mythic territory. Maurina's version of the story – some of which approaches stream of consciousness – is emotionally charged and frequently lurid. She insists that the frogchild was "the son of Papa God" (not Satan, as Evelina believes) and that his mother, Magdalena, was a saint. The proof lies in the fact – agreed to by everyone and confirmed by Johnny's father, Dr Domingo – that her hymen had never been penetrated: "Magdalena have this special veil of the church to protect her, that no wajank could never push heself inside no matter how hard he try."[63] The frogchild dies, is buried while still alive, is dug up and thrown into the swamp, is kept in a bottle in Uncle Olly's lab or is boiled in a callaloo[64] and served to the Domingo family for dinner – all depending on which account is "true". But it is Magdalena – as virgin, daughter and mother – not her child, who becomes the object of the cult, and Mother Maurina appears to be largely responsible for encouraging its growth, even asserting that Magdalena's name was given to her in a dream by an "oldman dress up head-to-toe in tin paper shining beautiful as the angel Gabriel".[65] The reappearance of the "oldman" in "tin paper" in this annunciation scene is highly significant inasmuch as the identity of the archangel impersonated by the old man shifts (through a lapse of memory on Johnny's part, or a mysterious imaginative transformation) from Michael to the more appropriate Gabriel – the angel who announced the birth of Jesus to the Virgin Mary.

The motif of the old man and his Corpus Christi costume in the novel is important for another reason as well. When he first appears, driving an oxcart as Johnny is making his way down the trace to dump the frogchild in the swamp, he is wrapped in aluminum foil, and Johnny mistakes him for a robot. The old man is indignant: "I is de archangel St Michael, dis my chariot going to battle."[66] Seventy-seven years later Johnny encounters him (or his latter-day avatar) again, looking for all the world like the same "angelic robot in the same Biblical rocket".[67] The angel/robot, chariot/rocket pattern is part of a dialectic between faith and science that occurs throughout Antoni's fiction, as early as "My Grandmother's Tale of the Buried Treasure", in which a tall tale about an angel competes for attention with a flashing metal detector.[68] In *Divina Trace* Johnny makes "the conscious decision to become a doctor"[69] on his sixteenth birthday, after being molested by the local Monsignor. "It was if," he recalls, "the world were suddenly divided, as if I could choose between science and religion and disregard the other."[70] He wants to learn "*daddy's language of medical science*" that "*understands everything clean clean*" so that he can "*forget that frogchild and this Magdalena*".[71] The dichotomy proves to be an illusion, as Johnny realizes when he sits behind Mother Superior Maurina in the convent chapel two years later. As he gazes at the back of her "white pasteboard-headdress", his imagination integrates the imagery of faith and science and intuits a common denominator: "The aluminium-white antennae of this angelic robot sitting before me ready now to receive and transmit some personal message from some master-robot by the name of *God*. Before my eyes. In my own ears."[72]

Adding to the Catholic element in the syncretic myth of *Divina Trace,* Antoni weaves into Mother Maurina's account a version of Bernadette of Lourdes, a saint to whom his real Granny Myna was devoted. Maurina's "St Bernadetta" is "a true true chupidee" and "a waterhead" who was brought to the convent by her mother and taken in as "an act of charity". Although the young girl had a "face fat like a football" and "big eyes always watching you dumb like a donkey",[73] she not only learns to read in record time but, after drinking water from the Maraval Swamp, she appears able to read in various languages. Some of the details of the Bernadette spoof overlap with those of Magdalena in Mother Maurina's earlier chapter, suggesting that the miraculous chupidee is yet another version of Magdalena. But it is Bernadetta who "discovers" the walking statue (presumed to be an effigy of Magdalena, if not the girl herself), initiating a train of events that ends with Mother Maurina's going to Rome in a broadly comical attempt to have Magdalena canonized. Instead, the "mammapoule Pope"[74] – identified by Mother Maurina as Pius IX and by Dr Domingo as Pius XI[75] – mistakenly declares "this USELESS WATERHEAD A SAINT",[76] and Mother Maurina, Evelina and Dr Domingo have to return to Corpus Christi and, in effect, canonize Magdalena themselves. By rewriting the "song of Bernadette" as a virtual Caribbean calypso, Antoni turns the Old World's cultural conquest of the New on its head (indeed, on its waterhead). And Mother Maurina's "invasion" of Rome, however farcical,[77] results in the empowering appropriation of Magdalena by the people of Corpus Christi as their own saint, not one imported from Europe.

During her sections of the novel, Mother Maurina's religious ecstasies are scarcely distinguishable from her sexual ones, and she (or Johnny's memory) also frequently conflates elements of her own story with those of her alleged daughter's. The most startling passage of this kind is Maurina's account of herself watching Barto and Magdalena make love. Syntax and memory alike take on new and strange forms as Magdalena's experience seems to become Maurina's own:

> . . . standing here at the end of this bed looking down again through the dark murky water of my dream with my feet to my knees in the mud of my own terrible passion without escape, here looking down again through the dark water seeing myself again my own beautiful daughter struggling helpless here in the mud of my own hopeless longing to lie again beneath my husband-father-son-of-my-son in nomine Patris Filii et Spiritus Sancti.[78]

The rest of this reverie resists expository analysis. Suffice it to say that Mother Maurina's imaginative appropriation of these events as she describes them is simultaneously orgasmic and sacramental. Barto, in her mind, is lover, father, son, angel, Holy Ghost and perhaps even Papa God himself.

Robert Antoni's unpublished paper on Joyce and Freud sheds some light on the psychosexual implications of the myth that lies at the heart of *Divina Trace.* In analysing the similarities between Freud's recreation of "the Primal History Scene" in *Moses and Monotheism* and Joyce's version in *Finnegans Wake,* Antoni concludes that the mother figure is "conspicuously missing" – or at least highly attenuated – in both. One of his purposes in *Divina Trace* is to restore "the absent mother" to her rightful place in the "earliest of primeval memories handed down to us as part of our phylogenetic inheritance". In Freud's formulation, social organization began with the sons' reinstitution of the father's prohibitions (against copulating with their mother and sisters) after they had killed and eaten him. Antoni argues that although Freud's emphasis is on the father and the sons, "the mother's position in the Oedipus complex is as . . . important as the father's, at least insofar as she is the forbidden object of desire". In Antoni's reformulation, the horde of sons, after killing the father, rape the mother. Later they repent and give the mother "an exalted status" equal to that of the dead father. These modifications of Freud's scheme, Antoni believes, would help explain the evolution of mother-goddesses from ancient times to the present, including Christianity's conception of the Virgin Mary as the quasi-divine Mother of God.

Antoni tries to rehabilitate the mother figure in *Divina Trace* by incorporating his revision of Freud's ideas into the genesis of his own Caribbean myth. For example, there are several accounts of a gang breaking into the convent and raping Magdalena. The gang is led by Gomez, St Maggy's chief of police, who may be the son of Mother Maurina and Barto. In this context the conflation of Maurina and Magdalena becomes very important, since Gomez and his "brother" policemen can be said to violate both their sister and their mother. Similarly, Johnny Domingo's recollection (or, more probably, his dream) of finding his grandfather Barto still alive and shattering his skull with a rum bottle re-enacts the murder of the primal father. The preoccupation with Magdalena's virginity and her imperforate hymen is just as pertinent. If the killing and eating of the father is ultimately expiated by the elevation of a totem meal to divine status (as in the Eucharist), then the original rape of the mother could have been expiated by having "the primeval mother declare herself eternally virgin". In this way "the Mother could dissolve our guilt for the primeval rape, since as Virgin she was herself proof it had not occurred".[79] In Antoni's multilayered myth Magdalena is both Mary and Magdalene, Mother of God and (in Papee Vince's words) a "consecrated whore".[80]

The two other principal strands of Corpus Christi's religious inheritance – those brought to the island from India and west Africa – are less pervasive than Catholicism in the fabric of *Divina Trace* but are just as integral to the novel. The Hindu element is concentrated in Magdalena's verse declamation, a syncretic and idiosyncratic retelling of the *Ramayana*. The *Ramayana* was first written down in Sansksrit by the poet Valmiki about two thousand years ago, but the legends it records are much older. Valmiki's "original" text tells the story of the noble lovers Rama and Sita, the ideal couple of Hindu tradition. Although the poem's length (some twenty-four thousand verses!) and complexity make it impossible to summarize adequately, a few words about the plot are essential to at least suggest its relationship to *Divina Trace*.

In the *Ramayana* Rama is the son of Dasaratha, the king of Ayodhya, by his wife Kausalya. Dasaratha also has two sons, Lakshman and Satrughna, by his wife Sumitra, as well as one, Bharata, by his wife Kaikeyi. When he attains adulthood Rama marries Sita, foster daughter of the king of Janaka. Sita lives in the city of Mithila, nicely transformed by Antoni into "Mythmythilia". Eventually Rama is banished for fourteen years through the trickery of the jealous Kaikeyi, who is ambitious for her own son. During their exile, Sita is kidnapped by Ravana, the demon ruler of the island of Lanka. The monkey demigod Hanuman and his monkey army help Rama rescue Sita, and during this incident Hanuman tells the embedded story of the monkey race – a subplot that parallels to some extent the main one but which is almost certainly much older, its presence here suggesting (among other things) the very origins of storytelling. Some versions of the *Ramayana* continue the story of the couple after their triumphant return to Ayodhya. In these accounts they are separated again because of unfounded suspicions that Sita was unfaithful while held captive by Ravana, but the couple is ultimately reunited in the heavens. To many *Ramayana* bards such a conclusion must have seemed appropriate, since Rama and Sita were incarnations of the gods Vishnu and his wife Lakshmi.

This is only a small part of the epic's plot, but it is enough to demonstrate the uses to which Antoni puts it in *Divina Trace.* Nearly all the characters in Magdalena's *Ramayana* are surrogates for figures in the novel, and Antoni has subtly shaped her retelling of the ancient poem so that its plot corresponds at many points to that of *Divina Trace.* For instance, since Rama and Sita parallel Barto and Magdalena, Sumitra and Kaikeyi are converted from stepmothers to wives so that they can serve as analogues to Maurina and her jealous sister, Granny Myna. Perhaps more significant than these kinds of modification is a change that is almost theological: in Antoni's version, Rama is an incarnation of Shiva, not Vishnu. This much more fundamental alteration of the *Ramayana* seems designed to emphasize the connection between Magdalena and Kali, who was the wife of Shiva. La Divina Pastora, the real-life prototype for Magdalena Divina, has been worshipped as a manifestation of Kali by the Hindus of Trinidad, and in *Divina Trace* she is said by Papee Vince to be one of Magdalena's avatars. It also seems fitting that Barto as Rama should be an incarnation of Shiva, the destroyer, rather than Vishnu, the preserver.

R.K. Narayan's short English rendition of the *Ramayana* begins, "Valmiki the poet explained to Rama himself: 'Owing to the potency of your name, I became a sage, able to view the past, present and future as one'."[81] In Magdalena's poem Valmiki dreams "heself a boychild again. / In he dream, de boychild toting an infant, / Same dream he dreaming again dat same oldman again." When the old Valmiki questions his dreamed younger self about the infant, the boy replies, "Dis popo is you and me together, / All we three persons in one. Father, body of we mummy, son."[82] If the boy holding the baby in Valmiki's dream can be construed as an image of Johnny toting the frogchild in a glass bottle, then we have a narrative scenario something like this: Johnny Domingo dreams, remembers and imagines *Divina Trace*, in which Magdalena ("body of we mummy") recites a version of the *Ramayana* in which the *Ramayana*'s "real" author, Valmiki, meets Johnny Domingo in a dream. The boy in the dream is Valmiki himself (as a child), his son (as his dream creation) and his father (as the metanarrator of the whole novel). Hanuman assumes additional importance by virtue of his connection with Valmiki: the two gaze at each other "as if in a lookglass", from this point on "spiritual father and son".[83] In Antoni's *Ramayana*, Hanuman, "through power of meditation deep" (or imagination), puts the story into writing and informs its voices "[w]ith he mirror-form",[84] so that Hanuman too is a version of Johnny Domingo (and, hence, of Robert Antoni). We shall return a bit later to a crucial consubstantiality, through the detached agency of the mirror, between monkey god, frogchild and narrator.

There are many other correspondences between Magdalena's *Ramayana* and the various accounts of her own story that form the rest of Antoni's novel; virtually the entire plot of *Divina Trace*, in fact, is retold by her (in Caribbean dialect and with many Caribbean references) as if it were the tale of Rama and Sita. As a literary act in itself, the poem brilliantly exemplifies (as, indeed, does the whole novel) Benítez-Rojo's dictum that a "syncretic artifact is not a synthesis, but rather a signifier made of differences".[85] In this part of the novel the figure at the centre of the novel's myth tells the story directly as a myth, incorporating into the texture of the ancient story elements that give it life for a new, composite culture. It is this cardinal theme in Magdalena's Caribbeanized *Ramayana* – the genesis of myth in storytelling and the power of myth to enter history and shape cultural identity – that binds the poem most closely to the rest of the book.

Evelina, the Domingo family's black servant, is the medium through whom Antoni introduces the novel's third major constellation of religious traditions. When Johnny is sixteen he is awakened in the middle of the night to accompany the old woman as she performs an "obeah spell" to protect the family against the curse (as she sees it) of the frogchild. She prays "to Ogoun in de old Yoruba language", but she tells Johnny it is the same as praying "to St Michael begging he thrust dis Eshu back in hell"[86] – which she also does, in Latin, a bit later. Both of her sections of the book are filled with talk of African gods, obeah and the calamity brought on the family by Barto and manifested by the birth of the frogchild. Although her grandmother Aiyaba may have worshipped the Yoruba gods alone, Evelina, the daughter of a "Shango priestess",[87] practises an even more syncretic religion that combines a modified Catholicism with African beliefs.

In the early days of slavery in the Caribbean, the displaced Africans tended to use Christian saints as surrogates for the African gods who were the true objects of their devotion. Over the years various kinds of amalgamations occurred throughout the region. The close association of Ogoun with Saint Michael and of Eshu with Satan, for example, is found both in Trinidadian Shango[88] and in some of the other African-derived syncretic sects. Eshu in particular is quite at home in *Divina Trace*. His connection with Satan probably derives from his reputation as a mischief-maker and lord of misrule. "The early missionaries and their converts," Philip Allison points out, "regarded Eshu as the Devil, but he should be more properly regarded as the spirit of chance and uncertainty."[89] He is "messenger of the gods, go-between for gods and mankind, ruler of communications and the marketplace, source of fortune and misfortune. Youngest of the gods, sometimes called the Great Trickster."[90] Henry Louis Gates agrees, finding that Eshu's characteristics include (among others) "parody, irony, magic, indeterminacy, open-endedness, ambiguity, sexuality, chance, uncertainty, disruption and reconciliation". Gates also argues persuasively that Eshu "is the Yoruba figure of the meta-level of formal language use, of the ontological and epistemological status of figurative language and its interpretation". He is, as well, "the guardian of the crossroads, master of style and of stylus, the phallic god of generation and fertility, master of that elusive, mystical barrier that separates the divine world from the profane".[91] Gates's characterization of Eshu and his many roles gives this playful African god as rightful a claim as any in the Christian or Hindu pantheons to be called the presiding deity of *Divina Trace*.

Evelina's version of the story is rather different from either Mother Superior Maurina's or Magdalena's. Instead of seeing Barto as a hero – Christian angel/lover or avatar of a Hindu god – Evelina portrays him as another kind of incarnation: a man possessed by the devil. The frogchild,[92] she tells Johnny, is "beget by dis wajank-diab who is Satan self, who . . . beget dis diab-crapochild and bring down he curse pon you, pon all Domingos, pon dis whole island of Corpus Christi, pon all de earth".[93] Evelina swears that Manuelito, who is indistinguishable from Eshu in her mind,[94] still lives beneath the ground in Domingo Cemetery, but that he cannot come out "to reap combruction"[95] if Johnny will come to the graveyard each year on the night of the crapochild's birthday (April 16, the same as Johnny's) and work the obeah spell that she teaches him. A good part of Johnny's fear in this scene derives from his conviction that he has already, three years earlier, dug up the frogchild and loosed him on the world – an event Evelina knows nothing about.

Evelina certainly comes naturally by her interpretation of the story, and her hostility towards Barto Domingo. She is, it seems, the illegitimate daughter of Barto, who was at least indirectly responsible for her mother's suicide. Evelina found her mother's body in a canefield, "and me", she says grimly, "could only always hate he fa dat".[96] Johnny also appears to learn from Evelina that her African grandmother Aiyaba was actually owned by Barto.[97] Not long after these revelations in the dream order of Antoni's narrative, Johnny Domingo remembers, or dreams, that he has killed his grandfather Barto – rapist, slaveholder and patriarch. The "confufflation" of religious, psychological and political implications involved in the ritual murder (whether real or imagined) of this man – a source of near-mythic authority and object of both fear and adoration – can scarcely be exaggerated.

The political power of the Magdalena myth as a whole grows directly out of its syncretic origins. Like the Cuban Virgin of la Caridad and the Mexican Virgin of Guadalupe, she is associated with both Christian and non-Christian belief systems. Because the cult of Magdalena in its very genesis partakes of the "density of codes"[98] that Benítez-Rojo astutely identifies as intrinsic to the Caribbean, it is able to speak to the culture in a language it already intuitively understands. The changing of the name St Mary to St Maggy, Mother Maurina's unsuccessful attempt to have Magdalena officially canonized and Magdalena's subsequent de facto canonization by the peoples of Corpus Christi – all are part of the process by which the culture produces the myth that will redefine and ultimately liberate it.[99] When the myth takes hold in *Divina Trace* (or, in Papee Vince's account, when Mother Maurina, as storyteller, brings Magdalena's story "to life"), the island is "miraculously transformed". It is "a single moment in history, a *rebirth,* not simply fa Mother Maurina's Magdalena in the black madonna, but fa Corpus Christi sheself".[100] The island, in effect, becomes Magdalena Divina's child.[101] And even though Corpus Christi continues to contend with the social ills resulting from "half a millennium of Colonial and Church subjugation", the people manage "to come back to life every year fa one day".[102] It is not irrelevant that the saint honoured on that day is a woman. Restitution of the mother figure to her rightful place of honour is the act that, at least for Corpus Christi, takes some of the sting out of those centuries of colonial/

ecclesiastical/patriarchal domination and perhaps restores to the culture a trace of its spiritual and psychic balance as well.

The nature of the holiday itself is significant, and it should be noted that virtually every major episode in *Divina Trace* takes place on, just before or just after it. The Magdalena/Corpus Christi fête is the novel's version of Carnival, complete with parades, steel bands and "playing mas".[103] In Trinidad, Carnival's ritual enactment of alternative reality has a powerful transformational effect on the whole society, as it clearly also does on that of Antoni's fictional island.[104] But Antoni is careful to make his carnival truly transformative only insofar as it transcends the officially sponsored Christian holiday and assumes, in Bakhtin's words, the attributes "of becoming, change, and renewal".[105] In his analysis of medieval European carnival, Bakhtin distinguishes between "the official feasts" of the period, which "sanctioned the existing pattern of things and reinforced it", and legitimate folk carnival, which "celebrated temporary liberation from the prevailing truth and from the established order".[106] This is the carnival that Corpus Christi Day becomes when it is infused with and regenerated by the power of the people's own myth. For Antoni, this is the carnival that lies at the very heart of creolization throughout the Caribbean: an open-ended, spontaneous and improvisational exaltation of the power of imagination to refashion reality.

As Papee Vince correctly insists, Magdalena's "most salient feature" is "she universality, the all-embracing all-comprehending expansiveness of she great love".[107] Her mysterious origins and ambiguous ethnicity only reinforce that universality; she is whatever her votaries need her to be. The Magdalena cult is specific to Corpus Christi, but its quality of "all-comprehending expansiveness" relates it to the essence of the Caribbean. Benítez-Rojo makes much the same point in his discussion of the Cuban devotion to the Virgen de la Caridad del Cobre. The Virgen, whose origins are as syncretic as Magdalena's, can be read as particularly or exclusively Cuban, but the cult can also be read "as a meta-archipelagic text, a meeting or confluence of marine flowings that connects the Niger with the Mississippi, the China Sea with the Orinoco, the Parthenon with a fried food stand in an alley in Paramaribo".[108] Johnny Domingo's journeys – to the swamp, into himself, into his past, to the world beyond the Caribbean and back again – are part of that dynamic, part of that confluence. But above all, it is his telling and retelling of the *story* that places him within the ceaseless meta-archipelagic ebb and flow of Caribbean culture. Evelina bestows the project on him almost as a sacred duty, making the boy who bore the bottle containing the frogchild now the bearer of both history and myth: "And if dere is anybody could explain all dis confusion to dose yankees, dat dey understand who we is and where we come from dat we can scarce even understand weself, it could only be you."[109]

THE IMAGINING EYE

Or could it only be "I"? The swampy matrix of storytelling in *Divina Trace* is human consciousness itself, and Johnny Domingo's journey into the mangroves and mud of his family's past carries him just as deeply into the thickets of his own mind. It is a passage that has cultural and political implications because the innermost being he confronts is creolized at its very core. This is a different kind of first-person narrative than familiar ones such as *David Copperfield* or *The Sun Also Rises*. Rather than an "I" that is integral and individuated, Antoni creates a compound "I", one that is innately plural and joined, in some primal way, to the minds and lives – the stories – of others. The passage in which Johnny grasps this is worth quoting at length:

> As though the story were forming itself now not out of the dregs of human time and memory, but out of the incense-filled air itself. The ancient, decrepit, candle-flickering air of that chapel breathed and

> rebreathing now not only by this ancient nun, by this boy of eighteen; not only by Magdalena and Barto himself, but by all of us sitting here together listening, interrupting each other occasionally sometimes two and three of us speaking together at the same time.[110]

There is no clear boundary anywhere in the text between Johnny's "own" thoughts and those of the voices he remembers. His understanding, on the day of Evelina's funeral, that his life story and Magdalena's are connected through a "mystery"[111] that he does not understand is an early step on his long trek through the inner landscape encoded in the novel's multiple-first-person point of view.

Johnny's exploration of the mystery of his identity becomes the unending dream/story of his life and is, of course, inseparable from the text of *Divina Trace.* Two years after Evelina's death, unable to decide whether Mother Maurina or her account of Magdalena is real, Johnny reaches out to touch Maurina's headdress and conceives that act as touching his "own imagination", which he calls the "farthest extremity of my deepest, most sacred self".[112] Only a few pages later, just before the beginning of Magdalena's poem, he elaborates on the nature of that deepest self. Recalling the night when he opened the bottle and watched the crapochild swim into the dark waters of Maraval Swamp, Johnny reflects,

> My aloneness had been suddenly violated, split in two by that swimming frogchild, as though in that frogchild I had suddenly seen myself, my other self, the constant companion of my ongoing silent conversation, my twin brother. I had seen the other I. Not the imagined I but the I of my imagination: the imagining I. The third eye in the middle of my forehead through which I saw myself – the Hindu tilak in the centre of my consciousness with which I heard myself, my essential self, God within. . . .[113]

The third eye is a recurring motif in *Divina Trace,* its manifestations ranging from the sober to the burlesque. Revisiting and refashioning

Mother Maurina's account of the frogchild's birth, Johnny envisions himself at eighteen and at ninety, "two of us watching together now through the same single cyclopseye".[114] Other variations include Dr Domingo's forehead mirror,[115] miners' hardhats with lights in the centre[116] and, most hilariously, a glass eyeball lodged in a man's anus. But the novel's most solemn manifestation of the third eye occurs when Johnny recalls Magdalena herself reaching into the swamp and bestowing a "mudspot-tilak" on his forehead – "a trace of its memory lingering in the fingerprint of mud" and making him aware that he is "being manipulated by some extraneous power manipulating [him] also from within".[117]

Johnny externalizes his imagining I as the frogchild Manuelito because it is such a monstrosity – a part of himself so unsuspected, so alien, so mysterious that it seems not even to belong to him. But it does belong to him, and Johnny instinctively understands that he must face it again: "Now . . . I know the only way to find that frogchild still hiding somewhere alive in the labyrinth of those innumerable mangrove banyans, is . . . to surrender myself up to this monkey of my imagination and let him speak, even in his own impenetrable monkey-language – to turn around and go back to the beginning once more."[118] The implicit association here of the monkey imagination with the frogchild/"imagining I" is reinforced many times in the text. Very early in the novel, as Johnny is carrying the bottle with the frogchild in it down Divina Trace to the swamp, a child looks at it and says, "See that, Daddy? Look the frog that boy hold up inside he glassbottle. He big as a monkey!"[119] Later signals include Johnny's reference to "this monkey of my imagination",[120] the repetition of the word "frogmonkey"[121] in Hanuman's tale of the monkey tribes, and the passage in Magdalena's poem when Valmiki and the monkey god Hanuman gaze "on each other as if in a lookglass".[122] In the second half of the poem, when Hanuman (who has previously served only as a scribe) is charged with completing it, he ponders its characters and realizes how to proceed:

"Only when Hanuman inform dem each, / With he mirror-form simple enough / . . . Did Hanuman begin to dress he story in Valmiki shacksloka."[123] That is to say, Hanuman can compose the rest of the epic himself only by reaching into his own monkey imagination, "informing" the story with it.[124] There is the suggestion here too that each story as read and interpreted is a new story told. Finally, Evelina's identification of the frogchild with Eshu, the lord of uncertainties, strongly hints that the meaning structures projected by the imagining I should always be taken as suspensive and contingent – not absolute.

Hanuman's "mirror-form" is only one of many in *Divina Trace,* all of them closely bound up with the questions of identity and consciousness that haunt Johnny Domingo. Quite early in the novel Papee Vince suggests that the crapochild is "the reflection of the viewer",[125] and Johnny's own strangely intuited kinship with it emerges most powerfully in the image of himself in the bottle that had contained Manuelito, "reflected on the silvergreen surface: squashed and mirror-ripple distorted, twisted on my back appearing now to float inside of the bottle myself".[126] The experience leads Johnny to a revelation: "[T]o question *Him,* now, at thirteen years of age, was to question my own existence. Because if *He* did not exist, then I did not exist either."[127] If any physical object can be construed as the centre of *Divina Trace,* it is this glass bottle. Magdalena's womb was the receptacle for the child, but the bottle – a shimmering, humanly conceived and fashioned work – is the only appropriate receptacle for the myth that is both a product of the imagining I and something inexplicably beyond it. In this sense the bottle in the book actually *is* the book. And like the glass artifact, the book's properties include the ability to contain and to reflect (through an aluminum mirror page in the middle) so that the reader sees himself in it, confronting the inexhaustible reflections of his own imagining I, just as Johnny does when he gazes at the bottle. The reader is contained by the bottle/book even as Johnny sees himself imprisoned within his own story. Speaking of

Papee Vince's recollected narrative, he says, "*this oldman have you hold-up on this cobo roost like that same frogbaby hold-up inside he glassbottle, with you toting youself now in this baddream to this place you don't want to go*".[128]

When Johnny faces the "farthest extremity" of his "deepest, most sacred self",[129] he moves into territory much stranger than the ancient legends lying behind the *Ramayana*. He calls it "a source deeper than my conscious mind, deeper than reasoning".[130] Antoni attempts, through Hanuman's tale of the monkey tribes, a direct literary representation of that wellspring of consciousness. It is possible to go through this section and string together enough phrases to form a reasonably intelligible account of the *Ramayana*'s Hanuman subplot. But those phrases are insistently interwoven with a dizzying welter of words and other signs relating in manifold ways to *Divina Trace* and the monkey imagination that informs its own characters (indeed, a version of the novel's plot is also contained in these thirteen pages). The various threads of this section (the Hanuman story itself, the plot of *Divina Trace*, references to the Caribbean and so forth) wrap around each other in such a way as to prevent the reader from apprehending the text in a linear way; indeed, the elements here assault the mind's ear in a manner that suggests the spontaneous sounds of the tropical rainforest. Many phases of Hanuman's story include subtexts relating to primatology or the history of evolutionary theory: "But Sugriva he vervet-vex, purplehowler you gibbon: 'Hanuman, you nasalis but a piltdownhoax! Tink is you dawson dis yana, stead of Valmiki? Is Rama wilberforse darwin! Is he to smash Bali! Tell me, Huxley, isntit you mummy a monkey? Mash you Bigfoot Mr Kingkong, yankeemoviestar-chimpanzee, watch, you ga chacma one cuttail with Bali!' "[131]

There are also more personal references. George Plimpton first published this part of the novel in *Paris Review* and was rewarded with a simian citation: "Allday at you writing desk, lefthandinyoupants, who ga publish dis monksense? garillaorgy! *Francoisi Review*?"[132] In this part of the novel Antoni squanders few (if any) opportunities to loop the monkey-tale pre-text into the large, intricate web of *Divina Trace*. For instance, the sequence "fireback a quick chalicewine, proboscis-blood mmmmm sapajou!" not only hearkens back to Dr Domingo's "firing back" several slugs of rum as he attempts to deliver Magdalena's frogchild but also suggests – through "chalicewine" and "sapajou" – the connection between the sapajou (or capuchin monkey, a New World species) and the Capuchin monks who brought the statue of La Divina Pastora to Trinidad from Spain. Some allusions are ostentatious, such as the design that, when reflected in a mirror, spells *alpha* and *rho* (as in Antoni + Robert)[133] along with a fish (suggesting Christianity) displaying a huge circle (suggesting the single "cyclopseye" of the imagination). But others are more arcane: a bar of music from an old calypso[134] that contained the phrase "When de baby born, half is mine", or a reference to "john gris"[135] – Juan Gris, who attached a fragment from a mirror to one of his paintings. Like many such "obscure" references, this last one is more than a clever joke. The use of collage by Gris and his contemporaries – and especially his placement of objects (not just paint) on a canvas – raised questions about the relationship between the work of art and the "real" world, questions that Antoni continues to ask nearly a century later, through the medium of a mirror placed within the printed text of a book

Possibly the passage that most directly links Hanuman's tale to the subterranean currents of *Divina Trace* occurs near the end, in a segment corresponding to the novel's account of the miraculous statue: "Monument it proboscis, lemurlike, poststructural. Monument it of feminist francosimarbre. Monument it of Luce, Kristeva, Cixous – Beauvoir as me potto black mummy!"[136] Antoni explicitly associates Julia Kristeva in particular with the stature of the Magdalena Domingo/Divina – the mother/matrix so close to the heart of the novel's myth and its ability to generate myth. While Hanuman's tale of the monkey tribes is saturated with signification, its meanings are not accessible to the usual strategies of reading and interpretation because it is a verbal facsimile of the disorganized preverbal flux that Kristeva calls the semiotic. At the very centre of Hanuman's speech is the previously mentioned mirror page: a startling objectification of the non-verbal core of consciousness and a means by which the reader must literally "inform" the story with his own "mirror-form".[137] The symbolic is, to simplify Kristeva's explanation rather coarsely, the regulation of the semiotic into the logic and order of discursive language and rational thought.[138] According to Kristeva, "the two modalities are inseparable within the signifying process that constitutes language, and the dialectic between them determines the types of discourse . . . involved";[139] but it is perhaps not too naive to view the semiotic, being necessarily preverbal, as a kind of matrix (from *mater*, mother) out of which the symbolic arises through struggle, and upon which it depends for its nourishment. The myth of *Divina Trace* fulfils itself in endless ways.

The cognitive acts produced by Kristeva's dialectic can be seen as storytelling at its most elemental: the means by which we define ourselves both as perceiving subjects and as objects within a wider reality that includes us but which we can know only through our perception of it. The entire vast concentric edifice of Antoni's novel is an elaborate attempt, or series of attempts, to extract a trace of definition from the formless semiotic swamp. By retracing in his mind stories he has heard or imagined about the island's history, Johnny Domingo constructs a composite cultural identity of which he is a part and which he in turn internalizes. The storytelling is collective because the Caribbean reality that those stories ceaselessly yearn to define is itself collective, a "multiple series of relationships",[140] and the telling must be speculative because the story of the past, like all other stories, can be fashioned only by the imagination. If the recuperation of a disputed past by multiple and mutually contradictory voices lacks the solidity of historical discourse proceeding from received authority, it also lacks official history's distortions. As Glissant explains, history as a linear, hierarchical formulation "is a highly functional fantasy of the West, originating at precisely the time when it alone 'made' the history of the World". To perpetuate the fantasy, "the collective memory was too often wiped out", and the Caribbean writer must "dig deep"[141] to retrieve fragments of it. The goal of this collective, tentative and distinctly non-authoritarian evocation of a scattered past is nothing less than the construction of a Caribbean consciousness, and the conception of history-as-story underlying the enterprise is not simply the restrictive, "othering" discourse of the West but a magically transformed one – fluid, changing and potentially liberating.[142]

"A magical notion of reality," Glissant points out, "is based on beliefs hidden deep in the collective past."[143] In *Divina Trace* Antoni's reading of human experience encompasses far more than the empirical; a vast reality of possibilities emerges from the recreation of the past by the imagining I – a reality incalculably enriched by ubiquitous encounters between the natural and the supernatural. It is worth recalling that in the *Ramayana* the god Shiva blesses Hanuman with the ability to transform himself into any shape, and also to become invisible. Antoni's mirror page in the middle of Hanuman's narration is the locus of both transactions. The mirror, empty of Hanuman's words and thus devoid of any verbal sign of his identity, reveals plainly the invisibility that precedes transformation: the no-thing out of which a new something can be generated. Cognition itself is the most elemental form of storytelling; in Antoni's ontology the world is born over and over again through the coitus of anticipation and memory, both acts of narration. Until looked into, the mirror page is blank, but when "read", it marks the transformation of Hanuman into the reader. The nexus of Shiva, Hanuman and this act of metamorphosis is a variation on the most significant sub-current of *Divina Trace*: the suggestion of a kind of consubstantiality between what we call the divine and the acts of "magic" performed by the imagination. The antiquity of humankind's insight into that link is encoded in the etymological relationship between the words *magic* and *make,* both having their root in the most primal act of transformation – the creation of the visible out of the invisible, something out of nothing.

The Christian doctrine of the Incarnation is perhaps the novel's most obvious manifestation of this idea, if only because it is implicit in every reference to the island's name. Corpus Christi is the feast that celebrates the Eucharist, in which the humanity of the participants becomes consubstantial with the divine nature of Christ. In a bizarre parody of the Eucharist, Granny Myna boils the frogchild in a callaloo (or so Johnny remembers her telling him) and serves it to her family for Christmas dinner. His name, Manuelito, is a diminutive form of Immanuel ("God is with us") – the name of the Messiah as prophesied by Isaiah.[144] But all sorts of gods, angels, diabs and demons (not just Christian ones) parade through the carnival of *Divina Trace,* and many of them are equally at home in heaven and on earth. Eshu, the trickster deity so feared by Evelina, is also the Yoruba messenger god, the guardian of crossroads and boundaries and the mediator between this life and the next. He crosses those boundaries at will. Rama and Sita, in Antoni's version of the *Ramayana,* are human incarnations of the gods Shiva and Kali. The very idea of incarnation (or the conjunction of this world with a dimension beyond it), so closely bound up with the novel's central myth of Magdalena and its effect on Corpus Christi, becomes a metaphor for all the ways in which the magic latent in imagination can transfigure human experience, bestowing on its meagre traces a kind of divinity.

The little statue of the black madonna with which Magdalena has been linked is believed to be the incarnation of several different goddess figures, including the Virgin Mary, but it is the coalescence of all these avatars into Magdalena Divina, a patron saint for all the people of Corpus Christi, that marks her story as a new myth belonging to a new creole culture. Papee Vince explains the process with reference to the relationship between Magdalena Domingo and the statue:

> Magdalena did not precede, or anticipate, or in any way inspire the creation of this black madonna. She did not give birth to this statue: the statue, or more precisely *history*, gave birth to Magdalena. And history took she life too – long before she was dead – only so that history could give Magdalena a *second* birth, could bring her back to life in this black madonna which preceded her.[145]

Born out of history, out of the stories ordinary human beings living within history tell, myth re-enters history through a tracery of beliefs and values that form the nucleus of culture, and it works as a cohesive force within culture precisely because it is seen to embody those same beliefs and values. But more than that, the infusion of history with the ahistorical impulse of faith has a transubstantiative effect, both within individual lives and in the lives of civilizations. That is why Papee Vince is deadly serious when he says to Johnny, "You see son, it is not so much the telling of this story. It is the *believing* in it"; a story told without belief is just "windballs and airfritters".[146]

This question of faith, so odd in a story told by multiple and contradictory voices, yet so palpably *imminent* in *Divina Trace*, has been addressed in an interesting way by Dean Karpowicz as part of "a paradox at the centre of the novel . . . that undercuts the all too common suppositions made about current postmodern texts: that the meaning is there is no meaning". Or to put it a different way, "The intention of the postmodern critic . . . appears to be an unraveling of narrative threads by revealing their own contradictions in binary opposites with a view toward a proof of the inability of narrative to represent an accurate reality." Karpowicz cites several such "contradictions" within *Divina Trace*, focusing particularly on the "two narratives" of Granny Myna. In the first, angry and vindictive, she asks Johnny to dig up the crapochild and throw it in the swamp, while in the second, penitent and forgiving, she asks him to go to the swamp to give her gold rosary to Magdalena.[147] Karpowicz convincingly argues that such conflicting versions, while seeming to resist in a typically postmodern way any determinate truth, actually "encourage the reader" to make the leap of faith advocated by Papee Vince. This is a Kierkegaardian leap "arrived at through a postmodern critical reading of the text, a reading that intends to nullify meaning within any system of representation and reveal that system's disunity". Karpowicz goes on to point out that in Kierkegaard, "the movement of faith must continually be made by virtue of the absurd" and ends in "union with the infinite or God".[148] Ultimately, then, the mirror page in the centre of *Divina Trace* embodies an inarticulable (because unknowable) mystery. It is not a message of non-meaning but a luminescent ideogram of meaning suspended somewhere beyond the frontiers of the word, remote and inaccessible.

Divina Trace re-enacts the process by which stories told collectively, as folktales, can gather into the contours of a myth, but it also probes, through the meta-narrator's relentless journey into his own psyche, the unfathomable source of storytelling – and belief – in the individual creative mind. A form of incarnation, or at least a variation on the concept, comes into play here too. Johnny Domingo looks down through the corridors of his memory at the living frogchild and sees a version of himself. Resorting to the lexicon available to him, he calls it, as we have seen, "the imagining I . . . my essential self, God within".[149] Johnny's characterization of his imagination as God (in addition to the Kierkegaardian association implied by Karpowicz) parallels other links between consciousness and divinity that can be found within the measureless mythologies of *Divina Trace*. Eshu – a god closely connected with language and interpretation (as well as with misinterpretation) – is frequently depicted holding, if not a glass bottle, a calabash that contains "the very *ase* with which Olodumare, the supreme deity of the Yoruba, created the universe". Gates translates *ase* as *logos*, in the sense of "understanding", or "the audible, and later the visible, sign of reason".[150] And in Magdalena's version of the

Ramayana, the very composition of the poem results from the conjunction of consciousness and divine intervention. Valmiki first hears the tale of Rama in a dream while dozing beneath a "sacred samaan tree"[151] but he is unable to cast it into poetry until the goddess Kali[152] gives him the ability to do so, suggesting that the raw matter of story can be articulated as art only through a catalyst believed to be extrinsic to the normal circuits of the human mind.

The branches of Valmiki's samaan tree spread over much of *Divina Trace.* The samaan, or rain tree, is native to the Caribbean basin and in Amerindian lore has long been linked with fertility, possibly because its leaves fold closed at night, allowing rain to fall (and therefore vegetation to grow) beneath it. For many in Latin America and the Caribbean, the tree evokes political freedom and rebirth as well because of its association with the liberator Simón Bolívar.[153] In Antoni's novel the samaan witnesses all forms of creativity – biological, religious and political as well as artistic. According to Evelina, Barto impregnated Magdalena under the samaan tree beside Maraval Swamp, thus hastening the birth of a myth that would galvanize Corpus Christi culturally and politically. And near the end, after he has spent the whole night remembering, Johnny Domingo goes for a walk, falls asleep beneath that tree and dreams the words that begin *Divina Trace*: "*The bottle was big and obzockee. I was having a hard time toting it.*"[154] Both the crapochild of myth and the crapostory that embodies/embottles the myth are engendered, appropriately, under the same tree on the edge of the same swamp. But the mysterious communion of consciousness, creativity and faith that Johnny finds in his own inner swamp is finally something that can be approached only through the obliquities of metaphor; all he can do is circle around this enigma, continuing to tell and retell the story that reveals itself to him as an endless orchestration of voices, filling "this empty glassbottle" again and again "with nothing less than reality itself".[155]

3

BLESSED IS THE FRUIT

A Feast of Becoming

An' it use' to have this Corpus Christi thing an' my grandmother use' to take me. An' I see all these little angels standing like sculpture, and they got white dresses. White, White everywhere! An' they got wings like they was birds. An' the faces like they all paint white. Or perhaps it is White girls: all the convent girls were White.
– Mother Earth[1]

Art gives life to what history killed.
– Carlos Fuentes[2]

WHEN THE BOOK READ

Granny Myna's gift of the rosary to Magdalena in *Divina Trace* leads directly into *Blessed Is the Fruit* – not so much because the second novel is arranged like the chaplets on a rosary but because it is animated by that kind of spiritual generosity. *Blessed Is the Fruit* does not venture as far into the territory of metaphysics as does *Divina Trace*, but it is nevertheless a signal achievement in the ongoing development of a literature that expresses the estuarial nature of Caribbean culture. "The ordinary thing," Benítez-Rojo explains, "the almost arithmetical constant in the Caribbean is never a matter of *subtracting*, but always of *adding*, for the Caribbean discourse carries . . . a myth or desire for social, cultural and psychic integration to compensate for the fragmentation and provisionality of the collective Being."[3] For Édouard Glissant the fulfilment of that desire is an evolving Caribbean identity in which the fundamental transaction is indeed not reductive or delimiting, but additive, "a *métissage* without limits".[4] In *Blessed Is the Fruit* fragmentation itself is the necessary starting point for the gradual mingling of the novel's twin streams of narrative: a delicate confluence of two cultures, two histories and, above all, two lives.

No less than in *Divina Trace*, the novel's form imposes itself at once on the reader's attention. The book is divided in two, with a sheet of transparent plastic – a "window" – in the exact centre. The first half of the novel is largely the narrative of Lilla Grandsol Woodward, the survivor of a once prosperous creole family on the Caribbean island of Corpus Christi. The other half is narrated by her black servant, Vel Bootman. Both narratives are spun out in the course of a single night in 1958 as the two women lie in bed together in the Grandsols' decaying family house, d'Esperance Estate – often called "Despair Estate" since the collapse of the sugar economy. Vel is pregnant with a child she has tried to abort, and whom both women in their recollections address as "Bolom", a Trinidad folk figure.[5] In the middle of the novel, on either side of the window page, each dreams her story again, recapitulating (in the case of Lil) and anticipating (in the case of Vel) the main plot. The dream stories are arranged on the page in couplets, with one line Lil's and the next Vel's, so that it is difficult for the eye to follow either story separately without noticing and absorbing part of the other. The combined dreams of Lil and Vel are also the dream of the fetus, Bolom, establishing a kind of cognitive link with the two women who will be its parents.

As if this were not structure enough, a glance at the table of contents reveals that the novel is divided into three "chaplets" of five "decades" each, with each decade further divided into ten subsections – the form of the Catholic rosary.[6] Antoni has told me that one of the inspirations for *Blessed Is the Fruit* was his maternal grandmother, Lilla Scott-Johnson Gonsalves, who used to say her rosary at night in bed until it dropped from her hand when she fell asleep. The design of *Blessed* thus completes a circle begun at the end of *Divina Trace*, when Granny Myna (based on Robert Antoni's paternal grandmother) asks Johnny Domingo to give her rosary to Magdalena. Through at least one lens of the imagining "I", *Blessed Is the Fruit* can be seen as that rosary.

These complicated structural arrangements are more dynamic and fluid than they might at first appear, because the novel's compartmentalization exists in a constant state of rebellion against itself. The two stories, so carefully apportioned into chaplets and so pointedly separated by the window page, keep finding ways to come together, until the narrative taken as a whole almost (to borrow Certeau's useful phrase) "becomes the saying of the other".[7] As the perspectives of Lil and Vel are woven together in the text, the estuarial mingling that takes place is adumbrated by the transformational motif of mas, or disguise, and encoded in the novel's central trope of childbirth. This *métissage* involves nothing less than the gradual necessary relinquishment of a definitive, locked-up concept of identity (both personal and cultural) in favour of one that is composite, borderless, fluid and ultimately unfinished. In the world of *Blessed Is the Fruit*, neither the human person nor culture nor even reality can be isolated, particularized, fixed – and the very form of the novel enacts a range of themes that prioritizes process over product, making the text itself, like Bakhtin's characterization of the quintessential mas – Carnival – a "feast of becoming, change, and renewal".[8] And Bolom, the yet unborn child to whom both women address their stories and in whose dream their own dreams and stories merge, embodies the creative potential that such a feast can unleash, as Caribbean society, no less than the house of Grandsol, is liberated from the oppressive and confining legacies of colonialism.

One of the most startling effects of *Blessed Is the Fruit* is the clarity with which the narrative structure displays each woman's story as a separate, distinct version of Caribbean experience while at the same time offering up a model for a new Caribbean reality that is an integrative or syncretic process. Lil Grandsol's life, prior to her meeting Vel Bootman, is a study in alienation, even from members of her own family and social class. As she lies in bed with Vel after Vel's bloody but unsuccessful attempt to abort her child, Lil's account begins with an effort to understand and put into focus that nearly tragic event. She reflects first on the immediate situation – two women in their early thirties living alone and virtually penniless in a crumbling plantation house – and those reflections lead her back, in the book's first two sections, through the past ten years. That period begins in 1948, when two disasters strike: Lil's husband, Keith "Daisy" Woodward, realizing both that he is gay and that his work on the island has been a failure, sails off to England with fellow cricketer Reginald DeBassier; and her trusted servant Di, finding herself pregnant late in life, leaves d'Esperance to settle among her own family on the other side of the island. Vel, hired to replace her cousin Di, in the course of time becomes Lil's closest companion – a replacement not only for Daisy but also for Lil's childhood friend, Di's daughter Dulcianne.

Among the events Lil recalls most vividly from the past decade are her mailing to Daisy, five years after his departure, a golden key to the house that she had made for him just before he left but had never given him. The key comes back, its envelope unopened, five weeks later. She also remembers a strange visit from a tall, homely woman claiming to be Vel's grandmother but who turns out to be her abusive former husband, Berry, dressed in drag. Berry's masquerade prefigures and counterpoints others in the novel, including the "high mas" of Daisy's struggle to be heterosexual. Berry, moreover, has also left his wife for someone else. These incidents begin a long process of interweaving threads from each woman's life story. Antoni's narrative strategy is subtle, leaving in the reader's mind an impression of two lives radically different but also alike in fundamental ways, stitched together by such common human experiences as betrayal and loss.

The rest of Lil's conscious memories, contained in the chaplet titled "d'Esperance Estate", drift chronologically from her childhood to Daisy's departure less than three years after their marriage. These recollections, particularly the earlier ones, form a pattern of references to race, religion and sex – matters that traditionally have tended to differentiate and divide people from one another. The full meaning of the pattern, as it evolves and unfolds in Lil's mind, reveals itself only gradually, but the essential significations can be detected from the beginning. During her girlhood, for example, Lil is kept for most of each day in a small, dark half-basement room, a torment she finds difficult to comprehend until she overhears a conversation between two of the servants. "Eh-eh", Cook says to Di, "but you see how the blight does always fall pon the fourth generation? Blat-blanch, eh? White *koo-ca-roach!* Ain't no wonder madam wouldn't let she in the sun."[9] The "blight" Cook refers to is the trace of African blood most visibly evident in Lil's "bad hair";[10] it is also from Cook that Lil learns of her French great-grandfather's marriage to his Yoruba slave. Racial categories are less rigidly defined in the Caribbean than in the United States, so a "white" landowning family such as Lil's can nevertheless have some African ancestry. But the idea of blight remains as a low-grade social stigma, and to those with a colonial cast of mind, a way of separating some people from others. For Lil the stigma is reinforced when she is sent to a Catholic girls' school in another part of

Corpus Christi, where the day students, most of whom are "pure English",[11] call her "*White cockroach*"[12] to her face.

Racial "blight" is not the only burden Lil has to bear. One Christmas Day she is sitting in church and hears the Irish Monsignor declaim, "*Every one of you who has performed a mixed marriage has committed a mortal sin!*"[62] Misunderstanding the Monsignor's words, she later asks her mother if she herself is a mortal sin because she "came out a blat-blanch", and Mrs. Grandsol slaps her twice, explaining, "It is *we* who have sinned because your father is a Protestant."[14] Lil's first awareness of racial and religious barriers is closely associated with their breach. Her French great-grandfather, her white father, her Catholic mother – all have willingly, purposely violated racial or religious taboos, and Lil's grasp of that is important to her acceptance of both "mixture" and rebellion as positive values.

The most vivid manifestation of Lil's openness to *métissage* is her friendship with Di's daughter Dulcianne, in which sexuality loops together with religion and race to form an intense emotional bond. At the age of nine, Lil realizes that whenever her right hand is "rolling beads" (her father's contemptuous phrase for saying the rosary or chaplet), her left hand is doing something else altogether. The two activities become virtually one in her imagination,[15] and before long she and Dulcianne are rolling beads together – Lil in her basement room and Dulcianne outside under the gallery, the two divided by a pane of glass. The form of the narrative as a whole springs from this tableau, with Lil's and Vel's stories separated by the window in the middle of the book, and much of the narrative power of *Blessed Is the Fruit* is generated by the text's determination to penetrate it.

Just before being packed off to the convent school, Lil stumbles onto a discovery that affects her life in several ways. She and Dulcianne have noticed for a long time "a small graveyard of rubbish"[16] under the gallery, and finally they set out to get a look at what they assume to be a lagahoo, or troll. Instead of that mythical creature they find a much more mundane two-backed beast: Lil's father and Dulcianne's mother, Di, "sleeping each night on the bed of old crocussacks".[17] Lil's father, although never much seen in the novel, is an important character behind the scenes. He runs his family into bankruptcy, eventually fleeing the island to avoid incarceration, and his philandering contributes in large part to driving his wife into alcoholism. But Grandsol's profligacy does have certain positive (though unintended) consequences. His fornication with Di, repeated years later when he secretly returns to Corpus Christi, is continued with Vel after Di's departure. Vel, afraid that she and Lil will entirely run out of money, fools the drunken Grandsol into thinking she is Di and – following Di's own example – makes him pay for her services. The unforeseen result is her pregnancy, making the fetus Bolom not only her offspring but also Lil's half-brother: a decidedly "mixed" child, incarnating both of their histories and cultures.

At the convent school Lil's education in sexuality continues, and it is here, amid a general atmosphere of repression and very specific instances of abuse at the hands of some of her classmates, that she resolves, albeit only half-consciously, to remain childless. Some of the other girls, the same ones who call her a "white cockroach", discover her "rolling beads" in the WC, and before long Lil finds herself being lectured by Mother Marie-Bernard, who warns her about the danger of giving birth to a *duen* – an unbaptized monster-child: "Continue touching-up yourself like that", she says, "and you going find youself pregnant with one of these duens! You hear? *Eh?* You going find youself haveen with a diab-*duen!*"[18] Lil survives several years at this unforgiving place and then returns home, where her mother, between bouts of heavy drinking, manages to groom her for a rather comical social debut. Within a short space of time she meets Daisy, a young cricketer and architect who becomes involved (much to his eventual regret) with a scheme to build cheap housing for the island's poor. After her mother's death and her father's flight from the island, with the bank on the verge of foreclosure, Lil marries Daisy, who buys the house and makes a number of much needed repairs to it.

Lil recalls her brief marriage to Daisy as happy, but the ambiguity of their sexual relationship suggests an element of make-believe. Their most passionate night together occurs during Carnival, when both are dressed in drag, and after that Lil never really enjoys sex with Daisy unless she combines it with "rolling beads". Emotionally unequipped to face motherhood (especially the possibility of giving birth to a "diab-duen"), she turns to Di for help after she misses her period for two straight months. When neither the quinine she takes nor Di's folk remedies seem to work, the two journey to "the small church in Suparee", an East Indian village beside the Maraval Swamp, to petition the "little madonna called La Divina Pastora".[19] Before leaving the church, Lil takes off her mother's gold chaplet with its little crucifix and slips it, as an offering perhaps, around the statue's neck. Only five days later Lil's menstruation begins again, and Di subsequently believes that she herself has become pregnant, the madonna having taken Lil's child and given it to her. After Di "miscarries", Lil chooses to believe that both their pregnancies were false – the product of overripe imaginations rather than ovaries. The whole tangled and slightly farcical episode, with its intimation of shared maternity, looks forward to the novel's primal scene: Lil and Vel lying in bed, only one of them physically pregnant but both of them expecting. When Di finally conceives a child in fact, just before Daisy leaves Lil, the stage is set for Vel's arrival.

Vel's story begins with a sharply etched childhood memory of her Granny Ansin's "big pot" that could "feed everybody" in the days when there was "plenty food".[20] Most of her recollections after that, however, are a litany of sorrows: poverty, physical abuse, back-breaking work, the deaths of four children and near starvation. The Corpus Christi that Lil Grandsol inhabits is known to Vel largely through inference, hearsay and speculation. The decline of the sugar economy affects the lives of Vel and her people just as surely as it does those of the landowning class, and even more ruthlessly. The reality and immediacy of hunger runs through Vel's recollections like a nightmare that will not go away, giving her narrative a distinctly darker tone than Lil's, despite the generous, open nature that informs it.

Adding to that darkness is the torment Vel suffers at the hands of men, particularly Berry, the man she eventually marries and with whom she has four children. One of those children dies from a scorpion bite, and another from the toxic effect of playing in the sewage that contaminates their house in the government's "Family Planning" estate – the shoddy project with which Lil's husband, Daisy, is affiliated. Vel recounts the loss of these and two other children with a directness that carries immense emotional force. Antoni puts to good use his command of the nuances of voice in this part of the novel, where Vel's linguistically rich dialect is a superbly effective instrument for the perfect pitch of her humour as well as for the many registers of her grief. After several years of relative peace at d'Esperance, she finds herself with child yet again, by old Grandsol, and recalls having heard from Di that when a servant "*find sheself pregnant she got to go, got to go home*".[21] Desperate because she has nowhere to go, she resolves on abortion as the only solution. "*Five months I trying to throw this child, Mummy!*"[22] she tells Lil after her last and bloodiest attempt. But Lil grasps immediately, and Vel comes to understand during the course of that night, that the child will not be thrown, will not die.

A number of elements in Vel's narrative are clearly meant to correspond to similar details in Lil's, forming a textual slipstitch for the interweaving of experience and consciousness most boldly realized in the dual dream at the novel's centre. Most of these parallels, paradoxically, call attention to differences between the two women's lives even as they suggest likenesses. Both women are childless when they meet, for example, but Lil's only pregnancy was a false one, while Vel has given birth four times. Similarly, Lil's beloved chicken dies and so does

Vel's pig Sue, but whereas the chicken is only a pet, Sue is Vel's "insurance"[23] against the day when there will be no more work in the cane fields. And the Family Planning estate, never more to Lil than a project that took up much of her husband's time and attention, plays a commanding role in Vel's life. It is Vel's decision to wed Berry and move into unsafe and unsanitary government housing (which accepts only married couples) that leads to her daughter Junie's death from cholera – a burden of responsibility that she finds nearly intolerable. Indeed, shortly afterward Vel goes into labour with her fourth child, and when she loses him as well, she attempts suicide. In the middle of the book Antoni juxtaposes Vel's dream version of these terrible events with Lil's dream of the panic she experienced when she thought she was pregnant:

> *fiery caterpillar crawling cross her upper lip oh I was so terrified knowing now sure*
> *tree behind the house and when I see the mid and Granny Ansin that they did bury*
>
> *that I was pregnant without a doubt even though I hadn't yet* **seen** *my menses even*
> *he too I just didn't want to be living after my four babies now* **gone** *dead and I just*
>
> *and that diablesse the mother-of-Satan herself the greatest fear in my life to*
> *go beneath the house in that shower-stall that we did had there I did take up that*
>
> *find myself pregnant again years later a grown woman suddenly a child again*
> *bottle of peroxide and I just drink it down straight all that peroxide and I out.*[24]

As the passage continues, Lil's remembered fears about having a baby flow in and out of Vel's remembered anguish at losing all four of hers, and their separate attempts at abortion are woven together also. Lil's dream (or, more accurately, Lil's part of their joint dream) occupies the first line of each couplet and Vel's the second; after the plastic window page, those positions are reversed, as if each woman has donned the identity of the other as they lie asleep, awaiting the birth of the new child that will belong to both of them.

Though most explicit (not to mention challenging) in the dream section, the integrative movement in *Blessed Is the Fruit* that I have associated with Glissant's conception of *métissage*[25] is also evident in other aspects of the novel's structure. The arrangement of narrative materials as set forth in the table of contents is a case in point. As previously noted, the book is divided into three "chaplets". The first one, "d'Esperance Estate", contains Lil's recollections of her life before Vel came to work for her; the second, "A World of Canes", contains Vel's memories of those years. But the novel does not begin with the first chaplet. Instead, it begins with Part Four (or, in rosary terms, the fourth decade) of the third chaplet, "Bolom", which contains both Lil's and Vel's accounts of their life together. The "Bolom" chaplet wraps around the rest of the novel, with Lil's two sections (parts 4 and 5) at the beginning, Vel's two (parts 1 and 2) at the end, and their joint dream account, part 3, in the centre of the book.

This circular organization of the narrative point of view – inspired by the form of the rosary – suggests not only wholeness but also the interlacing of one perspective by another, a notion that is further bolstered by the presence of two more versions of each woman's life. In the second section of Lil's portion of the "Bolom" chaplet there is a long letter from Vel summarizing her story, and in the second section of Vel's portion, near the end of the novel, there is a fragment from Lil's journal that does essentially the same thing, so that Vel's life in microcosm is contained in Lil's account, and vice versa.[26] Another, closely related way of looking at the interlocking of chaplets in the novel is in terms of time frame. The first two parts, or decades, cover events in the present day (1958) from Lil's point of view, but also that summary of Vel's past in her letter. The last two decades mainly recount the same present-day period from Vel's point of view, but with some summation of Lil's past in her journal. Bracketed within those sections of narrative are the first chaplet (covering Lil's past) and the second chaplet (covering Vel's past), and within *those* blocks of the story, at the book's core, is the decade titled "Sleep", relating in dream form both women's pasts and present. Because the presence of the past is also integral to the novel's structure and theme, these textual peculiarities deliver a strong message, not only about the personal and cultural dimensions of *métissage* but also about the interpenetration of the present by multiple pasts that must be acknowledged, not locked away. In the Caribbean consciousness, as Glissant argues persuasively, "the collective memory"[27] must restore a wholeness broken up by discrete and exclusionary versions of history.

The true Caribbean text, Benítez-Rojo maintains, depends upon and reflects such collectivity. It exhibits the features of the "supersyncretic culture from which it emerges" and appears "in its most spontaneous" manifestation as Carnival, "the great Caribbean celebration that spreads out through the most varied system of signs: music, song, dance, myth, language, food, dress, body expression", with "its flux, its diffuse sensuality, its generative force, its capacity to nourish and conserve".[28] Spontaneity, syncretism, creativity ("generative force") – all contribute to Carnival's unique role as both product and producer of Caribbean culture, continually re-enacting the centuries-long struggle to achieve liberation from colonial categories of thought and to form a new, composite cultural identity out of disparate contexts. Some of the same elements can be found in Bakhtin's broader analysis of carnival as a subversive force within European history. Bakhtin's idea of carnival, outlined in *Rabelais and His World*, is part of a dialectic between oppressive authority and irrepressible popular culture: "As opposed to the official feast, one might say that carnival celebrated temporary liberation from the prevailing truth and from the established order; it marked the suspension of all hierarchical rank, privileges, norms, and prohibitions. Carnival was the true feast of time, the feast of becoming, change, and renewal. It was hostile to all that was immortalized and completed."[29] At its root, carnival – "playing mas" – has been revolutionary, defying official discourse and undermining the very distinction between "truth" and fiction. It "belongs to the borderline between art and life. In reality, it is life itself, but shaped according to a certain pattern of play."[30] And, just as significantly, it is not just a spectacle "seen by the people" but an event in which they participate and which embraces all of them. If Carnival is construed as a recreation of reality – life shaped into a new pattern collectively and somewhat spontaneously by the people themselves, in all their clamorous diversity – it is little wonder that successive generations of authorities, from medieval European aristocrats to corporate sponsors of calypso bands in present-day Trinidad, have attempted to exert control over it.

Daisy's role as a cricketer may also, somewhat indirectly, be one of the novel's ways of playing mas. Although the game has long been associated with propriety and (British) tradition, it has become more populist in the West Indies. In a fascinating commentary on C.L.R. James's analysis of Caribbean cricket, Michael Dash points out that Carnival "can be seen as an extreme and explicit manifestation of what is implicit in cricket: the discontinuous text, the free play of signifiers, the primal nature of sensation and the transgression of boundaries".[31] If these characteristics can indeed be attributed to cricket, and if cricket in the islands is, like Carnival, "a phenomenon of the street",[32] then Daisy's ultimate transgression of boundaries – accepting his homosexuality and following his teammate Reggie to England – should be seen as an action that, while hurtful to Lil, is part of a liberating process that the novel as a whole celebrates.

The irreducible component of Carnival – disguise – figures even more prominently in *Blessed Is the Fruit* than in *Divina Trace*. Throughout the text there are numerous instances of characters costuming themselves or playing roles, and in nearly every case the deeper meaning of the mas has to do with trading places (social, racial, sexual) and, however momentarily, liberating the self by assuming part of the selfhood of another. Lil recalls an incident five years before – when she attempted to mail the gold key to Daisy in England and found herself locked out of her own bedroom – almost as an opportunity to become Vel: "Wearing Vel's clothes now, then, for five weeks. The feel, smell, the texture of Vel's clothes against my skin. Like living *inside* another's skin."[33] And letting her thoughts take her further back, she remembers playing a game with her childhood friend Dulcianne – Vel's precursor – in which mistress and servant exchanged roles. Berry's penchant for disguising himself as Vel's Granny Ansin, like the wolf in "Little Red Riding Hood", not only parodies Daisy's sexual confusion but also parallels to some degree the two major scenes in the novel in which characters don masquerades and exchange genders. These two episodes in turn parallel each other as part of the plot's elaborate skein of cross-references.

In *Divina Trace* the feast of Corpus Christi unites all of the island's religious and ethnic groups in celebration of Magdalena Divina, making the festival an expression of collective cultural identity. Carnival serves a similar function in *Blessed Is the Fruit*, though Lil reflects that in the past "whites did not take part . . . . They considered carnival something vulgar. Something for blacks and East Indians."[34] This attitude on the fictional island of Corpus Christi has its analogue in the real Trinidad. According to Peter Mason in his definitive study of Trinidad carnival, Carnival remained a "lower-class Afro-Trinidadian preserve until the last 30 years or so".[35] Lil's participation in it on this occasion is another small step towards a more plural sense of her own identity and heritage. The couple's choice of costumes (Lil as Uncle Sam, Daisy as Miss Liberty) is highly ironic considering that the *métissage* outwardly dramatized in Carnival is part of a process of cultural self-definition. This detail, as well as references throughout the novel to American military bases, indicates that Antoni is not unaware of the danger of neocolonialism, specifically in the form of American economic and cultural influence, to that process.[36] When the couple return home exhausted after the festivities, they fall asleep, wake up the next morning still dressed in their cross-gender garb, and make love more fervently than they ever have before. Lil attributes the passion only partly to the idea of embracing a person of the same sex, insisting that "it was more the idea, somehow, of making love to ourselves. Of embracing our own *self*. Our own selfsame *other* – own inverted mirror-image, separated from us by the pane of glass."[37]

The cognate incident in Vel's memory is the night of the Firemen's Ball, when she and Berry cross-dressed and, like Lil and Daisy, experienced a feeling of freedom and euphoria: "We just didn't care about nothing, cause we was so happy then. I say, 'Good thing we ain't got no neighbors living beside, cause they would say we crazy in truth. They would send we in the mental first thing!' . . . . We did living life so good then. That time."[38] In each instance the emancipatory effects of playing mas are fleeting, but the exchange of identities through masquerade constitutes a small movement in the direction of a more comprehensive *métissage* that can more fully liberate both women.

No aspect of *Blessed Is the Fruit,* however, more clearly (or more literally) embodies *métissage* than does Vel's pregnancy. The choice of 1958 for the present-day action of the novel, and thus for the birth-year of Bolom, is not accidental. In that same year Robert Antoni was born – suggesting a rather close connection, perhaps even an exact correspondence, between creature and creator – and the definitive version of Derek Walcott's *Ti-Jean and His Brothers* was first performed in Port of Spain, Trinidad. The play concerns a woman whose three sons each in turn accept a challenge from the devil, in the guise of a white planter. The challenge is conveyed by Bolom, a fetus whom the mother addresses as "Child of the Devil"[39] and who does indeed make his first appearance as part of a troop of fiends. Both of Ti-Jean's older brothers fail their tests and are killed, but Ti-Jean (following his mother's advice to rely on instinct, conscience and good sense) manages, with the assistance of the creatures of the forest, to best his foe. Bolom appears again and begs Ti-Jean to force the devil to grant him a normal birth and life in this world. If Bolom represents, as Theodore Colson contends, "aborted human potential, in a world of black mothers and white planters",[40] his birth must signal some hope for the future, even though Ti-Jean is careful to warn that the life into which Bolom is born will be filled with pain and disappointments. But it is the possibility of hope that most closely ties *Blessed Is the Fruit* with Walcott's play.

Antoni's Bolom – the living, growing, *dreaming* child – is the heart of the novel. Neither the diab-duen that Lil feared nor the aborted fetus that Vel tried to make him, he is the evolving future for both women – and a future for the Caribbean, as their dream at the middle of the novel makes plain:

because society says two women together black-white with a child of their own
cause the people say two womens together white-black with a child of they own

in the same house and happy also let us not forget this happiness also more than
in the same house and happy too that we can never forget happiness too more than

ever *before in my life I say let us dream now of our two races black and white*
ever *before in this life I say let we dream now of two peoples white and black*

together *in one child let's dream of birth shattering this invincible glass pane*
together *in one child let we dream of birth swallowing this invisible glass pane*

be-
be-

[plastic window page]

tween we forever ***you*** *Bolom melt from out we mouth in broken glassbottle of words*
tween us forever ***you*** *Bolom smash it now to hell and let us kiss one another at last*

let we wake from this old-age nightmare and live side by side happy here in this
let us awaken from this age-old nightmare and live happily together here in this

big old board-house two peoples two language two race to cleave together in one
old colonial house two people of two languages two races brought together in one

child one hope for all the world unite up here under this galvanize-tin roof the
child one hope for all the world united here under this corrugated-zinc roof the[41]

Several details in this remarkable sequence require commentary. First, the women's two dreams resemble each other more and more as they approach the window, ultimately becoming identical at their conjunction. The only identical lines they utter are the first syllable of *between,* which thus becomes a joint affirmation of the child and the world to come: "Be. Be." It is also here that the voices shift positions within each couplet (Lil/Vel switching to Vel/Lil) – the textual equivalent of exchanging identities by playing mas. As for the window that so ostentatiously divides them at their point of contact – the point where their twin sensibilities merge into Bolom's dream – that piece of plastic, unlike the famous mirror page in *Divina Trace,* is removable; the reader who takes it out can participate in the syncretic process, joining in the feast of becoming that the novel celebrates.

For Glissant, this kind of evolving cultural consciousness constitutes an "identity . . . in which the relationship with the Other shapes the self without fixing it under an oppressive force".[42] The Other can become part of the self because they intersect by choice, not through conquest. That idea is grounded in certain epistemological assumptions, since the perception of such a cultural identity cannot be divorced from a model of reality that is itself dynamic and processive rather than fixed, as Wlad Godzich explains:

> Against a notion of the truth as the instrument of a mastery being exercised by the knower over areas of the unknown as he or she brings them within the fold of the same . . . there is a form of truth that is totally alien to me, that I do not discover within myself, but that calls on me from beyond me, and it requires me to leave the realms of the known and of the same in order to settle in a land that is under its rule.[43]

This is the model of reality, and of culture, that the mechanics of

Blessed Is the Fruit dramatizes: a calling from beyond and a voluntary yielding to it, a continual recomposition of the self in a rich dialectic with the Other. Two incidents in the novel epitomize the necessity of relinquishment to the success of that project. When Lil places her mother's gold chaplet around the neck of the statue of La Divina Pastora, she is giving back to Corpus Christi – "an island ruled over as much by the Catholic Church as its own colonial government"[44] – a token of its long subjugation. And similarly, when she finally slips the gold key to her house around Vel's neck, she describes it as "letting go, after long last, letting go. The gift given. After long last".[45] It is an act that carries an even greater weight of significance than the relinquishment of the chaplet, for the key is "intertwined inextricably" with Vel's own silver crucifix and the charm given her long before by an old obeah woman – emblems of colonial ownership, the Catholic Church and the traditions of Africa linked together as one. And Vel is fully aware of the gesture's meaning: "Right here tied round my own neck pon the same length of fishingtwine with Ansin little silver cross and the shard of obeah-mirror. The golden key. *We* golden key. We life together, hers and mine and yours! *You* golden key, Bolom!"[46]

Although the circumstances of Bolom's conception hardly conform to Godzich's model (any more than do those of that primal molestation, the colonization of the New World), Bolom's real coming into being results from just such an act, as the two women invest in his consciousness their merged dreams and their lives together and thus create the child that will be. That voluntary (if subconscious) process of joint relinquishment, like the slow construction of a new, creolized culture following the initial shock of European penetration, initiates his gestation as the Caribbean child. The key *is* Bolom's, and he is the key that can unlock a future that neither Vel nor Lil has ever dared to imagine until now: a feast of becoming, change and renewal. "Happy-ever-after, like a story out the pictures!" Vel muses happily. "That's just how this story bound to end, Bolom. Like a story out the pictures. How this story bound to *begin,* cause truth is we only reach the beginning part. We go through all this commess only to reach the beginning part." The golden key, her proof that she has reached the "happy-ever-after beginning part", glitters "like a prayer for waking. For waking up inside a sweet dream." Saying "Amen! to that", she places the key in her mouth so that Bolom can taste it too, and concludes her prayer – the key between her lips impeding her speech – by affirming her impending motherhood: "Ah-mum! Ah-mum! Ah-mum!"[47] The text also ends here, but the novel's structure, embodying the dynamics of *métissage,* demands that its most consequential event, the birth of Bolom, occur outside the text, or, as the title of the last decade suggests, "When the Book Read". Only then will the "*dream of birth shattering this invincible glass pane*"[48] be actualized, allowing "*two peoples two language two race to cleave together in one / old colonial house two people of two languages two races brought together in one // child one hope for all the world*".[49]

THE HOUSE OF THE FUTURE

The Caribbean plantation, a projection of European power, depended from the start on the importation and subjugation of non-European peoples. That strategy, of which the central component was the African slave trade, optimized the degree of European dominance and, as Sidney Mintz observes, "produced a deeply divided social structure in each colony", leaving "little or no room for the growth of alternative economic activities, or for the rise of substantial middle classes".[50] Although Mintz's analysis focuses on the plantation's socio-economic dimension, his remarks – notably the phrases "little or no room" and "deeply divided" – are also relevant to the totality of space occupied by the plantation in the Caribbean consciousness. Many of the events recounted in *Blessed Is the Fruit* occur after the sugar economy (and, indeed, the whole colonial edifice) has fallen into decline. However, Vel and Lil's recollections still bear the indelible imprint of a time when the plantation seemed to crowd out all else, every other conceivable mode of being, imposing such a disposition of divisions, separations and erasures that, even long afterward, Olive Senior could write, "There was nothing left of ourselves / Nothing about us at all."[51] To a considerable extent Antoni's novel is a response to this apparent vacancy, a record of the Caribbean's subterranean history: one of resistance to the imposition of divisions and erasures, a counter-chronicle of *métissage* which might ultimately succeed the divisive "totalitarian philosophy of history"[52] dictated by colonialism.

While the structure of *Blessed Is the Fruit* enacts an integrative, estuarial process, it also participates, through the function of narration itself, in the production of postcolonial space – more specifically, in the repossession of social and psychic space formerly occupied by the plantation. That a literary text can perform this kind of transaction is hardly a revelation. In his well-known essay on Montaigne, Michel de Certeau investigates "both the text's power of composing and distributing places, its ability to be a narrative of space, and the necessity for it to define its relation to what it treats, in other words, to construct a place of its own". The capacity to compose and distribute places, "a spatializing operation which results in the determination or displacement of boundaries delimiting cultural fields",[53] is rather close to Edward Said's claims for the novel-text in particular: "The appropriation of history, the historicization of the past, the narrativization of society, all of which give the novel its force, include the accumulation and differentiation of social space."[54] *Blessed Is the Fruit* is one of the texts that enacts Said's "voyage in"[55] because Antoni's textual space (and the dynamic of *métissage* that fills it) evokes, and at the same time supplants, a social space (the plantation) that has lost its essence. And if the novel's two skeins of narrative loop closer and closer to each other in anticipation of a post-textual merger, the individual stories that the women tell – especially their characterizations of the physical and conceptual spaces in which they find themselves – make it clear that the struggle to liberate and repossess those spaces has not been an easy one.

As Said masterfully demonstrates, nineteenth-century English novels such as *Mansfield Park* have to be read "in the main as resisting or avoiding that other setting": the colonial plantation. This observation comes during a commentary on a brief reference in Austen's novel to the slave trade. Fanny has asked Sir Thomas Bertram about it, and his reply is "a dead silence". Said goes on to say that eventually "there would no longer be a dead silence when slavery was spoken of, and the subject became central to a new understanding of what Europe was",[56] but the process took a long time. For all of the nineteenth century and a good bit of the twentieth, "the metropolis" derived "its authority to a considerable extent from the devaluation as well as the exploitation of the outlying colonial possession".[57] Whether suppressed by silence or casually dismissed with phrases such as "the coral reefs and cocoanuts and all that sort of thing",[58] the unspeakable space was kept at a distance from the arena where life was thought to be truly lived.

"That other setting" was sometimes even demonized. Novels as disparate as Thackeray's *Philip*, Wilkie Collins's *Armadale* and, most famously, Charlotte Brontë's *Jane Eyre* identified the Caribbean in particular as a source of moral degradation. If in *Wide Sargasso Sea* Jean Rhys attempted to fashion not only an "answer" to *Jane Eyre* but also the beginnings of a newly imagined non-European world, Antoni's novel in a sense takes up where Rhys left off. It expands her repossession of colonial space into the twentieth century and frees it even further from European definition by foregrounding Vel's discourse more completely than Rhys did Christophine's. Indeed, after the Hail Mary that begins *Blessed Is the Fruit*, the book's first words are Vel's, quoted by

Lil. Lil's life echoes to some degree that of Antoinette in *Wide Sargasso Sea.* Her loneliness, the erosion of her family's prosperity, her preoccupation with mirrors and dreams and even the epithet "white cockroach" all suggest the parallel. But by assigning half the narrative responsibility to Vel, Antoni also gives voice to a part of Caribbean history, a vector of post-plantation space, that Rhys leaves less than filled.

Since Antoni's entire text is narrated from a bedroom of the old Grandsol estate, the logical point to begin a "reading" of colonial and post-colonial spaces in the novel is the house itself, an architectural enclosure that also functions metonymically as a figure for the noumenal structures of family and society. Gaston Bachelard's identification of the house as "a veritable principle of psychological integration"[59] linked with our deepest cravings for "well-being"[60] can be usefully extended here to the broader notion of cultural integration (and hence, security) so important to the structure of *Blessed Is the Fruit.* The Grandsol home, like other "great houses" in the West Indies, was an extension of colonial control, one of many subsidiary replications of a "Government House" that itself replicated a more distant architectural embodiment of supreme authority in Europe.[61] As twice-removed surrogates for the palace (be it Buckingham or Versailles), the great houses on small islands must have fit Bachelard's formulation admirably. For the privileged whites who inhabited them, they were the objectification of a stable, orderly, prosperous world.

But the situation in which Vel and Lil find themselves in *Blessed Is the Fruit* is more evocative of Derek Walcott's ruined great house, where "A smell of dead limes quickens in the nose / The leprosy of Empire".[62] The Grandsol family has fallen apart, its fortune has been dissipated and the house itself is in an advanced state of decay. Yet as the women lie in bed recounting their stories to themselves and to the unborn Bolom, they perform a remarkable act of recuperation. The house, Bachelard reminds us, "is one of the greatest powers of integration for the thoughts, memories and dreams of mankind",[63] but we must constantly reimagine its reality.[64] For Lil and Vel, the reimagining of their "house" necessitates a reconstruction of the locus of authority so that they themselves are, in their own minds, the true possessors of the space they inhabit. "One of the basic impulses of Caribbean thought," as Michael Dash remarks, "is undeniably the need to reconceptualize power."[65]

Even early in the novel, Antoni makes pointed references to the larger implications of architectural dilapidation, as Lil's succinct summary of her situation attests: "Three of us, here together in this old, broken-down Colonial house. In this room with the rusty tin ceiling, the moss-eaten rotting rafters. That huge maidenhair-fern leafing out bold-faced above our heads. Three of us here together in this bed: somehow that strikes me as perfectly West Indian, Bolom."[66] What is "perfectly West Indian" is not only the racial composition of the new family but the fact that it is being formed, literally, in the place of – and in place of – the "broken-down" house of colonialism. Somewhat later in Lil's narrative she recalls a letter sent to her by her mother when she was at boarding school, which included a "detailed description of the estate's financial problems, of the falling prices of sugar and cocoa and copra, of how my father had been forced to sell off another plot of land in order to stave off bankruptcy".[67] By the time Lil marries Daisy several years later, nothing much remains of the family estate but the house itself. Its physical deterioration visually reinforces the disintegration of the family and, as Mrs Grandsol's letter suggests, of the economic and political underpinnings of the entire colonial society.

In the hierarchical arrangement of power that defined the plantation, each level had its source of authority, from metropolitan government to colonial governor to head of household. In *Blessed Is the Fruit* the failures of authority figures at the family level are indicative of the rottenness of the whole system. When the "troll" or "lagahoo" that

Lil and her childhood friend Dulcianne suspect has been sleeping under the house's gallery turns out to be Mr Grandsol (copulating with Dulcianne's mother, Di, the family retainer), there is little doubt that the legitimacy of colonial order is being questioned. "*Please Dulcianne!*" Lil later tries to pray. "*Forgive me my father . . . OUR father, who will one day burn in hell!*"[68] Grandsol is indeed a troll, a monster: he squanders the family fortune, drives his wife to drink, sleeps with servants, gets children out of wedlock (including Dulcianne herself, as well as Vel's baby Bolom much later) and eventually, an exile and fugitive from justice, degenerates into what Vel scornfully calls a "bacra-johnny".[69]

As for Daisy, when he marries Lil, he saves the estate from foreclosure and he also makes an effort to repair the house, but his departure leads to an acceleration of both financial and physical collapse. Vel's husband, Berry, never fulfils the protective function of husband and father for any sustained period of time; indeed, his most striking role in the novel is as the Big Bad Wolf dressed, not very convincingly, as a kindly grandmother. When he sneaks into the Grandsol house to try to win Vel back, Lil in her delirium perceives him as "the phantom Bazil, the Jab-Jab, Satan himself";[70] that same night Vel tells him to get himself "to hell" and not ever "to soil this sacred ground again".[71] In the end, all of these patriarchal figures have to go if the women are to succeed in constructing a place where authority is not imposed from without, and by force. Lil's expulsion of Dr Curtis, who is quite prepared to kill Bolom in the womb, eliminates the last serious threat (as well as the last and most odious male authority figure) from the repossessed house. Mr Grandsol, Dr Curtis and, in their sadder ways, Berry and Daisy, are all parts of a power structure that belongs in the past.

The most important of these keepers of the house is Mr Grandsol, whose corruption baldly reveals that of the system in which he has played a key part, but who is also the catalyst for the new order embodied by Bolom, the "*hope for all the world*"[72] awaiting birth in Vel's womb. This paradox is perhaps the principal source of the Caribbean's social complexity: that the rape of Africa by Europe, a primal act of miscegenation and violence, can result in the ultimate birth of a society so mixed as to be liberated from the mind-forged manacles of colonial history. There is such an abundance of riches in Antoni's work that it is easy to pass lightly over the racial issue, but racial divisions and mixtures are an inescapable part of Caribbean life, and they lie at the very heart of *Blessed Is the Fruit*. The barriers and boundaries of plantation space, which have endured well into the vaguely defined post-plantation years, delineate much of the space of Antoni's novel as well. Underlying Lil's early awareness of her father's actions lies an intricate pattern of racial secrets and half-acknowledged truths. Whites and blacks are publicly presumed to be separate groups, and this fiction is necessary for the perpetuation of the plantation, but even families like the Grandsols – "high whites" – often have African ancestry. Lil knows from a very early age that she is, like Dulcianne, mixed. She even comments at one point, "I didn't dare say it; I was the only girl in the convent with visible negro blood",[73] but the system nevertheless ordains that she is white and Dulcianne black, and that disposition of racial categories is made concrete by the basement room in which Lil is kept out of the sun during the day. This space, so evocative of a prison or tomb, marks the boundaries of Lil's whiteness. Outside, looking in, is her black sister Dulcianne.

In *Faulkner, Mississippi*, Glissant discusses Thomas Sutpen's downfall in terms of his pursuit of "filiation", defined as "the intergenerational relationship between a father and his sons, and its continuity",[74] on which the whole plantation edifice depended. In Glissant's reading of *Absalom, Absalom!* "it is a matter of fierce obligation for Thomas Sutpen to establish a family seat, a lineage, a dynasty", but his efforts are doomed: "Not only is it true that he is not of aristocratic descent or a traditional Planter, but he has also suffered (in Haiti) the disturbing onslaught of *métissage*." Late in the novel "Sutpen convinces Henry . . .

that the family relationship between Judith and Charles Bon is nothing; but the tiny, invisible drop of African blood blots out everything else."[75] In more general terms, Glissant argues, the "real failure of filiation becomes apparent little by little when we discover that the bloodline is menaced and corrupted by black blood",[76] and that perception of corruption, of the invasion of white space by black, can lead only to a society-wide disaster. In Glissant's view the rejection of "miscegenation and Creolization" is a problem that emerges with crystal clarity in *Absalom, Absalom!*

What "offends" Faulkner is creolization: "*métissage* and miscegenation, plus their unforeseeable consequences".[77] Because the racially "inextricable" (which Faulkner accepted) is "not the same as mixture",[78] Faulkner appears to be repelled by the Caribbean. Haiti, at least in *Absalom*, is "a place where . . . the stain of miscegenation marks every corner of the Plantation".[79] And the refusal of creolization amounts to nothing less than refusal "of the Other".[80] While Faulkner's novel expertly exposes a society with these values (whether or not he personally shared them), the beatific vision of Antoni's text, adumbrated somewhat nakedly by the book's title, suggests a somewhat different artistic strategy.[81] *Blessed Is the Fruit,* even in its warp and woof, rejects not mixture but filiation. Indeed, the breach of filiation embodied by old Grandsol's illegitimate child Bolom is essential for the creation of a new post-plantation space in this insistently anti-plantation novel.

Many enclosures in *Blessed Is the Fruit* can be seen as part of the complicated evolution of post-plantation space. The water closet in which Lil hides at boarding school to "roll beads" becomes a "place of refuge"[82] from the cruelty of the other girls. Lil's unsuccessful attempt to create, out of the most unlikely structure, her own safe interior – a home – is echoed again and again throughout the novel. Vel's miserable sequence of abodes, culminating in her superficially modern "Family Planning Estate" house, forms an important part of this pattern. This project, a well-intended enterprise meant to improve on the makeshift shanties in which most of the island's poor live, can be seen in a more candid light as a government-sanctioned perpetuation of the plantation's spatial divisions. Like Di's "little mudhut"[83] on the Grandsol estate, the projects are set apart from the spaces reserved for the plantocracy. And the liberal impulse that seemed to prompt their construction was not sufficiently liberal to ensure that they were constructed soundly and safely. Nowhere in the novel is Antoni crude enough to say so, but from the point of view of an establishment still shaped by the plantation, these houses were good enough for blacks. In fairness to Daisy, he does at last recognize that they are building "ready-made tenements"[84] and that his role as principal architect for them is a joke.

Nevertheless, when Vel first moves in with her worthless husband, Berry, she briefly makes a home out of the place, even coping with daily leakage from the adjacent WC: "Bolom," she recalls, "I buy a mop, and I just get used to mopping out the floor."[85] Just as she did at her grandmother Ansin's house and at the little hut in the canes where she previously lived with Berry, she takes possession and constructs a refuge. But, as is the case with many of these enclosures in *Blessed Is the Fruit,* the refuge proves to be transitory and ineffectual. One day her daughter Junie scrapes a hole in the thin wall separating the house from the toilet next door. Despite Vel's blocking the hole with a boulder, the little girl manages to move it and get through, exposing herself to the waste. She dies of cholera shortly afterward. Admitting defeat, Vel exclaims, "We *living* in extrement! Where we *living* is extrement!"[86] Towards the end of the novel even d'Esperance Estate is labelled a WC by the taxi driver who takes Vel there: "Embassy of the WC," he calls it, "them French white-*culs*."[87] White-*culs,* white creoles, white cockroaches, world of canes: the association of waste with both Vel's and Lil's attempts to create a safe space indicates rather bluntly how futile those endeavours can be.

Vel's domestication of the cane fields is still more interesting, both because the notion of interiorizing the outdoors is so conceptually bold and because the canes in particular are the plantation's fundament and reason for being. Vel's attempt to make the canes *her* world is an assault on the system, though she does not think of it in those terms at the time. Even as a child of twelve, however, she understands that the canes can be made a place of refuge, a kind of temporary home: "I *couldn't* go at school. You pregnant you can't go at school. Don't be no schoolchildren at school pregnant. I just look for place in the canes and I just sleep."[88] When she moves into the first little house she shares with Berry, which is almost surrounded by the cane fields, he says to her, "We got the whole world of canes for we backyard",[89] and in fact she and Berry have often used the canes for a bedroom. But if this conquest of the canes strikes a note of liberation or decolonization, on another level it must be recognized how consistently such tenuously subdued spaces morph into prisons: Lil's basement room (her "own" room, but one she cannot leave), the WC at the boarding school, Vel's Family Planning house and the canes themselves. The "world of canes" is finally not so much a world Vel has made within the canes as a world imposed on her by the plantation. All of these refuges, including Lil's upstairs bedroom in the Grandsol house, are traps, because none has yet been truly repossessed. That pivotal achievement still lies in the future of these two women, who for most of their lives continue to be dominated by the plantation's lingering deployments of social and economic authority.

Structures too small to function as human shelters – miniature containers such as drawers and boxes – figure prominently in *Blessed Is the Fruit* as covert repositories of the self: spaces compact enough, presumably, to be under one's own control. Both boxes and chests, as Bachelard points out, "are very evident witnesses of the *need for secrecy*, of an intuitive sense of hiding places". There is "a homology between the geometry of the small box and the psychology of secrecy".[90] In the transitional world recollected by Vel and Lil, as we have seen, the struggle to create a safe, liberated space often ends in failure, so when the ego is so relentlessly threatened by forces that would subjugate it, the smallest of spaces where the self can secretly hide become intensely important. In Paul Bowles's *The Sheltering Sky*, for instance, the farther Kit Moresby drifts from herself, the more she is preoccupied with the contents of her handbag. Similarly, in *Blessed Is the Fruit*, Vel's description of the box in which she keeps a few cosmetics eloquently attests how important it is to her sense of identity:

> I hide them away secret in a little box. I had my little white shoebox, all my things wrap nice in tissue, that I uses to keep hid under a bush side the house. It was my secret, but even so once I get a pencil and I write my name cross the lid, tall clean capital letters, VELMA CLARINE DOWNS BOOTMAN, BASSETERRE TRACE. And that writing did make my secret more special still. I had my little white shoebox . . . .[91]

The box encloses a space that is hers – something not controlled by anyone else. Vel clings to it as she does to her sanity in those early years, but it is telling that the shoebox also contains objects closely linked to tragedies in her life and, in a larger sense, to her subjugation by the plantation system: the mirror that Junie used to scrape the deadly hole in the wall separating their Family Planning house from the WC, and the sewing scissors that Vel much later uses to try to abort her last baby, Bolom.

Drawers function for Bachelard in much the same way as boxes. "Wardrobes with their shelves," he says, "desks with their drawers, and chests with their false bottoms are veritable organs of the secret psychological life." Here is "a centre of order the protects the entire house [read 'psyche'] against uncurbed disorder".[92] In *Blessed Is the Fruit* the drawer is a small, inviolable space in which both Vel and Lil have inscribed not just their names but also accounts of their experiences. Close to the beginning of the novel, Lil, rummaging through a drawer, finds along with her diary and expired passport "Vel's large brown tattered envelope"[93] containing the letter Vel wrote ten years before asking for employment and describing some of the catastrophic events that had brought her to that point. Having only glanced at the letter when she first received it, Lil settles back into the bed beside Vel and examines it carefully for the first time. This is also the reader's first introduction to the details of Vel's many hardships. Near the end of her narrative, Vel, in a parallel scene, recalls the day when she discovered Lil's diary in that same drawer. So for Vel and Lil, Bachelard's "secret psychological life" consists fundamentally of the stories of their lives, and it is ultimately there – in their telling (and our reading) – that the liberation of plantation space will occur. As Glissant aptly puts it, referring to the plantation, "The place was closed, but the word derived from it remains open. This is one part, a limited part, of the lesson of the world."[94]

No structure in *Blessed Is the Fruit* more clearly marks the border between plantation and post-plantation space than the basement room in which Lil is kept during her early childhood. The room's purpose is to keep Lil as white as possible, and it also keeps her apart from Dulcianne. But for "nearly a year" the two of them meet at the window that separates them and masturbate – Dulcianne outside, under the gallery, and Lil inside, standing on a stack of books. "Dulcianne and I shared this secret life together", Lil recalls.[95] That picture of the half-sisters kept apart by the architecture of the great house (while still attempting valiantly to share a "life together") stands in contrast to the novel's prevailing image of Lil and Vel lying in bed in the same house, which belongs to both, awaiting the birth of a child that will belong to both, and telling their two stories that in the end will become one. Bachelard calls the cellar or basement "the dark entity of the house, the one that partakes of subterranean forces",[96] but in *Blessed Is the Fruit* this formulation has two rather contradictory implications. Certainly the room functions as the foundation of the plantation house and promotes its values, in that its purpose is to keep Lil as light as possible and to segregate her from Dulcianne. She internalizes that room and feels an "acute and profound sense of loneliness"[97] for many years as a result. But the room is also the subterranean foundation of Lil and Vel's repossessed house of later years, because it is here that Lil realizes the urgency and inevitability of her bond with Dulcianne, whose roots are much deeper than that of the colonial edifice: "In my eyes she was more beautiful than all the Creole girls in the convent. More beautiful and stronger. More alive. More *real*. Dulcianne was part of the tall cedar trees and the glittering river and the smoky, musty smell of the forest. She was connected to that life force, part of that world."[98] Not long afterward, when she has been sent to "the closed-in world of the convent"[99] – another colonially imposed prison – Lil is taken to the beach by the nuns and submerges herself in the shallow water. She looks up at her distorted reflection on the surface and sees her "twin sister" Dulcianne: "As I lay on the white sand I'd dream that I would never have to breathe again. Never again have to leave the cool world of solitude and silence beneath the water. The world of my imagination and of Dulcianne."[100] Although Lil does not realize until boarding school that Dulcianne is her "twin" and her "own distorted reflection",[101] the window of the basement room has been a double-sided mirror from the beginning, violating the plantation's boundaries by coaxing the inside out and the outside in. Lil's understanding that she and Dulcianne are somehow the same is indispensable to the novel's gestalt because it incorporates the Other (including especially the cultural Other) into her conception of the self.

From a Lacanian perspective, this insight would seem to be much healthier than construction of a fictional ego through a true mirror image. In *Blessed Is the Fruit* the reflected self really is the Other.[102] Antoni is careful not to let the reader miss the importance of this idea. When Lil and Daisy make love dressed in drag, she thinks of it as "embracing our own *self.* Our own selfsame *other* – own inverted mirror-image, separated from us by the pane of glass."[103] And when Vel arrives at the Grandsol house in 1948, Lil writes in her diary: "*Gazing into the eyes of this woman I had known for only an instant, but whom I felt sure I'd known all my life. Whom I had always believed was my own twin sister. My opposite. My own inverted mirror reflection separated from me only by the pane of glass. The pain of glass.*"[104] As Emmanuel Lévinas has explained at great length, true transcendence can be achieved only when "the *event of being,* the *esse,* the *essence,* passes over to what is other than being", and "it is because newness comes from the other that there is in newness transcendence and signification".[105] Something like this happens in *Blessed Is the Fruit.* Lil's initial recognition of Vel as her "twin" is matched by Vel's characterization of Lil's gaze as "so familiar",[106] and the result, as Lil says in her diary, is their "*unexpected, unasked-for life together*".[107]

The plastic page in the middle of the book functions, no less than the basement window of Lil's childhood, as a virtual mirror, with the text's deeply embedded pattern of parallels, echoes and interconnections making each half of it – like Dulcianne and Lil – a "distorted reflection"[108] of the other. Arranged on either side of the window page, as I have discussed earlier, are the entwined dreams of Lil and Vel, where their two narratives come closest together, forming a textual space shaped by *métissage.* At their point of conjunction – the window/mirror – the novel registers its most persuasive note of harmony and peace. "Human life", Bachelard comments, "starts with refreshing sleep. . . . The experience of the hostility of the world . . . come[s] much later."[109] When "we reach the very end of the labyrinths of sleep, when we attain to the regions of deep slumber, we may perhaps experience a type of repose that is pre-human . . . approaching the immemorial".[110] For Vel and Lil, however, the dream is more than an achieved feeling of integration, serenity or safety; it is a blueprint for their waking lives and a way of imagining a different kind of future.

What they are finally able to imagine (after ten years) is a new, shared world no longer maddened by the plantation's demarcations and estrangements. Without articulating it, they are joining in the collective Caribbean longing "for one island that heals with its harbour / and a guiltless horizon, where the almond's shadow / doesn't injure the sand".[111] Because of the house's iconic status as a centre of power in the plantation scheme, it is not inconsequential that, near the novel's chronological end, both women casually muse about its wider connections. Lying in bed with Vel, Lil sees the mildew on the ceiling as "little islands of fuzzy, bluegreen moss", and the picture is completed by Vel, who gives it a local habitation and a name: "Open my eyes slow now, very slow, and see the first light of morning breaking in through the blinds. . . . Lighting up all that multitude of miniature islands growing long the rafters. A whole Caribbean of islands, floating tranquil pon the sea of the sky, light up, coming back to life."[112]

The mossy map of the West Indies on the ceiling – "islands . . . coming back to life" – nicely coincides with Vel's determination to resuscitate the house itself, turning it into the healing island of Walcott's poem: "*Open up all the doors!* Oh, yes. Every *one*. Open up all the doors and all the windows. All together. Get some *air* to blowing through this old house. Some fresh air."[113] In her dream Lil admits that she herself "*could never understand . . . this obsession with this golden key*" or why every morning for ten years she has turned it in the lock and made her bedroom a "*self-imposed prison-sanctuary*".[114] But our primeval image of the house – be it nest, hut or even womb – is a place that should be safe without being locked. Vel realizes this: d'Esperance Estate (and, by extension, the Caribbean), so often locked in the past, is to be brought to life, opened up, liberated and transformed. And though Vel now holds the house's key, voluntarily relinquished by the last Grandsol, she acknowledges that the key and the house belong to all of them now: "We golden key. Hers and mine and yours, Bolom."[115]

There is another house in *Blessed Is the Fruit*, and equally essential to the novel's design – Bolom's home within Vel's womb. Like the totality of Caribbean space during the claustrophobic rule of colonialism, Vel's body has been occupied by a foreign power: Mr Grandsol – big sun, the Sun King of d'Esperance – and she knows all too well that his was only one of many such invasions. The most recent offensive has occurred just before the women tell their stories, when Dr Curtis attempts to complete the abortion that Vel in her desperation began. His initial diagnosis, in which he condescendingly dehumanizes Vel by lumping her into an anonymous "they", so angers Lil that just a few moments later she physically ejects him from the bedroom: "Shoving him backward. *Bodily* backward. Actually lifting him up off the flooring for an instant an enormous sea-wave lifting him up bodily into the air. Shoving him backward. Backward. Sweeping him out of the room."[116] This is literally repulsion of an alien enemy, as the repetition of the word "backward" plainly indicates. Lil's conquest of Curtis prevents "those hairy little hands" from making one last assault on Vel's womb.

The house of Vel's body, like d'Esperance Estate, can finally be set free by the dynamic process of relinquishment and *métissage* encoded in Antoni's text. Even as Vel emerges from the novel's long night of sleep, she grasps the context and magnitude of that liberation: "Lie here and feel my own body waking up. Slow. Slow. My busted-up, exhausted-out body that feels five-hundred years old! Waking up after a sleep of five-hundred years. A nightmare lasting five-hundred years long."[117] Five centuries of occupation and oppression, Lil might well say, as she does after surrendering the key to Vel, "After long last."[118] *Blessed Is the Fruit* enacts with startling clarity Benítez-Rojo's characterization of the "phenomenon of the slaveholding plantation" as "the womb of the Caribbean".[119] In Antoni's unique iconography, Vel's womb-space (containing the heir to the conjoined traditions of Africa, Europe and the Caribbean) is a newly repossessed reality that will continue to evolve "When the Book Read" and Bolom is born – a living ideogram of the world to come.

Vel, praising the psychiatrist who helped her at her lowest point, writes in her letter: "*Is Dr B teach me how to read my life. What it is to be a human being again.*"[120] In *Blessed Is the Fruit* Lil and Vel read their lives to each other through Bolom and teach themselves how to be human again. What they appear to gain, by rehearsing in such detail the stories of their lives and sinking into their extraordinary joint dream/story, is a serenity that neither of them has yet known and that can come only from the achievement of psychic wholeness. At one point in her reflections, Vel comes close to capturing that feeling of repose, as she thinks about listening to the waves crashing on the shore not far from the Grandsol house:

> And think how long since you stop to listen for that sound. How, when you first reach here in the house, you couldn't sleep nights only for listening to the sound of the waves turning. . . . How you didn't *want* to drop asleep, only for fear that somehow that sound, and the waves turning, and the sea sheself might go way. Turn back into fields of ruined canes. Villages of smoking rubbishheaps, and dust, and falling-down patched-up shacks. You fear of losing the sea! And listen first thing every morning before you open you eyes to make certain, that sound of the waves turning over gentle pon the shore. Still there. . . . And think how for so long, years now, since you forget to listen for it. Forget to remember. Like all good things, after a time you forget to remember.[121]

The sea looms large in Caribbean consciousness. It is the ultimate tributary and the ultimate estuary – a link both to all pasts and to all futures. When Vel forgets to remember to listen for the sound of the waves, she has finally learned to take its reassurance for granted, to incorporate it into her own sense of being. The ruined canes and tumbledown villages that she dreads recall a past scarred, divided and distorted by colonialism and its aftermath. For five centuries, half a world was broken and divided. Its repossession in the way Antoni's novel envisions is not necessarily a foregone conclusion, but a post-plantation Caribbean is at least possible. As a seat of colonial power the Grandsol home belongs to history; fresh air will certainly blow through its newly opened doors and windows and, as Bachelard reminds us, "Sometimes the house of the future is better built, lighter and larger than all the houses of the past."[122]

4

MY GRANDMOTHER'S EROTIC FOLKTALES

The Real Treasure of El Dorado

Because the collective memory was too often wiped out, the Caribbean writer must "dig deep" into this memory, following the latent signs that he has picked up in the everyday world.
– Édouard Glissant[1]

A structural idea appears to be Robert Antoni's virtual starting point in his first two novels, each of which is, in a different way, a model of what Antonio Benítez-Rojo calls "Caribbean Being" attempting to "rediscover its lost form". Likening that effort to the search for El Dorado, Benítez-Rojo conceives the novel of the Caribbean as travelling "along many and varied routes by various means . . . toward a hypothetical centre or origin" which is "in continuous displacement".[2] The seven voices of *Divina Trace* embody the multidiegetic nature of the region's ongoing self-discovery, their harmonies and dissonances often wafting close to unchartable vectors where consciousness and myth converge. Through its schematically simpler but still insistently dialogic structure, *Blessed Is the Fruit* enacts the integrative process of *métissage* that is for Robert Antoni the hallmark of Caribbean sensibility. If neither novel arrives at Benítez-Rojo's "impossible"[3] destination, that is plainly because the construction of a Caribbean reality must be a progression, not a finished product or an achieved goal. It is no accident, then, that Antoni's third book, *My Grandmother's Erotic Folktales,* came into the world as a short story collection, seemingly much more miscellaneous in its arrangement of narrative material than its predecessors. But the book's format is deceptive, because this archipelago of tales (all told by a single teller) is yet another of the "varied routes and various means" towards the continuously deferred, always evolving El Dorado of Caribbean identity.

If structure is so important, what kind of book is *My Grandmother's Erotic Folktales*? I have used the word "archipelago" deliberately to place it within that ambiguous category of fiction that lies between a collection of unrelated short stories and a continuous long narrative. Both Benítez-Rojo's "repeating island" metaphor and Édouard Glissant's characterization of the Caribbean as an estuary postulate that a central dialectic (not to say paradox) in Caribbean life is diversity coupled with unity, separateness with connection.[4] The region itself, as Mark Kurlansky implies, is neither a scattering of distinct and self-contained islets nor a monolithic land mass but rather a "continent of islands" – Lawrence Scott's "archipelagic rosary of the Caribbean".[5] For Benítez-Rojo this "island bridge" takes on "the character of an archipelago, that is, a discontinuous conjunction (of what?): unstable condensations, turbulences, whirlpools, clumps of bubbles, frayed seaweed, sunken galleons, crashing breakers, flying fish, seagull squawks, downpours, nighttime phosphorescences, eddies and pools, uncertain voyages of signification".[6] In these senses, all of Antoni's fiction is archipelagic as well as dialogic. While his novels (his fictional "continents") at times seem to bud off into a multiplicity of islands – stories, versions, retellings, digressions and dreams – the third book's "autonomous" stories seem almost equally bent on knitting themselves into the land mass of a novel. For Antoni, both types of "discontinuous conjunctions" – novels in which there is "no end"[7] to the generation of stories, as well as stories integrating themselves into a larger pattern – are projections of the most fundamental transaction of the human mind. The "imagining I",[8] embarking on "uncertain voyages of signification", tells stories to structure and understand inchoate experience, and in doing so actually creates experience, including history, myth and all the other elements that comprise what we call culture.

The "mixed" genre of interrelated stories is hardly unique to Caribbean literature,[9] but Antoni puts it to a uniquely Caribbean use, as can be seen by contrasting the most prominent formal elements of *My Grandmother's Erotic Folktales* with those of the best-known archipelagic collection from the West Indies, V.S. Naipaul's *Miguel Street.* Naipaul's book is a series of vignettes focusing on people who create distinct impressions in the narrator's imagination as he grows up in Port of Spain, Trinidad. Although those impressions are so foregrounded that each approaches a kind of autonomy with its own protagonist and plot, they are linked to each other through the muted but persistent motif of the narrator's growth and development. There is no extradiegetic dimension as such – no framing narrative apart from the separate stories – but the narrator's presence as a character throughout serves as a kind of internal frame or skeleton. It is difficult, however, not to conclude that the real life of Naipaul's book lies in its vibrant individuated narratives, the colourful tales of the denizens of Miguel Street.

The frame narrative of *My Grandmother's Erotic Folktales,* on the other hand, is conspicuous. The narrator, Granny Myna, appears throughout the book as the teller of the tales, while within the separate tales she is the protagonist in three and merely the heterodiegetic narrator of two. The narratee is not the vaguely defined "you" of *Miguel Street* but her grandson Johnny Domingo, and the passing down to him of both the stories themselves and the art of storytelling is of utmost significance. Her autodiegetic presence in the frame reinforces that role: by repeatedly addressing Johnny directly, often with brief embellishments, she directs the reader's attention to herself as storyteller. The crucial difference between Naipaul's and Antoni's strategies, then, is that in *Miguel Street* the narrator's separate stories take on a life of their own, eclipsing (though not erasing entirely) the story of his life, whereas in *Erotic Folktales* an outwardly disparate handful of stories is welded together by the force of the narrator's personality. Even in the tales that have nothing to do with her life, Granny Myna's voice – her speaking style, her opinions, her exaggerations, her asides and digressions – is the real protagonist, and through Antoni's identification of that voice with the culture, Granny Myna becomes a folk figure herself and a repository of the elusive and fragmented Caribbean Being that is the West Indian writer's El Dorado.

Antoni's arrangement of the volume's five stories is symmetrical, which should come as no surprise to readers of *Divina Trace* or *Blessed Is the Fruit*. Papee Vince's speculation about God in the first novel – "*that oldman . . . has something of a propensity for symmetry and balance*"[10] – could just as easily apply to his actual creator, Robert Antoni. In *Erotic Folktales*, Granny Myna's accounts of her adventures during the Second World War, when American troops were stationed on Corpus Christi, occupy the most striking positions (first, middle and last), enveloping the two shorter tales she tells from the "old-time time".[11] In fact, the story of her life – increasingly focused, as the tales progress, on her role as defender of Caribbean cultural integrity – is the ur-novel that lies beneath the diegetically variegated design of the book as a whole. It reveals itself not only in the interconnected autobiographical stories but also in countless smaller, less obvious ways, particularly when she addresses Johnny directly as frame narrator, each time adding to her authority as storyteller. Moreover, her narrative's luxuriant growth of subsidiary stories strongly suggests that the *process* of storytelling, as much as the personality of the teller, is the source of the book's deepest rhythms.

Like a living organism, *My Grandmother's Erotic Folktales* displays an almost endless capacity for regeneration, a characteristic that is evident even in the bountiful title and the table of contents. The full title virtually stands as a minimalist story in itself: *My Grandmother's Erotic Folktales: With Stories of Adventure and Occasional Orgies in Her Boarding House for American Soldiers During the War, Including Her Confrontations with the Kentucky Colonel, the Tanzanian Devil and the King of Chacachacari.* The descriptive table of contents is a time-honoured device, of course, but in Antoni's hands it becomes a garden of narrative fecundity, including as it does not only summaries of the main tales ("Further Adventures of the Kentucky Colonel and the King of Chacachacari, and How My Grandmother Became a Disk-Jockey and the First Female Calypsonian, and Managed by Accident to Decode a German Message so America Could Win the War") but also synoptic versions of embedded tales ("*including* Gregoria la Rosa's Story of the Time She Got the Pin-Cushion Stuck Inside Her Bamsee, and My Grandmother Attempted to Operate and Almost Pulled out Her Whole Asshole"). These preliminary pages seem scarcely able to contain the stories they announce, as if the stories are trying to burst out of the book before the narrator has a chance to tell them.

The fact that Johnny Domingo narrates the title and table of contents, which places "my grandmother" in the third person, confirms his status within the book as legatee of Granny Myna's gift. But just past the second title page he recedes into the role of silent listener, absorbing not only the content of her tales but also her techniques and, most important, her purpose. She knows full well (though she never says so explicitly) that storytelling as an essential agent of culture construction derives much of its energy from the inherent magic of language and the power of rhetoric to alter perceptions, often in defiance of hegemonic dispositions of power. Glissant comments that the "Caribbean folktale focuses on an experience suppressed by decree or the law",[12] and Granny Myna is quite alert to the subversive, even rebellious, nature of her enterprise, including not least its pervasive eroticism and exuberant scatology.[13] (Roland Littlewood, in his discussion of the Earth People of northern Trinidad, has remarked that in various stages of history obscenities have been viewed as " 'natural' and 'earthy', demotic and carnivalesque subversions of social power through the intrusions of nature into social life".)[14]

Granny's very first words are "Yes, that is a story! It's a very good story that I can tell you if you want, but Johnny, don't tell nobody I told you that thing that is a very *bad* story, like you mummy and daddy."[15] Like the influence of Zoe and Jook Jook on Addy in "Two-head Fred and Tree-foot Frieda", Granny's stories presumably violate the letter of parentally imposed law. But the new Caribbean world can be created only through the authority of a fearless, rebellious Caribbean voice, utterly free to challenge and demolish earlier received realities. The Caribbean storyteller must not shrink from a reassemblage of both time and space, and Granny Myna is up to the task, weaving a world in which the "experience of time does not keep company with the rhythms of month and year alone", in which the landscape of the word is the world's landscape, and its frontiers are indeed open. It is hardly an exaggeration to state that the book's greatest treasure, its own "golden man", is the imaginative force that generates it: the ability to shape reality, to extend the space of human experience beyond the limited frontiers of the physical.

Many details in *Erotic Folktales* tend to blur unequivocal distinctions between an empirically verifiable world with clearly defined borders and an imagined world with a "frontier" that is "open". An important feature of magic is its capacity to break the most elemental rules of everyday life: those governing space and time. Benítez-Rojo's characterization of Caribbean culture as "not terrestrial but aquatic",[16] not fixed but fluid, applies almost as aptly to space as to time, particularly as space is re-formed by the Caribbean writer. The setting of Antoni's first three books is Corpus Christi (truly a "repeating island"), a place not on any map yet intensely, vibrantly real. Like the Body of Christ for which it is named, this land comes into being through an act of transubstantiation – from a geographically and historically recognizable Trinidad (with its Pitch Lake, its Sangre Grande, its American military base during the Second World War) to a transcendent space that is "neither static nor localizable".[17] There is something within Caribbean sensibility that "struggles against"[18] mimesis, as Glissant notes, and Antoni repeatedly reminds his communicants that Corpus Christi's identity as Host encompasses but also extravagantly exceeds any "factual" Trinidad of atlases and gazetteers.

If the spatial coordinates of Antoni's fiction extend beyond the boundaries of geography, its temporal dimension breaks free from the constraints of history. J. Michael Dash points out that "History attempts . . . to fix reality in terms of a rigid, hierarchical discourse" and to "systematize the world".[19] Consequently, Glissant argues, Caribbean communities' "quest for the dimension of time will be neither harmonious or linear" but "will be marked by a polyphony of dramatic shocks" originating, ultimately, in "a collective memory".[20] In *Erotic Folktales* Granny Myna is the conduit for that memory, especially in the more fabulistic "old time" tales of "How Crab-o Lost His Head" and "How Iguana Got Her Wrinkles". But even in the autobiographical stories she does not hesitate to bend time – doubly reconfiguring it, in fact – to suit her purposes. There are many examples of what may be called external anachronisms, or dislocations from the chronology or history of the "real" world. Ernest Hemingway shows up on Corpus Christi (and leaves it on American Airlines!) during "the old, old-time time"[21] of Caribs and Yoruba slave women. A character named Dr Jewels is "a Socialist"[22] in a story that takes place near the end of the sixteenth century. And "Elizabeth the Segunda one"[23] is queen of England during the Second World War. This last reference, while anachronistic on the surface (Elizabeth II did not become queen until 1952), conceals a more subtle embedded anachronism: Granny Myna's insistence on "the Segunda one" implies that this must be made clear, as if the temporal frontiers of her fictional world are so elastic that she could well have been Elizabeth I.

Even more radically, Granny's stories contain temporal "derangements"[24] even within the context of Antoni's fictional world. Any close reader of *Divina Trace* will be familiar with its numerous anachronisms as well as its internal chronological inconsistencies – easy to dismiss as errors, perhaps, but essential to the conjuring of a reality that is not fixed by history. Antoni takes these derangements a step further in *My Grandmother's Erotic Folktales.* Granny Myna is an important character in *Divina Trace,* and in *Folktales* she mentions other characters and incidents from the earlier work, such as the story that Johnny's father, Dr Domingo, told about "the physician who looked inside the asshole of he patient to find the eyeball looking out".[25] But in *Divina Trace* (to cite just one rather obvious instance), this same Dr Domingo, fresh out of medical school,[26] delivers a child born in April 1899, whereas in *Erotic Folktales* he is just five or six years old[27] during the Second World War. Similarly, according to the calculus of *Divina Trace,* Granny Myna would be dead before the war ever begins, and certainly not alive to tell stories about it many years later. In the volume's final story Granny Myna herself acknowledges that this time-scrambled word-world is not subject to the laws that govern quotidian experience. When the Kentucky Colonel announces his new "namenick" to be "Wolfman Jack", Granny declares, "[T]hat was the most blatant, ridiculous, *upsetting* anachronism or whatever the fuck they called it that I had ever heard in all my life! 'Because the real life Wolfman Jack probably isn't even *born* yet'."[28] Truly, as Benítez-Rojo crisply notes, in the Caribbean, "time unfolds irregularly and resists being captured by the cycles of clock and calendar".[29]

The volume's first story, "My Grandmother's Tale of the Buried Treasure and How She Defeated the King of Chacachacari and the Entire American Army with Her Venus-Flytraps",[30] is an account of a near-epic confrontation between Granny Myna and an outrageous mountebank[31] who exploits her twin faith in science and religion. The imposter "King" of Chacachacari turns up at Granny's house one day "dressed up like he was playing mas in Carnival", with "one big set of cloth wrapped up around he head" and "a big ruby upon the forehead flashing, and earrings dangling, and rings rings rings". She notices at once that "even with all the jewels and paraphernalia he had, the only clothes he was wearing were dirty old dungarees, both the pantaloons and the shirt".[32] Carnival does not play so important a part in *Erotic Folktales* as it does in *Divina Trace, Blessed Is the Fruit* or, obviously, *Carnival*, but the juxtaposition of "paraphernalia" and "dirty old dungarees" here does set up a pattern of engagement between the real and the imagined that runs throughout the entire book and forms its most significant subtext. The King tells Granny he has come "from he country across the sea in search of the long lost treasure of Chacachacari"[33] – stolen by the Spanish in 1776, taken to Corpus Christi and buried on land belonging to her "in a place called Chaguarameras".[34]

Like much else in the *Folktales*, this yarn contains some threads of "real" history. Both of these locales are fictional versions of places in Trinidad. Chaguarameras was originally called Chaguaramos ("Farmingland of Flowers") but was renamed "Farmingland of Prostitutes" after "half the whores in Venezuela" flocked to the American military base established there during the Second World War.[35] The proliferation of prostitution during this period in the actual Trinidad was enough of a social problem to provoke the commentary of calypsonians. As late as the 1950s, in fact, when the American base in Chaguaramas closed down, the artist who became known as the

Mighty Sparrow commemorated the event with his first famous calypso, "Jean and Dinah":

> No more Yankees to spoil the fete
> Dorothy have to take what she get
> All of them who used to make style
> Taking their two shillings with a smile
> No more hotel and Simmonds bed
> By the sweat of thy brow shalt thou eat bread.[36]

The island of Chacachacare (as it is usually spelled), which lies off the northwest tip of Trinidad, was long a haven for smugglers, pirates and brigands, so its fictional version here makes a rather appropriate homeland for the bogus king.[37] When Granny explains that "the American soldiers . . . took that estate away a long time ago to build they Base", the King proclaims her "the rightful owner of everything *below*" the ground and produces a map. The argument is unconvincing; Granny tells him, "I was not about to fight no American Army – not even for forty-two gold bricks!" Moreover, the map "was only saying that the treasure was buried *somewhere* near Chaguarameras, but it didn't tell me where was the place to dig". But the King has a trump card: a metal detector that actually appears to work. After witnessing a demonstration of the machine's powers, Granny sends him off to Chaguarameras to find the treasure, admitting, "I was ready to do *anything* the King told me."[38]

The King, accompanied by an entourage of "little baboo-boys" (East Indians),[39] appears as a figure out of remote times, legendary places and buried treasures – or such is the impression he wishes to convey. But he is also the suspicious stranger in dirty dungarees, and Granny Myna has seen too much of hard Caribbean reality to be easily taken in by this parody of Caribbean romance. After the King returns about a month later, he tells Granny that an angel guards the treasure and can be propitiated only by burning ten thousand dollars in his presence. Granny carefully questions him about this heavenly being. Is it male or female? she asks. The King replies that it is a "man angel" because "he saw the *parts*". Although the angel is a fabrication, part of an elaborate scheme to trick Granny Myna out of her money, the reality of angels, from her point of view, is never in doubt. In fact, she suspects the King of lying because she *does* believe in them: "Now I told the King that was all I wanted to hear . . . now I knew not to believe *nothing* this King said . . . . Because the truth, if you've ever seen an angel – and I have seen plenty in my time – the truth is that they are all *smooth*."[40] The family scientist, Uncle Olly, is called in to confirm this point, but both he and Granny Myna, captivated by the "magic" of the King's flashing and winking metal detector, are ultimately drawn into his scheme and surrender all the cash they can scrape together. After several farcical twists in the plot involving counterfeit money, prostitutes, American soldiers and two local eccentrics, Granny realizes that her initial instincts were correct. She brings all her wit and experience, including knowledge of a plant with "magic sexual powers",[41] to the task of defeating and humiliating her foe.

The association of imagination with magic in the story, and the imagination's clear primacy over rational, hierarchical paradigms of thought, constitutes an assault on the colonization of both culture and individual. Although the King of Chacachacari is a storyteller too, his stories are instruments of manipulation and control, not liberation. He is a comic variation on the outsider who comes to deceive, exploit and plunder. Attempting to envelop Granny Myna in his far-fetched yarn, he is instead ultimately contained within hers. The traditional Caribbean folktale described by Glissant evolved as an act of cultural survival in a distorted reality of extrinsically imposed identities and enforced speechlessness. As a political utterance it strives "to express something it is forbidden to refer to": "Everywhere that the obligation to get around the rule of silence existed a literature was created that has no 'natural' continuity, if one may put it that way, but rather, burst forth in snatches and fragments."

Antoni's reconstruction of the traditional folktale in this book constitutes, in effect, a deconstruction of official historical discourse. Glissant goes on to call the storyteller "a handyman, the *djobbeur* of the collective soul".[42] That is Granny Myna's role as well. In the three long autobiographical tales she is a comic-heroic protagonist, vanquishing her (foreign) enemies, the King and the Kentucky Colonel. But the telling itself is of even greater consequence, because she cobbles together, like Glissant's *djobbeur*, pieces from the "collective soul" of her island and transforms them into a kind of counter-history that approaches myth. Hesiod's notion that a sparing tongue is the greatest treasure finds its living antithesis in Granny Myna. By the time she has finished, she has not only told the story of her struggle with the King but has also woven into it three major embedded stories, references to several other stories left untold (for the time being) *and* her version of the Second World War (in which "factual" history is displaced into her own tale and subordinated to it). This ascendancy of story over fact parallels her victory over the King within the narrative.

But the task of the Caribbean *djobbeur* never ends, and the magic must be transmitted from one generation to the next. Returning again to her autodiegetic role in the frame, she tells Johnny, "Papa God . . . always makes sure I have plenty of children around me to hear my stories. And that is the other thing Papa God gave me, that maybe you have a little bit of it youself? This love for telling stories."[43] If this Johnny is the same Johnny Domingo who discovers the link between his "imagining I" and his "essential self, God within" in *Divina Trace*,[44] Granny's supposition is something of an understatement.

The middle story, "My Grandmother's Tale of the Kentucky Colonel and How They Made Their Fortune Selling Pizzas to the American Soldiers, Before Their Parlour was Raided by the Chief-of-Police for Prostitution and Illegal Trafficking", continues in a similar vein, though touching more lightly on the first tale's preoccupation with storytelling and expanding its exploration of American influence in the Caribbean. Throughout the book, unwanted representatives of colonial powers intrude on Corpus Christi: English and Spanish explorers, "Portugee" planters, pirates, American military personnel and, here, Colonel Sanders of Kentucky Fried Chicken fame.[45] Once again Granny Myna, in the middle of the Second World War, finds herself waging her own battle against a clever swindler.

At first not believing her son Amadao, who announces his arrival, she declares that "Colonel Sanders wasn't a *real* person, he was only the story those Americans thought up to sell they chicken". But when she sees him, dressed in a "white suit with the little black ribbon tied in a bow around he neck for the tie" and "sitting behind the wheel of he big white Cadillac motorcar", she is sufficiently impressed to invite him to dinner.[46] Reasoning that Americans eat only fried chicken and pizza, she enlists a young man from New York City (one of several American soldiers she has taken in as boarders) to help her. During the next few rollicking days the Colonel and his sidekick, the Tanzanian Devil, convince Granny and her adopted daughter, Gregoria la Rosa,[47] to turn her house into a pizza parlour. To this end they steal an oven from a "rich Syrian"[48] to whom Granny has previously sold her smaller house.

The pizza restaurant, however, quickly becomes a front for a brothel in which soldiers are provided with young island boys. Looking for Gregoria one morning after an especially riotous night, Granny finds "an orgy of bullers going on with five or six of those American soldiers in the bed – and some more on top the bureau, down on the ground and posted up against the wall – and each soldier had for he partner one of those poor helpless half-starved little baboos".[49] The chief of police has earlier extorted money from Granny for operating a restaurant without a licence, but after he tries the same trick again – this time charging her with prostitution and illegal trafficking – she discovers that he is in league with the Colonel, the Tanzanian Devil and the Syrian. With the help of Gregoria, her Italian-American boarder Tony and her friend Sergeant Warren from the military base, she manages to recover all her lost money, forcing the Syrian to open up a home for underprivileged boys who will later be trained to serve on the police force.

Even this somewhat turgid summary cannot begin to include all the characters, incidents, plot reversals and comic asides in the story, much less the two embedded narratives: "The Tail of the Boy Who Was Born a Monkey" and "The Story of How Gregoria la Rosa Got Her Name". Amid the nonstop action and over-the-top slapstick, however, Antoni manages to sharpen his political focus considerably, chiefly by making the outsider/scoundrel figure not just an American but an icon of American commercial and cultural imperialism. During one of the story's several wild parties, Tony sings "in he American twang Lord Invader's famous calypso, "*Rum and coca-cola / Down to Point Cumana, / Mothers and they daughters / Working for the Yankee dollar!*"[50] Caribbean writers are well aware of the threat posed to the region's evolving cultural identity by what Olive Senior calls "a new center-periphery system"[51] based in the United States. As one of Caryl Phillips's characters remarks, "I guess if you really want to make some money in this country you best butter up your backside with some bendover oil and point your arse towards New York."[52] The Mighty Sparrow put it even more bluntly:

> Well, the day of slavery back again!
> Ah hope it ain't reach in Port of Spain.
> Since the Yankees come back over here
> They buy out the whole of Pointe-a-Pierre.
> Money start to pass, people start to bawl,
> Pointe-a-Pierre sell, the workmen and all.[53]

In Antoni's burlesque treatment, the Kentucky Colonel implicates local people (the Syrian, the police chief and the buggered boys) in pursuit of that Yankee dollar, but he is sent packing by Granny Myna. She outmanoeuvres him in another way too. As in her confrontation with the King of Chacachacari, the events of the tale are complemented by its telling. When the Colonel first appears at her house, Granny thinks he is only a story fabricated by Americans to sell fried chicken. By the time she finishes her account, she has reduced him to a character in her own ongoing story. Near the end of the tale, she comments, "I told Gregoria she had a brilliant mind when it came to business – that if Columbus had met *her* on the dock instead of she grandparents *we* would own the whole of Europe by now and America too, instead of the other way around."[54] The conclusion she draws here seems unduly pessimistic. Through that one small word "we" Granny Myna identifies herself explicitly as a Caribbean voice and a defender of its culture against the "ownership" of Europe or America, a point she makes again, much later, when she asserts, "In my heart of hearts I am nothing but pure West Indian."[55] As the protagonist of her own story she expels the Kentucky Colonel from her island, but as storyteller, she incorporates him (like the King before him) into her world, making him a part of it. Her strategy in all three autobiographical stories beautifully exemplifies Benítez-Rojo's contention that the "literature of the Caribbean seeks to differentiate itself from the European not by excluding cultural components that influenced its formation, but . . . by moving toward the creation of an ethnologically promiscuous text".[56]

Both of Granny Myna's nemeses turn up in the third autobiographical story – "Further Adventures of the Kentucky Colonel and the King of Chacachacari, and How My Grandmother Became a Disk-Jockey and the First Female Calypsonian, and Managed by Accident to Decode a German Message so America Could Win the War". While the tale's structure follows that of its predecessors quite closely, it amplifies still further their political implications. The King arrives first, followed by the Kentucky Colonel and his sidekick, the Tanzanian Devil, and all are greeted warmly by Granny, whose hospitality far exceeds her good sense. The King and the Colonel immediately plunge first into a fistfight, then a war of words that Granny calls an "Elizabethan tournament of caca-pelting", calling each other such choice names as "the fattest, flabbiest, pulpy-fleshed, milk-dripping, banana-peeling fruit-of-a-soursop ever to stuff heself into a three piece suit"; a "brassfaced, big-mouthed, blue-striped, balloon-bellied son-of-a-peacock" with "lilies in he liver and quaileggs inside he pants"; and a "frufru, a beggar, a thousand-pound pussywillow that don't remember the last time he showered with soap nor sprayed deodorant beneath he arms".[57]

Granny calms them down with an invitation to one of the West Indian dinners she often cooks for her boarders, and after the meal she performs the usual ritual of telling them all a tale. This story – her recollection of the time Gregoria la Rosa got a pincushion "Stuck Inside She Bamsee"[58] – appears to incite the Tanzanian Devil to force himself on Gregoria. During the Colonel's and the Devil's previous visit Granny had to warn Gregoria to be "*very* careful with a good-looking man like that Tanzania".[59] These details assume further importance as the story unfolds, taking their place in the book's extensive network of deceptions and disguises that begin as early as the King's scam and Uncle Olly's "*fluke* money"[60] in the first tale.

As in the companion stories, the great deception on which the plot turns is a scheme hatched to trick and exploit Granny Myna. The day after the dinner party she learns that the Colonel has sold the Kentucky Fried Chicken business to the King so that he can realize his life-long ambition to be a disk jockey – "a *Houdini* of the higher frequencies" and "an *artiste* of the airwaves".[61] Of course he needs space in Granny's house for a radio station, and to gain her agreement, he promises her a singing career. Unable to resist the opportunity to become "the world's first female *Calypsonian*",[62] she lets the Colonel and his cohorts set up their electronic gear in her upstairs garret and place an antenna on her roof. After two weeks of nightly calypso performances, Granny manages to discover that her singing is being broadcast only to her own radio, and that the King and the Colonel are using their equipment to intercept information from General Eisenhower and pass it on to the enemy. When she hears a German voice attempting to confirm when the "Zee Day" operation will take place, she instinctively gives them the wrong date, thereby insuring the success of the Norman invasion and hastening the end of the war. In the story's denouement the Tanzanian Devil turns out to be "Secret Agent Tyrone Davis",[63] an American intelligence officer pursuing the King and the Colonel. Far from being the dangerous lecher that Granny supposed, he is actually secretly engaged to Gregoria. The King and the Colonel, having earlier been knocked out by a couple of Granny and Gregoria's "homestyle BBQ Baked Bean farts",[64] are arrested, and Granny stages a wedding for Gregoria that is attended by none other than General Eisenhower himself.

All the comic radio business in this story (and there is a good deal more of it) has its serious side. The Colonel, anxious to convince Granny Myna that she will not lose the money he is asking her to contribute for the purchase of equipment, is quick to remind her "that radio stations make they fortunes selling *advertisements*" and "the American army is already mobilized to announce all they endless Uncle Sam propaganda exclusively on *we* radio station".[65] She well understands the "official" function of the medium, signing off each night with the words "*Uncle Sam wants you and the Colonel has you fried chicken too!*"[66] But scattered moments of American commercialism and propaganda are outweighed and subverted by the hours of calypso tunes she and Gregoria sing into their microphone – songs as authentically indigenous as Granny's own tales.[67] Granny's efforts to broadcast her songs are part of the same estuarial impulse that motivates her storytelling: a flowing outward and mixing with the wider world.

The strength of "peripheral" Caribbean culture in surviving and even extending its influence to the "centre" manifests itself even more vividly in the tale's concluding tableau. Traditionally the protagonists of comedy overcome a series of obstacles (often imposed by authority figures) and establish a new, youthful society, liberated from unreasonable restraints and obsolete rules. This is exactly what happens at the end of "Further Adventures", as the Tanzanian Devil – now revealed to be Tyrone Davis of Oklahoma – marries Gregoria la Rosa, who is one of "the last people of Carib blood" and "mixed with African blood too".[68] The new society that the story happily envisions includes both the Caribbean and a newly Caribbeanized America. And Granny Myna, proclaimed "*Official Adopted Mother of all the American Troops*",[69] blesses the union by drawing the wedding guests (including Ike, the living symbol of American hegemony) into her spell as she prepares to tell yet another tale, incorporating all of them – and the reader/listener as well – into the ever-expanding current of her narrative.

If the autobiographical stories enhance Granny Myna's authority as narrator by elaborately foregrounding her experience and linking it closely with that of Corpus Christi, the two "old time" tales of Crab-o and Iguana allow her to display fully her skill as *djobbeur*, digging deep, as Glissant says, into collective memory, retrieving and recreating treasured fragments of Caribbean identity. The two tales have much in common. Set in a remote past (but laced with anachronisms that mock linear models of human experience), both incorporate fables involving animals into larger, more complicated narratives involving island "history" and the transformational powers of storytelling.

Granny Myna places the first story[70] firmly within the landscape of the word almost as soon as she begins to describe the main character's origins: "She wasn't an oldwoman. Still, even the oldest oldmen in the village could never remember a time when she didn't live in the big estate house, perched high on top the mountain looking down over the village."[71] Her true identity is lost in a web of yarns about Carib

Indians, Portuguese planters, English pirates and Yoruba slaves, and her true name is known to no one, so she is called Blanchisseuse by the locals because she does her laundry in the river below her house; in time the village takes on that name as well.[72] Every day she makes her way down the hill, strips naked, bathes herself and washes her clothes while all the village "wadjanks" hide, "crab-o in hand", and watch her.[73] Believing her to be "an obeahwoman – or worse still a sukuyant, a lagahoo, or a diabless", they are afraid to make themselves known to her, and their fear is only increased by the sharp cutlass she keeps "tucked beneath she jackspaniard-nest of hair". Their fear is well grounded, as the embedded story of Hax the Butcher confirms. According to local lore, Blanchisseuse had caught Hax looking, his "crab-o standing up stiff like a standpipe", and "with little more than a flick of she slender wrist, she swiped he standpipe off clean at the base!"[74]

In Granny Myna's story-shaped world, words can have multiple referents. Throughout this tale, the lowercase crab-o denotes the penis, while the capitalized Crab-o is the name of an animal who, like the village men, watches Blanchisseuse at the river. Crab-o, who "in those old days . . . still had he head sure enough", listens to the woman sing each day in "the old Yoruba tongue" and finally manages to "decipher the meaning of she words" – which are also her true name.[75] Two plot lines are entwined from this point on. Blanchisseuse takes a series of lovers (allowing Granny Myna a golden opportunity to describe in detail their crab-os) and an orphan girl, Moyen, comes to live with her and help her with her laundry. Blanchisseuse tells Moyen she can eat all the mangoes she wishes, but none of the fruit from her many other trees unless she can guess her true name. In the course of time Moyen learns the name from Crab-o, whom Blanchisseuse promptly decapitates in a fit of fury. But her anger is not assuaged by this act of vengeance. "Still vex and hot up with sheself",[76] she whips out her cutlass and slices the head off the crab-o of Mr Chan, her Chinese lover, then does the same to all the others: Felix the African, Clifton the Englishman, Pierre the Frenchman, Ram-sol the Hindu and Orinoco the Amerindian.

Blanchisseuse's serial butchery seems almost to enact, in the form of farce, Benítez-Rojo's articulation of a problem perhaps unique to literary production in this region. "The Caribbean writer" – unlike the European – "feels himself always in need because European languages and traditions, although indispensable to him, are insufficient for the narration of the carnivalesque context which surrounds him." This is a milieu, heteroglossic on a massive scale, in which "dismembered signs from all corners of the world coincide".[77] If the comparison seems fanciful, it is worth recalling that both *language* and *lingam* (Sanskrit for penis, as well as for "distinctive mark") derive from the same Indo-European root, *dnghü*. In Antoni's comic variation only Ernesto, the "Yankee tourist from the windy plains of Illinois",[78] writer and "mariposa-collector",[79] escapes, because his already "dismembered" sign – his circumcised American crab-o, a "little pencil-eraser, poking out so sad between he two fuzzy quaileggs" – is just too small. The sight of his tiny, flaccid crab-o displaying its head (as the other men's crab-os do only when erect) makes Blanchisseuse hesitate to decapitate it, so in effect his symbolic castration saves him from a real one. Ernesto – a wicked sendup of Hemingway – later goes on to write "this story of how he'd survived he adventure in the jungles of the savage Caribbean, without losing he head like all the rest"; he calls his account "*The Sad Story of the Savage American Practice of Circumcision*".[80]

The role played by Ernesto in this tale also pertains directly to the notion of storytelling as an act of transformation. Granny Myna begins by describing Blanchisseuse according to the stories handed down about her. Phrases such as "some said" and "most people said" occur frequently in the first few pages, but soon the simple indicative mood begins to predominate: "She was a very tall woman. Some said as much as seven feet, but it was difficult to tell, because she always wore she hair piled in the tall jackspaniard-nest on top she head. She was very particular about she clothes."[81] The assurance of *always* reinforces the declarative certainty of *was*. For the rest of the tale Granny confidently assumes the authority of eyewitness narrator: what was "said" becomes what was; word becomes world.

Several other elements in the story confirm the magic of language and storytelling. Knowledge of the Yoruba words that constitute Blanchisseuse's true name, for example, will enable Moyen to eat the previously forbidden fruits in the older woman's Caribbean Eden. Blanchisseuse herself, when she takes the village men as lovers, is less interested in "the range and shape and size of they crab-os" than "in the particular *verbal* response each of them made at the moment of he greatest excitement", because she is "a little bit of an apprentice *linguist* on top".[82] Most revealing of all is Granny's characterization of Ernesto's Caribbean story – "the very same tale", she tells Johnny, "that you have just finished hearing". Almost in the same breath, however, she qualifies that assertion: "Of course, Ernesto could only relate it with all those same careful, real-life newspaper details that have become the trademark of all the famous Yankee writers."[83] The word "only" speaks volumes. Excoriating "belief in the powers of realism", Glissant argues that the "surface effects of literary realism are the precise equivalent of the historian's claim to pure objectivity".[84] By contrast, a "magical notion of reality is based on beliefs hidden deep in the collective past",[85] and it is this reality, "with all its many deceptations, and cumbructions, and confufflations",[86] that Granny Myna's storytelling conjures up.

Just as the Crab-o fable reinvents and satirically dismisses a figure embodying the restrictive premises of literary realism, "The Tale of How Iguana Got Her Wrinkles, or The True Tale of El Dorado" recreates the early history of Corpus Christi, reducing the "official" account – with its own "careful, real-life newspaper details" – to a prefatory episode in Granny Myna's more expansive and colourful one. According to her version, in which Antoni typically rearranges elements from the actual history of Trinidad, Fernando de Berrío, competing with Sir Walter Raleigh to find the legendary city of El Dorado (the Golden Man), sends for his business partner, Don Antonio Sedeño, to be made the first governor of Corpus Christi.[87] Don Antonio sets sail for the island right away, later sending for his devout wife, Doña María Penitencia, and their daughters, María Dolores and María Consuelo, who arrive shortly, "bringing with them they old Archbishop". Their first American discovery is Don Antonio in bed with "he little Amerindian slavegirl".[88] This girl, an Arawak princess, is found to be pregnant by Don Antonio. When the child is born, the mother is sent back to her people and the baby, named Iwana (iguana in Arawak), is cared for, more or less, by her two half-sisters.

This part of the tale comes very close to a Caribbean version of Cinderella. Although the child is born ugly – with "shiny red eyes like those of a salamander" and "tiny cups like the suckers of a frog" on the ends of her fingers instead of nails[89] – she grows up to be quite beautiful, and the more beautiful she becomes, the more she is mistreated by the three Marías. Eventually it is time to find husbands for Don Antonio's legitimate daughters. But among all the island's "wadjanks and badjohns looking to get theyselves rich", not to mention assorted prisoners, criminals and scoundrels, there is only one suitable match, a champagne-swilling French dandy with the absurdly comical name "*Dr Jewels Derrière-Cri de Plus-Bourbon*".[90] Consistent with the Cinderella motif, this dubious Prince Charming chooses neither of the two Marías but rather the lowly Iwana – primarily because she has not been baptized; he, as "a Socialist", does not believe "in Papa God" and cannot possibly marry a Catholic.[91]

After the two are wed, Dr Jewels locks Iwana in a tower and favours her with his presence only when he wants to indulge his "unusual *culinary* habits" – the sole type of sexual activity he enjoys. But Iwana is befriended by an iguana that leaps into the room from a nearby silk-cotton tree. One day, hearing Dr Jewels approach, Iguana crawls into Iwana to hide. Because "the tail of an iguana doesn't taste so different from the legs of a crapo" and Jewels is a lover of frog legs, he is delighted, having "never tasted a pussy so *sweet* as that in all he life!"[92] Here Granny Myna pauses briefly to list all the types he has sampled, paralleling her catalogue of crab-os in the companion story and freely indulging in what Glissant terms the Caribbean storyteller's "taste for excess".[93]

As the years pass, Iwana continues to live in the tower and her husband, now "a rickety oldman", develops proclivities that even Granny Myna considers "too nasty to name".[94] One day he brings with him Anaconda, a handsome young African slave, and demands that the two have sex while he watches. But Anaconda, who is a Yoruba prince well versed in "those special powers that he had brought with him across the sea", takes pity on Iwana and changes into the snake that is his namesake. He does this repeatedly, each time changing back into human form, until one evening he pauses on the branch of the silk-cotton tree and happens to see Iguana crawling out of Iwana. Learning that both are in love with him – each "with the appropriate shape" – he hatches a plan.[95] Shedding his snakeskin, he tells Iguana to put it on so that Dr Jewels will experience the "sour taste" of Anaconda instead of the customary flavour of iguana. Repelled by both the sight and taste of the wrinkled snakeskin inside Iwana, Jewels is suddenly overcome with sympathy for the beautiful young couple and hurls himself "from the tower to he death down below". Iguana wriggles out of Iwana, leaving half the wrinkled skin inside, which explains, as Granny Myna tells Johnny, not only how the iguana got her wrinkles but also why there are "all those wrinkles folded up inside" women.[96] The next morning, Anaconda teaches Iwana how to change her own shape so that she becomes an iguana. Here Antoni strongly implies that these two animal figures, although they come from different parts of the world, have in common a holistic connection with the natural world that rationalist Europeans (represented by Dr Jewels) have long ago lost. They live together forever in the forests, changing back only occasionally so that they can make love the human way. Their continuing metamorphoses, as well as their union, embody the fluidity of Caribbean culture, or, as Glissant calls it, an "unceasing process of transformation".[97]

The final sentences of this tale merit some scrutiny because they hint at the serious purpose that lies within the book's cornucopia of eroticism.

> They disappeared inside the forest, where they have lived happy together to this very day. Only on occasion, when the moon is full with the scent of the forest green like the first day Papa God breathed life in the earth, do Anaconda and Iwana feel a longing to change they shape. Only on occasion do they surrender, and only to make love together like human beings.[98]

This passage, though uncharacteristically tasteful and restrained, strikes the perfect note for the end of a tale about creolization and the coming together of the Old World with the New. In *My Grandmother's Erotic Folktales* the erotic is alternately comedic, farcical, satirical, but its semantic common denominator is always desire for the Other. Although Anaconda and Iwana are both natives of the island in their animal forms, their human bodies are African and European/Amerindian. They voluntarily return to those human incarnations so that they can fully enter into each other's alterity. At the close of the tale there is no mention of procreation. As so comprehensively and eloquently enacted in *Blessed Is the Fruit*, the calling out of "a form of truth that is totally alien" from "beyond",[99] and the response to that call (Antoni's "surrender"), is sufficient in itself. Even Granny's many disparaging references to homosexuality are part of a broad pattern of Other-seeking that the text endorses and celebrates. Quite opposed to that movement is the behaviour of the colonialist Dr Jewels, whose interest in Iwana is lascivious but not erotic. Objectifying her, keeping her locked away, walling off her Otherness as a defence against it, he is unable to cope with the ineluctable consequence of true eroticism – *métissage* – and therefore has no choice but to kill himself when he is faced with it.

In an earlier reimagining of Caribbean history, one of Antoni's storytellers remarks, "In fact, when Sir Walter Raleigh told them back in England that on the island of Corpus Christi, where he was convinced he'd discovered El Dorado, oysters grew on trees, they took him fa madman."[100] Raleigh's actual account of his travels in Trinidad and northern South America, among the earliest surviving descriptions of that region, was met with some scepticism when it appeared in the late sixteenth century. "On the basis of his own extravagant and materially uncorroborated claims", Jeffrey Knapp explains, "Raleigh's detractors decided that he had never sailed farther than Cornwall . . . , that his golden empire existed nowhere but in his book."[101] Knapp and others have documented Raleigh's exaggerations and outright fabrications. Whatever his motives for embellishing *The Discovery of the Large, Rich and Beautiful Empire of Guiana* with the stuff of fiction, Raleigh's narrative serves as a rather appropriate template for Granny Myna's tales, and not just the one in which he appears as a character. Like Raleigh, Granny Myna "takes pride in lying",[102] and like him she subverts the distinction between the experienced and the told.

More than three hundred years after Raleigh's death, V.S. Naipaul revisits the original story of a "golden man" who annually "rolled in turpentine, was covered with gold dust and then dived into a lake" as "an Indian memory that the Spanish pursued; and the memory was confused with the legend, among jungle Indians, of the Peru the Spaniards had already conquered". In the course of time, Naipaul continues, "[t]he legend of El Dorado, narrative within narrative, witness within witness, had become like the finest fiction, indistinguishable from truth".[103] Beginning with the alleged gold bullion of the first story, *My Grandmother's Erotic Folktales* contains many references to monetary wealth (the King's fake jewels, the gold bars, the Yankee Dollar, the gold of El Dorado), and its pursuit – no less than for the Spaniards of several centuries before – generates both action and dreams. But it is clear that the real treasure is Granny Myna's capacity for storytelling, and just as Naipaul's storied El Dorado – and, indeed, Raleigh's *Discovery* – her narratives within narratives, laced with memory, legend and the occasional "fact", become a kind of truth, a small, living precinct of Caribbean Being.

When Anaconda first sees Iguana emerge from Iwana, he almost dismisses it "as another one of those meaningless magical events common enough in folktale-stories like this".[104] But in Antoni's narrative landscapes the magic is far from meaningless; it is no less than the power of the *djobbeur* to bring forth "a magical notion of reality" from the "collective past" and make it live in the Caribbean present. Granny Myna's version of island history at the outset of this tale suggests the protean character of that magic, as well as its origin in the "imagining I" of *Divina Trace*. The search for El Dorado, she says, was complicated by the fact that no one even knew what it was, much less where. Hearkening back to her technique in the tale of Crab-o, she offers a number of hypotheses drawn from the collective consciousness.

> Some said how it was the long lost city of those Chibchas . . . . Some said how it was the mausoleum of a great Arawak king, or the emperor of those Incas from Peru, hidden high in the mountains. Others said it was not the creation of a man, but some marvel of the earth . . . . Others said that it was a secret fruit, or flower, and if you ate some you shit would come out in shining bars.[105]

Granny's conjectures, placing both the location and the very nature of El Dorado in a highly subjective realm, lead her to conclude that "all this El Dorado business wasn't nothing more than the fantasy of everybody's imagination", although Fernando de Berrío himself, she concedes, believed that the fabled city "was hidden somewhere right here on this island of Corpus Christi".[106] But those two propositions do not actually contradict each other, since "this island of Corpus Christi" is itself a fantasy of the imagination, a noumenal rather than a phenomenal point. As the subtitle – "The True Tale of El Dorado" – intimates, the truth of El Dorado lies somehow within this story of renewal and change, an imagined centre on an imagined island in an imagined tale, and the search for it, like the search for Caribbean Being in Caribbean storytelling, is a process of transformation and re-creation that never ends. In Benítez-Rojo's words, "Such is the inexhaustible treasure so fervently sought in this place at once mythic and utopian".[107]

5

CARNIVAL
The River's Return

Steel voice of a steel god
commands the groined shuffle and shake
man beat man beat she hard
holy rum and roti host
up and down the profane aisles
of this tin pan city
clinking clanking
pilgrimage in disguise
to cleanse the past from terror
and from fury what is to come
– Henry Beissel, "Pans at Carnival"[1]

All the rivers run into the sea; yet the sea is not full; unto the place from whence the rivers come, thither they return again.
– Ecclesiastes

My Grandmother's Erotic Folktales concludes with a significant estuarial event. Granny Myna, whose whole carnivalesque outpouring of narrative has subverted the received authority, official history and conventional morality imposed on the Caribbean by powerful outsiders, prepares to send her beloved Gregoria la Rosa into that same outside world – almost as her counter-colonizing emissary – on the wings of yet another story. Just before she bestows this final gift on the departing wedding guests, she says to them, "But now it is time for *us* to make we *own* return trip home, whether we are prepared for this voyage or not. And even though *we* voyage is the shortest distance, even though we own is the quickest, it is the longest and most difficult journey of all."[2] In a sense *Carnival* begins here; his fourth book is Antoni's shortest and quickest journey, at least in terms of narrative complexity, but it is also his longest, darkest and most difficult because it takes him so much closer to the vicissitudes of his own life than any of his earlier books, and much more into the world beyond the West Indies of ancestors and legends. In doing so, however, it also traces subtle connections between personal experience in the here and now (its narrator aspires to be a novelist) and the more distanced, mythic material of Antoni's previous work, with its wellsprings in the oral tradition. As different as it seems from the earlier books, *Carnival* is linked to them in many ways – not least in its association of diaspora with discourse. The conclusion of *Erotic Folktales* makes clear that emigration and storytelling are currents in the same river flowing out of the same complicated culture, and in *Carnival* those streams still carry along with them much of the often dangerous and disturbing detritus of Caribbean history. Like Gregoria la Rosa, *Carnival*'s William Fletcher has relocated in the United States; like Granny Myna, he attempts to tell his story; and, like many others, he seeks "to cleanse the past from terror / and from fury what is to come".

Antoni has commented that *Carnival* is about "always fleeing from home, and returning home. The characters don't quite fit in where they live, nor where they return to. Identity becomes something fluid; something you pack in your suitcase. That's an essential part of being

Caribbean. It's about geography, but the geography that we carry with us."[3] That ebb and flow – simultaneously physical and conceptual – gives the Caribbean imagination such elasticity, allowing it to push constantly outwards, extending its frontiers, though it can also be a source of the kinds of anxieties that trouble the characters in *Carnival.* For Antoni, diaspora is integral to Caribbean identity, not just a peripheral characteristic. Virtually everyone in the region has either lived in "foreign" or knows someone abroad. Because expatriation has figured so prominently in his own life, it should come as no surprise that in *Carnival* he finally focuses on the dilemma of West Indians carrying the islands in their luggage, or that he chooses as his paradigm that quintessential narrative of exile and anomie, *The Sun Also Rises.*

This is particularly plain in light of the narrow but deeply significant diasporal current running through his earlier work. As early as *Divina Trace* there is a clear interface between Caribbean identity and the fact of expatriation. During the long night preceding his ninetieth birthday, Johnny Domingo recalls scenes from his two periods of exile: his years as a medical student in the United States and the time he spent doing his residency there. The two passages, which occur at different phases in his nocturnal reverie, flow into each other the way dreams often do. One of their several common features is Johnny's self-proclaimed quest for "the definition of the Caribbean".[4] For a medical student newly arrived from the islands, that amounts simply to "*the way we suck an orange*",[5] but by his second tour of duty in New York the definition has become decidedly more ominous: "*whatever America wants you to be*".[6] A Jamaican peddler flashes briefly into both scenes – a fellow West Indian trying to make his way in the larger world. Underlying and shaping both memories is Domingo's distinct sense of displacement in America and his struggle to understand who he really is in that strange setting: what his place is there, and what place *there* will have in his own evolving imaginative landscape. The fact that *Carnival* begins in New York City is no accident; in an early manuscript version of the novel, the character who became William Fletcher was called Johnny.[7]

These scenes, remembered as nightmares within a larger nightmare, are as surreal as any in *Divina Trace.* They bring to life, with just the right mixture of "realistic" memory and slightly deranged hallucination, a world outside the Caribbean that remains on the horizon of Johnny Domingo's mental terrain, even though he lived in it for several years. Antoni's next two books continue the incorporation of "foreign" into the landscape of the Caribbean imagination. In *Blessed Is the Fruit* that external world figures primarily as a place of escape or asylum. Young Dulcianne, after becoming pregnant by Lil's father, has "no choice" but to "take-off running for America".[8] Old Mr Grandsol is forced into exile first because of his shady business dealings and later by his own daughter because of his sexual depredations. As Vel testifies, "She make it so *he* got to run from this island, just how he do to Dulcianne, and Mistress Lil make it so he can't come back neither. Put a charge pon he head before the magis."[9]

Lil herself spends only eight weeks outside the West Indies. Sent to England by her mother for "polishing", she experiences acute alienation from her surroundings, which is exacerbated by the cold weather and her English grandmother's disapproval of her island ways. Of all the characters in the novel who travel abroad, only Lil's husband, Daisy, does so with any degree of enthusiasm, though his is a special case. Born on the island of Corpus Christi of British parents and reared mostly in England, he is less West Indian than European. More important, his homosexuality is a secret country that he inhabits constantly, regardless of his physical location. His return to England with his lover Reggie is an attempt to make himself whole by bringing his inner and outer geographies into some kind of alignment. Antoni remixes this brew in *Carnival*: William Fletcher's psychosexual confusion becomes (because he is the narrator) a lens through which other forms of dislocation are viewed.

My Grandmother's Erotic Folktales, with its expansive historical/legendary scope, treats "foreign" more broadly than do the first two books: as metropolitan world, mother of the colonies and latter-day source of economic plunder and political manipulation. But, as in his previous work, Antoni continues to play (though still in a minor key) with variations on that bigger world's place in the construction of Caribbean identity. In Granny Myna's two stories from "the old old time" she touches on the history of the region as a New World "found" – and to a certain extent created – by the European powers. The tale of Crab-o begins with references to "Spanish explorers" and "English pirates"[10] and ends with the triumph of Granny Myna's scornful dismissal of the American outsider Ernesto and his reductive attempt to tell the story with "careful, real-life newspaper details".

Both the vivid portrayal of the West Indies as a neglected economic backwater in *Blessed Is the Fruit* and the canonization of Magdalena by the people of Corpus Christi in *Divina Trace* (after the "mammapoule Pope" refuses to do so) demonstrate that Antoni has always been aware of the political dimension of the Caribbean's relationship with "foreign". In *Erotic Folktales* this motif becomes more insistent, woven as it is throughout the whole book. In the tale of Iguana, the Europeans' search for wealth in the region morphs gently into the story of a single, especially cruel case of abuse before evolving once again into a parable of liberation through *métissage* – the incorporation of "foreign" into a developing Caribbean sensibility. The story concludes, like any traditional comedy, with a new, non-restrictive society being brought into being by the union of the Euro-Amerindian Iwana and her lover, the African Anaconda. The European (and later North American) conception of the West Indies as a place to get rich is paralleled by the scheming of the King of Chacachacari and the Kentucky Colonel in Granny's autobiographical tales. The chicanery of these two brings the familiar theme of economic exploitation up to date. Yet no matter how elaborate the King's and Colonel's plots to deceive and plunder, Granny Myna outsmarts them in all three tales. This profoundly comic book concludes, as we have seen, not only with the rout of the neocolonialist villains but also with the flowing of the Caribbean estuary into the wider world, through Gregoria's marriage to the American Tyrone Davis.

The twin traumas of repeated incursions from abroad and continuing large-scale emigration have stitched themselves into Caribbean consciousness over the years. Certainly the heart of *Carnival* is its meditation on the confluence of the Caribbean with the outside world, broadly worked out through William Fletcher's narration of his life in New York and his brief return home. But in *Carnival* the geographical separation of exile also becomes a way for Antoni to talk about many other disruptive forces, such as the breaches that open up between past and present, between men and women and between white and black. All of these issues arise in the earlier books, of course, but in *Carnival* Antoni makes a concerted attempt to address them within a contemporary framework: the framework of his own life and times. The facts that William allows to emerge in the book's first chapters – his own sexual dysfunction and the nuanced racial difference that separates him from friends and relatives – are not incidental. These elements take on greater and greater magnitude as the story moves to the island where William and his friends seek at least temporary restoration – or escape – through the transformative cacophony of Carnival and, afterward, their visit to the Earth People.

Caribbean writers, however, have always tended to reflect their peoples' scepticism about the durability of the changes wrought by this annual ritual, as any reader of Earl Lovelace's *The Dragon Can't Dance* (1979) or Sam Selvon's *Moses Migrating* (1992) can attest.[11] Within Antoni's own work, Daisy and Lil's carnivalesque cross-dressing in *Blessed Is the Fruit* does little to alter the sexual realities that make their marriage ultimately impossible, and in *Divina Trace*, Magdalena's festival on Corpus Christi Day brings the island "back to life" – in Papee

Vince's words – only "fa one day".[12] *Carnival* examines much more fully the darker side of mas, where deep divisions are partially concealed by communal revelry. And when the celebration is over, those divisions and barriers – racial, social, sexual – manifest themselves all too clearly, even in the pastoral setting of Mother Earth's mountain refuge.[13]

The formal complexities of *Carnival*, such as they are, lie more in the interweaving of its skeins of narrative – the story of expatriation, the story of mas, the story of the Earth People and their mythology – than in the plot itself, which is as sequential and straightforward as that of *The Sun Also Rises*. At first glance it may appear that *Carnival* is a highly compartmentalized work, with section one taking place in New York, section two in a fictionalized Port of Spain and section three in the mountainous countryside. But rather like *Blessed Is the Fruit*, the novel intentionally undermines its own structure by allowing the seemingly disparate narrative elements outwardly defined by those geographical markers (exile, Carnival, Earth People) to flow into one another, suggesting a deeper tendency within the text to blur frontiers, both literal and psychic ones. The characters talk about Carnival and the Earth People while they are still in New York; when they arrive on the island, they find that the theme of their carnival band is Mother Earth; their subsequent excursion into the mountain forest leads back to exile; and so on.

The sole narrator is William Fletcher, a young West Indian who has been living in New York for some years, initially as a student, later as an adjunct professor and aspiring novelist. The first part of the book takes place over about eighteen months, from one summer into the autumn of the following year, as William becomes reacquainted with his childhood friend Laurence de Boissière. They have been separated for ten years, with William attending Fordham and Columbia universities in New York and Laurence going to Oxford on a scholarship. During that time William, the product of a privileged white family,[14] has been unable to whip his MFA thesis into a marketable novel, while Laurence, who grew up in a poor, predominantly black neighbourhood, has become a noted poet and playwright. William recalls that on the occasion of their first meeting, when they were nine, "I knew that I adored and despised this boy even as much as I did myself."[15] These ambivalent feelings towards Laurence (and towards himself) are indivisible from his equally complicated and even more emotionally fraught ties with his cousin Rachel. Almost from the beginning of the novel, both relationships are bound up with William's own sexual ambiguities. When Rachel shows up in New York with a young Spaniard (the most recent of several men she has married), they all agree to meet again for Carnival on their home island, an unnamed, lightly masked version of Trinidad.

The first seven chapters are anchored in an easily recognizable – though considerably Caribbeanized – Manhattan.[16] On the day of his reunion with Laurence, William Fletcher is wearing a T-shirt advertising the Desperadoes, the steel band of Laurence's old neighbourhood, Laventille. Fearing that Laurence will think he is reminding him of his humble roots, he turns the shirt inside out – the first of numerous masquerades in the novel. That same day they meet a young Jamaican bartender, an aspiring actor who plies them with cold Red Stripe beers and Mount Gay Barbados rum. The following summer Laurence casts him as the lead in his play about the Haitian revolution. And in the fall, when Rachel arrives, they attend a "pre-carnival jump-up" starring David Rudder, "our most popular calypsonian".[17] It is at this rum-soaked party that they hatch their plan to reunite on the island for carnival. William also invites the others to accompany him afterwards on his annual trek into the forested northern range, perhaps to see a great leatherback turtle crawl up on the beach to lay her eggs, and perhaps even to visit the mysterious Earth People, who have isolated themselves from the corrupt social world they call Rome.[18] These and many other such details certainly provide a realistic glimpse into how much Caribbean space there is in New York City today, but more than that, they suggest how much of the Caribbean is packed into William Fletcher's mental suitcase.

When the scene shifts to the island, the book's long central section follows the three main characters and their friends through five days of frenetic celebration. Antoni brings the festival to life with the accuracy and relish of a true aficionado, but beneath the revelry lie persistent racial and sexual tensions that refuse to go away. Moreover, a sense of dislocation continues to cling to William's narrative, as if he no longer fully belongs to the island he calls home. The novel's final movement takes Rachel, Laurence and William into the northern mountain range, where they encounter not only the peaceful Earth People but also three extremely nasty policemen and more than one shocking reminder that the traumas wrought by history upon the Caribbean will not be easily healed.

Unquestionably the most striking technical characteristic of *Carnival* is its "cross-dressing" – as Antoni likes to say – in the garb of *The Sun Also Rises.* His appropriation of Hemingway's novel will undoubtedly be compared to latter-day engagements with other canonical texts such as Jean Rhys's *Wide Sargasso Sea* and Peter Carey's *Jack Maggs.* But if *Carnival,* broadly speaking, can be categorized as counter-discourse, it is not exactly a case of the empire writing back.[19] Unlike Rhys, Carey and others, Antoni does not revisit the characters, or even the historical period, of the earlier book. He uses it in a different (and wholly original) way to tell a different story. In his previous work he maintains a certain control over his material through the distancing of mask. *Divina Trace, Blessed Is the Fruit* and *My Grandmother's Erotic Folktales* are largely told in voices that are not Antoni's own. They emerge out of the depths of family history and island folklore or, as Johnny Domingo puts it, "out of that vast storehouse of words and images constantly disassembled and reassembled and surfacing again mysterious, new".[20] In *Carnival* the voice must be a modern one, and the narrator is a character who resembles the author in many respects. He needs a voice, but not the ornate, highly figurative and often hyperbolic one of Granny Myna, Vel or Mother Maurina.

For Antoni, telling this story through the technique of cross-dressing is a way to maintain the distance and objectivity that came naturally in his first three books, but with a style appropriate to William Fletcher, his time and his place. *The Sun Also Rises* also provides Antoni with a language – sometimes symbolic, sometimes literal – that enables him both to express the anomie of the West Indian expatriate and to examine the interface between expatriation and the deep roots of Caribbean being. If Hemingway confronts the trauma of a generation unmoored by the First World War, Antoni explores the disorientations of a post-colonial world, focusing on the part of that world he knows best.

Many of the outward trappings of Hemingway's story are used by Antoni to shape his own, as he himself acknowledges: "My thievery extends to the skeletal: I even utilise the same number of chapters and sections as Hemingway."[21] The plot of *Carnival* parallels that of *The Sun Also Rises* in myriad ways. Paris becomes New York; the Pamplona fiesta becomes a Caribbean one, described in even more intricate detail; and Jake Barnes's fishing trip becomes William's trek into the mountains with Rachel and Laurence. Readers will at once notice similarities between various characters in the two books. William is Antoni's Jake Barnes; Rachel, his Brett Ashley (unattainable for quite a different reason); and Laurence, his Robert Cohn. These links, however, are not exact; Antoni freely reshapes, recombines and transforms elements from Hemingway's novel.

In *The Sun Also Rises*, for example, Brett Ashley arrives on the scene accompanied by a "crowd of young men" with "white hands, wavy hair, white faces, grimacing, gesturing, talking".[22] Early in *Carnival* a group of gay men also appears, but they are with Laurence's fiancée, who is prankishly named Ashling Worthington. Rachel's young Spanish husband, Javier, initially fills the role of the bullfighter Pedro Romero, but later in *Carnival* Rachel sets her sights on Eddoes, one of the Earth People who has come down to the city to play mas. Echoing Brett's remark about Pedro, she says of Eddoes's Carnival costume, "I'd love to see how he gets it on!"[23] And there are many other traces of *Sun* in *Carnival* that are harder to categorize, as when an eatery in the island's capital is described as "one of the best restaurants in the world",[24] or when Rachel, attending church on Ash Wednesday, says to William, "I'm no good for this anymore . . . . Let's get out of here!"[25] Even the town of Carmel, California, is mentioned near the beginning of both novels.

But by far the most important element in Antoni's cross-dressing is the channelling of Jake Barnes's voice into the personality of William Fletcher. In keeping with the best Carnival costumes, it is a masterpiece of mimicry, from the first sentences of the novel to the last. William begins, "Laurence de Boissière was once the tennis champion of Oxford. Don't think I'm too highly impressed by that as a tennis title, but it meant something to Laurence",[26] and he ends speaking wistfully to Rachel: " 'Yes.' I said. 'Isn't it happy to think so?' "[27] No one who has read *The Sun Also Rises* can fail to recognize these lines, and the rest of the book is filled with them – small areas where the costume's stitching is laid bare. Some of them are more subtle, as when William says, "It was funny to think about", or when he expresses satisfaction at having "things under control".[28] Perhaps most usefully for Antoni, William, like Jake, frequently addresses the reader directly. He says at one point, "The rest of that night remains a blur. So don't hold me responsible for the accuracy with which I recount it",[29] and in a later chapter, "You won't believe me, but I got to NYU an hour early for my class the following morning."[30] There are many sentences like that, and they are extremely evocative of Jake Barnes, but they also link this book to Antoni's earlier ones, and to the oral roots of Caribbean literature, reminding the reader that this too is a story being told to an implied listener (or reader).

Telling those stories, as we have seen, is intrinsic to the construction of cultural and personal identity. As if to emphasize the point, near the beginning of *Carnival* Antoni distinguishes his first-person narration from Hemingway's by repeated references to "us" as William speaks for himself and the people back on his native island. The significance of that multiple first person is implicit in William's reaction when he meets Francis, the Jamaican bartender: "Another one of us, I thought."[31] In a similar vein, he characterizes some of Laurence's early professional successes and romantic exploits as big "news for us at home".[32] Jake's "I" is a wholly individuated, quintessentially American *I*. William's strives to be a collective Caribbean *we*.

Hemingway is not the only presiding deity of *Carnival*, however. If *The Sun Also Rises* provides a kind of language with which Antoni can record the registers of William's alienation, the mas bands of Peter Minshall inform William's effort to narrate himself into the culture of the Caribbean. William's account is itself an elaborate narrative jump-up whose theme is his yearning to join in, connect, take part in what Lawrence Scott calls (in a fine short story about Carnival) "the ritual and the fact of his belonging".[33] Minshall, one of Trinidad's best-known Carnival impresarios over the past thirty years, is widely respected for the extravagance of his talent and for his artistic integrity.[34] He has, as Peter Mason notes, "tried to bring messages to his mas, pursuing complicated themes with many different sections and giving teams of designers free range".[35] Just as he borrows parts of his *Carnival* costume from Hemingway, Antoni also raids Minshall's closet, using bits and pieces from several of his past mas bands. In 1982, for instance, Minshall's band was in fact called River and featured characters recycled in *Carnival,* Washerwoman and Mancrab. Unlike her fictional counterpart, Minshall's real "*Washerwoman* queen, the embodiment of purity and harmony, was symbolically raped and murdered by his king, *Mancrab,* a devil-like creature representing greed and evil technology."[36] Despite significant differences, this early Minshall work is a major source for the Earth People's mas in *Carnival.*

Antoni's novel as a whole, however, appears to owe more to a much later Minshall creation, the Lost Tribe of the 1999 carnival.

> There once was an island place that was blessed with many riches. Mountains, valleys, clear rivers, warm seas. The greatest of its blessings, though, was its people. They were a people whose ancestors had come from many different places, who had come together to make one tribe, in a new world. . . . They traveled together toward a wonderful new destiny. To know the direction in which they must travel, they followed a great map. No one man could have drawn this map. It was a map that had been assembled from the knowledge of all the ancestors of all the people. But one day . . . the leaders of the different families within the tribe quarreled amongst themselves. In their foolishness, the map was torn into pieces. . . . The island place became a spiritual wilderness. The tribe lost its way. Until the pieces of the map are put together again, the people will squander their riches. Their destiny will remain distant and obscure. And they will wander aimlessly.[37]

All of Minshall's Carnival concoctions have strong story lines. I have quoted this one at length because it is a plot that *Carnival* seems to follow almost as carefully as it does that of *The Sun Also Rises.* William's story is virtually a narrative performance of Minshall's 1999 presentation. More than a clever echo of Gertrude Stein's "You are all a lost generation", Antoni's epigraph, attributed to Minshall – "We are all a lost tribe" – sounds the opening chord and the dominant motif of a mas enacted in words.

After attending a New York production of Laurence's play about Toussaint L'Ouverture and the Haitian revolution, William admits, "Suffice to say that L'Ouverture's problem, his confusion, no different from any of us, was that he could not make up his mind which of the tribes he'd come from. And there were so many he'd lost count."[38] Once again William rhetorically binds himself to the islands through a pronoun that pluralizes his very being, but in doing so he also associates himself with an iconic Caribbean figure whose alienation at the end of his life was absolute.[39] The urgent problem for William, then, is how to make that "us" a reality, how to learn which of the tribes he really belongs to. All of his "confusions" – political, racial, sexual – are forms of psychic dislocation, but literal expatriation is the semantic template that gives the novel its shape. *Carnival* is above all a novel of exile and return. From the beginning, even though enjoying his exile in New York City as much as any young man would, William is preoccupied with the idea of home. His first references insistently (perhaps a little too insistently) equate home with the island of his birth. When he refers to "[p]eople at home" or those of "us at home",[40] there is no doubt as to his meaning. As narrator, he is careful to include his friends in this formulation, recalling Rachel's comment "The plan is to meet at home in three month's time" and observing that "other than a few brief visits" Laurence "hadn't been back home himself".[41]

But the question of nationality turns out to be much more complicated. When asked by the ringleader of a group of drunken "frat-boys" whether he and the others are "Brits", William replies with more historical awareness (not to mention irony) than his interlocutor can possibly absorb, "We used to be. . . . Now we're from the West

Indies."[42] And he describes the David Rudder jump-up as "packed with raucous, bawling, thoroughly happy West Indians. And we were among them."[43] But when they arrive in the rainforest after Carnival and are asked by a veterinarian they meet if they are British, William's response is, "We're Americans", though he admits it is "an odd claim to make".[44] Odd indeed, and of not much consequence to the menacing policeman who brands them "foreigners" and later orders them to go "back to wherever you come from, England or America or wherever the fock it is!"[45] The angry exchange almost exactly echoes a New York peddler's words to William and Lawrence months before: "Fuck-off back to wherever you come from."[46]

"What is foreign", Certeau writes, "is that which escapes from a place",[47] but in the unmoored world of *Carnival,* escape is not always voluntary. William, Laurence and Rachel find themselves perpetually off balance, always remaining, in Antoni's own analysis, "both outsiders and insiders, wherever they happen to find themselves".[48] Their sense of dislocation is further complicated by family, and especially by family history. Rachel, like William a member of the wealthy elite, has not "been back to the island in years"[49] and stays at a hotel with her friends rather than with her parents. Laurence is on closer terms with his immediate family, but it is more scattered than either Rachel's or William's. His mother, an accomplished and educated woman, was abandoned by her husband when their son was only seven. The elder de Boissière went "to foreign", William recalls – not, like William or Laurence, to attend university, but to pursue economic opportunities unavailable in the West Indies. At the time *Carnival* takes place, he has recently been fired from his job as counsellor in an English orphanage after being implicated in a scandal that has a homosexual (and possibly racial) dimension. All three have stayed in touch over the years, however, and both Laurence and his mother are trying to come to terms with this latest crisis.

For William, studying in New York has been a way to break with his family's "blood money";[50] his disaffection from his father (who once had an affair with Rachel's mother) is, he says, "by now . . . pretty much official".[51] And one reason why he returns "home" only for Carnival is that he knows he will not have to see his parents then: "My mother and father regularly 'escaped the rabble' by flying off to Barbados for the week, together with their groups of proper English friends." They consider the festival "vulgar and barbaric. . . . An event, at best, to be tolerated for the 'blacks'."[52] William's situation throws the novel's broader concerns into bold relief. The family is such a fountainhead of identity in part because it is a link between the individual and a wider society, but it is also a link between consciousness of the present and understanding of the past. Like identity itself, family is both a spatial and a temporal construct, encompassing ancestors as well as immediate kin. Antoni touches very lightly on the racial and social injustices that went into the making of the Fletcher fortune in years gone by, but they clearly fuel William's estrangement. The paradox for him, as Antoni puts it elsewhere, is that he and his friends need both to reclaim history and to escape it. Their psychic movement is always both towards and away from a conception of home that includes a past still not cleansed from terror.[53]

For William and his friends, race is a present-day issue, but one framed in a peculiarly West Indian way. Their racial identities are ambiguous because they are multiple, like Toussaint's tribes. None of them "belongs" to any one race. They are all of both European and African ancestry, in differing degrees – "divided to the vein", in Derek Walcott's words.[54] William's and Rachel's ethnic heritage in particular encapsulates the indeterminacies of race in the Caribbean, which is often more a matter of context than of genetics. Although several times in his narrative William casually refers to himself as white, he qualifies that designation when recalling his acceptance into Columbia University's MFA programme:

> Of course, there was a bit of a fiasco when I arrived at Columbia, and they took a look at my face. Because my being West Indian had led them to certain assumptions – which were not altogether false – though they were not true enough, either, to enable me to fulfill their prescribed quota. Not very easily. At least, not in the clear-cut way they liked to envision it.[55]

Back on the island, an immigration officer at the airport puts his own spin on the incident: "I hear this story bout how you did pose as a negro-man. To get some kinda scholarship they was giving-way in one them fancy writing schools in New York."[56] Clearly this man, an East Indian Caribbean named Ganish Ramsumair, regards William simply as white, and that impression is reinforced somewhat later when Laurence introduces him to a famous novelist from the island (obviously V.S. Naipaul). The great man advises William, tongue in cheek, not to let them put his picture on the jacket of his novel when it comes out, because "nobody's going to pay much attention to a West Indian writer who happens to be a wealthy white boy".[57] The issue of William's "whiteness" appears to be Antoni's way of confronting the problematics of his own family's identity in the context of Trinidad: racially white and economically privileged. Socially William comes from the same class as the Antonis, but it is worth reflecting that Antoni gives William a bit of African ancestry while he has never explicitly claimed that heritage for himself.

Rachel is more visibly "mixed" than her cousin, a fact established with considerable humour in an early scene. William has been waiting for Laurence in the Bar None when Laurence appears with Rachel and her new husband in tow. Some time afterwards, a drunken college student "scams" Rachel, earnestly telling her, "Lady . . . you got more class in your earlobes than most white chicks got in their whole freaking cadavers. I mean, I ain't prejudiced or nothing, gimme a classy negress over a washed-out white chick any day a the week."[58] William has already described her in detail: red hair, green eyes, "café-au-lait cheeks" and "extravagant lips".[59] From the perspective of the white American boys she is simply black, however light her skin tone might be. To Laurence, keenly aware of her family's wealth and social status back home, both she and her cousin are "rich white West Indians"; much later, on their trek into the mountains, Rachel is contemptuously derided as "white pussy" by one of the three belligerent policemen they encounter.[60]

These and many other similar references to racial demarcations and combinations – some funny, some ominous – add to the sense of "constant masking and . . . unmasking" that in Lawrence Scott's words makes "the whole book . . . a carnival".[61] But there is also, running right through the novel, an undercurrent of anxiety. While Carnival is in large part a celebration of the Caribbean's ethnic multiplicity, William and his friends seem to intuit that an individual whose family history is one of both slaves and slave owners bears a burden that does not get any lighter when the music stops. Clearly the broad cultural *métissage* that Antoni's books celebrate has not eradicated, even in his fictional world, the Caribbean's racial barriers, inequities and tensions.

William Fletcher's most damaging "confusion", however, is psychosexual. His "wound", unlike that of Jake Barnes, is not physical, but it is just as debilitating. He is exiled from a part of himself and has no idea how to find his way back. Antoni brings the reader into William's problem gradually, scattering enough hints to leave plenty of room for interpretation. The first clue to his problems with women is so faint as to be nearly unnoticeable. When Laurence, joking with William and Francis, the Jamaican bartender, points out that the map of Barbados on the Mount Gay rum bottle looks like an erect penis, William admits, "[E]ven I had to laugh."[62] The implications of that little word "even" ripple throughout William's narrative. Shortly afterwards he recalls an attempted affair with an older woman in one of his classes. Once again addressing the reader/listener directly, he asks, "Have you ever had somebody try to put a condom on your flaccid penis?" Ksenga, like most of the "sensitive, speculative women" he has tried to date, finally concluded that he was gay.[63] She even sent a band of young gay men (embarrassingly, all of them William's students) to usher him out of the closet.

This is not a solution that William readily accepts, but it is a question that increasingly bores its way into his story. He does admit that what he knows best about women is a "look of frustrated expectation",[64] and during Carnival week that frustration is put on display three times. On Friday night Rachel begs him, "At least allow me to try", but he stops her.[65] Two nights later a girl named Jennifer puts her hand in his pants and then pulls it back "[l]ike she'd shoved it into a coalpot", exclaiming hotly, "What happen? . . . You ain't like me?"[66] And two days after that, on Fat Tuesday itself, yet another girl tries to take William to bed. He closes his eyes, "[f]ighting to find a focus", but soon he hears Monique shouting "something in French – exasperated, angry".[67]

The relationship with Rachel is the one that most torments William. When they were children, he explains, everyone expected them to grow up and marry, and their emotional bond, despite everything, has remained strong over the years. On that first Carnival night, when Rachel wants to try one more time, she calls their situation "[o]ur lifelong predicament".[68] Like so much else in this novel of glittering costumes and surfaces, that predicament has a dark history. Antoni introduces it very gradually, first through a cryptic remark William makes to Rachel outside the Bar None in New York: a reference, which quite upsets her, to something that happened in their past. In subsequent chapters the unmentionable incident comes slowly into fuller focus – first as the account of a recurring dream, later as a direct and more detailed recollection – but Antoni saves the final revelation for William and Rachel's reunion at the Queen's Park Hotel back home.

About fifteen years earlier, when both were in their mid-teens, they planned to have sex for the first time while their parents were celebrating Old Year's Eve at the British Club and the younger siblings were in bed. Just a moment or two after they began, the two of them "fitted together" as one, "three wajanks" carrying cutlasses and fuelled by cocaine broke into the house and attacked them.[69] All three were black, one wearing dreadlocks and the other two, identical twins, sporting shaved heads. The assault was so traumatic that Rachel, even years later, is not fully aware of what happened – she had kept her eyes shut throughout the entire ordeal. In the hotel room during Carnival, William finally reveals the whole truth: "What they did to you, they did to me, too."[70] William was sodomized by all three intruders, and he remembers with particular vividness the sensation of being raped by one twin and glancing over to see Rachel being raped by the other, almost as if he were looking into a mirror: "The twins merged, they became one, and I became them." Although William adds, "Whatever it means, if it means anything at all, I do not know",[71] the tableau he describes suggests not only his own bifurcated sexual orientation but also an identification of victim and predator. William and Rachel's family tree, we are obliquely reminded here, contains the blood of both.

On his first day back on the island, the Friday of Carnival weekend, William runs into Rachel almost accidentally. As they kiss, he finds his thoughts racing back to his last summer on the island with Rachel, two years after the rapes. Even before she left convent school she had planned a special reunion with William at Huevos Beach, a meeting that would turn back the clock to a time before that terrible night. "Rachel had written me a long letter from school as the end of the year approached, describing in detail how it would happen. 'A symbolic Extreme Unction,' she wrote, 'for both of us.' According to Rachel this ritual would restore us. Instantly. Magically. Back to before. Both of us, pure, unwrecked, practically – 'technically,' she wrote – virgins again."[72] They would splash naked in the sea after each of them buried in the sand something important. But the magic failed. However intently William struggled to concentrate on his desire for Rachel, images of the rapes flashed through his mind, and all he could find within himself was an "absent center".[73] Rachel told him then, in so many words, that although they loved each other like "no other two people ever", she could not, and would not, "wait any longer".[74] Eleven years later, when the main events in *Carnival* take place, Rachel has already experienced four failed marriages, mute testimony to the "absent centre" in her own life.

As for William, this sequence in the novel plainly suggests that his impotence stems from the rapes. After all, he and Rachel were in the midst of intercourse when the "wajanks" burst into the house. Yet that explanation seems hardly more credible than that of Laurence's mother when she writes to a British newspaper that her husband's relationship with a young man is "a response conditioned in him by the history of his race".[75] The etiology of sexual confusion rarely has a single clearly identifiable source. It may be worth pointing out here that in an earlier draft of *Carnival* Rachel and William (then still called Johnny) were half-siblings. Antoni eventually dropped the legal and ecclesiastical barriers between them and substituted a more ambiguous one. The taboo against incest is nakedly unequivocal, while the vagaries of sexual identity are very difficult to trace, much less demarcate or pin down.

William is candid enough to note that, even in his youth, some people back home had considered him "a buller".[76] When Ksenga had her "indefatigable posse" of young gays virtually raid William's apartment, he claims he "demurred", which can mean either "objected" or "delayed".[77] Antoni leaves it at that for the time being. But near the end of the novel, in the seclusion of the rainforest, William impulsively kisses Laurence. The scene is intense, shot through with anger on the part of both men as they trade insults. Laurence calls William a buller, and William responds by alluding to the homosexual scandal that cost Laurence's father his job at the orphanage. Laurence hits William, then walks off, leaving William to stare in shock at his penis – erect at last.

Perhaps the sexual assault on William and Rachel, coming as it did at such a fragile moment in their adolescence, intensified and brought to the forefront of William's consciousness an inclination long present but largely dormant. This explanation of William's "problem" strongly suggested by the text may for many readers lack plausibility. Most men of William's age and education living in an academic environment in New York City would not take fifteen years to figure all this out. What can be said with certainty is that William does love Rachel desperately on some level, but his conflicted sexual makeup (whatever its origins) will never permit consummation. Their "lifelong predicament" – an ever-frustrated need for each other – is only the most dramatic and poignant of many variations on yearning in the novel, a longing for some kind of connection, be it with another person, a place, a family or a history. It is that impulse, always flowing just beneath the surface of their collective consciousness, that has brought William Fletcher and his friends home for the annual bacchanal.

One of the purposes of Carnival is the liberation from fixed identities so that new ones can be assumed, at least temporarily. The *mas* in "playing mas" is short for *masquerade,*[78] but there is also an underlying suggestion, both in the word and in the activity it denotes, of Mass, the Catholic liturgy of the Eucharist, or transubstantiation of bread and wine into the body and blood of Christ. The Carnival mas is transformative also, but it is transitory as well; no sane celebrant expects the metamorphoses to extend into the rest of the year. Nevertheless, Carnival is more than just a tension-releasing purge. It stands for something real: the potential not just to be but also to become, both for individuals who jump up and for the society as a whole. It is also an elaborate, chaotic performance of creolization – the estuarial process of mixing, flowing together and growing that Caribbean culture embodies and enacts. For Antoni's characters, to return to the island at this particular time for this uniquely participatory event makes perfect sense. They can throw themselves into the celebration, join with the extended family of their compatriots, abandon inhibitions and perhaps, just perhaps, find some of the connections they long for.

The long midsection of the novel follows the characters through five orgiastic days, from the Friday before Shrove Tuesday (Mardi Gras) to Ash Wednesday, the first day of Lent, when reality is supposed to reassert itself. During these days they are swept up in the music and masquerade, the wining and jamming, the drinking and sex, revelling in the ethos of *métissage*: "All o' we is one."[79] But reality repeatedly peeps around the edges of their masks during the festivities, from the first day to the last. William's three encounters with women (Rachel, Jennifer and Monique) only intensify his anguish. Rachel's frustration also continues unabated, working its way out in the form of an increasingly predatory attraction to the handsome dreadlocked Eddoes, a young son of Mother Earth who has come to town to play mas in Peter Minshall's band.[80] And the fault lines of race and class show through as well. Gordon Rohlehr characterizes the quintessential Carnival moment as an "illusory neutralizing element . . . when anonymous under the mask, boss man and servant pretend to forget, to be free of their history, and sometimes even to exchange their normal roles".[81] Yet in the very midst of the celebration, on Carnival Monday, William finds himself in an altercation at the British Club, where the bouncer refuses admittance to Eddoes and even to Laurence: " 'No dreads inside here,' the guy shouted. . . . And no upstart niggers, neither!"[82]

There is more to carnival than mas itself (dressing up in the costume of a particular band), and Antoni chronicles every detail of it in this novel, following his characters through every phase of each day. Although he has said he did not want "the book to become some sort of travelogue or tourist guide" (and to avoid that cut many pages from an earlier draft),[83] readers looking for an intimate eyewitness account of the total Carnival experience, including such details as costume changes for different phases of the celebration, will not be disappointed. William abundantly records the parts of the festival in which he participates – which is most of it – but he obviously cannot be everywhere at once. On Saturday the big event is the Panarama steel band finals. Every year (on this fictional island as in the real Trinidad) the best bands enter this competition. During preliminaries the dozens of bands are whittled down to a few of the best, which then compete on the Saturday before Carnival Tuesday. This is normally one of the highlights of William's visit, but this year he misses it. He has been summoned to the Hilton by Laurence, where he is introduced to the "novelist and travel writer" easily identifiable as V.S. Naipaul.[84] Several bottles of whisky later, when William and Laurence finally stagger out, the finals are over. William has managed, earlier that day, to make his way to Peter Minshall's mas camp on the outskirts of the city to pick up his costume and touch base with the band. He learns that for this year's Carnival Minshall's band will be based on the beliefs of the Earth People who live in Hell Valley, high above the island's northern seacoast, and that its name will be River.

On the next day, Sunday, William and his friends have an enormous lunch at his favourite restaurant, then attend the calypso competitions and the judging of the various bands' kings and queens, "the finale of Dimanche Gras".[85] In the pre-dawn hours of Monday morning, called *jouvert*, "dirtymas" – contrasting with the "prettymas" of the two main Carnival days – takes place. William describes it vividly:

> The night was alive with people, flashing in and out of the streetlights. Most, like us, dressed in rags – dirtymas, mudmas – their faces and bodies blackened. Or painted head-to-toe in devil-red. Bright baby-blue. Some wearing oldtime jouvert costumes: mokojumbies on tall stilts, caped Midnight Robbers, Dame Lorraines in frills and petticoats – flipped up to reveal stiff pink dildos. . . . Fire-and-smoke breathing dragons. Bats. Imps. Pitchfork-stabbing jab-jabs.[86]

Peter Mason explains that jouvert displays "the dark, demonic flip side of mas" and goes on to call it "good-natured but . . . definitely more aggressive, more extreme, more macho than the pretty mas it precedes".[87] It is during this "more macho" phase of the celebration that William disappoints Jennifer when she puts her hand in his pants – one of several signals that Carnival's powers to transform are limited indeed. He fares little better on Monday, the day of the ugly incident at the British Club, and on Mardi Gras day itself, when he experiences yet another humiliating sexual misfire. This unpleasant episode with Monique also causes William to miss the final big event of Carnival: the appearance of Minshall's band on the main stage of Queen's Park Savannah at sunset. "I wasn't among them," he reflects. "But despite it all, or in spite of it all, I did not feel that I was far away, either."[88] Sadly for William, he feels closer to the band he can hear only distantly across the Savannah than to the girl who was, until a moment before, lying in his bed.

Lawrence Scott calls Antoni's portrayal of Minshall's mas camp "a memorializing, recording part of the book",[89] and while this observation is certainly apt, it is incomplete, because it is through Minshall's mas that the Earth People's mythology enters the novel in full force. When William and his friend Shay-lee first arrive at mas camp, he learns that Minshall, true to his reputation for innovation, will have two kings heading up his band this year, but only one queen. The queen will be arrayed as Mother Earth herself, but in the guise "of a popular West Indian folk character, washerwoman, always depicted in white".[90] Astute readers may remember a variation on this same figure in "The Tale of How Crab-o Lost His Head" from *My Grandmother's Erotic Folktales*. One of the kings will be played by Eddoes, the naïve country boy who has come down from the Earth People's mountain redoubt to take part in carnival – an actual member of Mother Earth's family playing a king in a mas that dramatizes her belief system. His costume will evoke the natural world, especially "the river at sunset",[91] while that of the other king (played by a white man) will be a "bulky and ominous" affair with "mechanical claws, rockets" and even a television set, representing modern mankind, whose "science and technology has cut him off from Mother Earth, bringing his slow destruction".[92] The first and most startling layer of Eddoes's equally elaborate costume is the "skin-tight latex" bodysuit so admired by Rachel, with airbrushed gold paint highlighting every anatomical detail.[93]

On Sunday (Dimanche Gras) William is back at mas camp to help prepare for the competition back in town at the Savannah. When they arrive there, his friend Oony tells him "the story of River" – the narrative of Minshall's mas – which is, with minor alterations, the myth of the Earth People, which Minshall has learned from Eddoes. William, already familiar with it from his previous visits to Hell Valley, includes a summary version in his narrative. What follows is an even briefer paraphrase of William's account: Mother Earth had twin sons to whom she gave their own planet, the sun. After a while they returned to earth and entered into her womb, causing her to bring forth the black and white races. The stronger white son invented science and went with his people to Europe and America; the weak son went with his black people to Africa and Asia. The strong son called himself God and attempted to control nature, creating a religion based on science and materialism. Eventually almost all people, both black and white, came under the sway of this God, in whose name wars were fought and the seas were polluted. He nearly destroyed the world, but his brother survived under the protection of the Mother. The white son came to their hidden valley, called Eden, and tried to kill his brother. But the black brother, standing on his side of the river, hurled a small stone at his enemy and killed him.[94]

Roland Littlewood provides a fuller rendering of the myth of Trinidad's actual Earth People, and it is easy to notice areas in which Antoni exercises a bit of poetic licence.[95] Littlewood says nothing about twins, for example; the struggle as he explains it is between the Mother and the Son. But twins representing white and black, technology and nature, nicely enrich the motif of divided identity running throughout *Carnival*. The fundamentals of the Earth People's cosmogony presented in the novel are consonant with Littlewood's research – hardly surprising in view of Antoni's own first-hand knowledge of the Earth People.

Minshall's mas, River, is an artistic construct that attempts to interpret, and presumably to celebrate, Mother Earth's world view. To this end he enlists Eddoes, and it is one of the novel's finest ironies that Eddoes, himself one of the Earth People, becomes a part of an effort to aestheticize and thus domesticate his own belief system. But the Earth People, though living peacefully and harmlessly in a remote region of the island, are philosophically in a state of open rebellion against the rest of the country and, indeed, the whole modern world. They consider the Christian god to be "the principle of Science and Death";[96] they eschew all clothing while at home in Hell Valley and wear very little even when they visit nearby villages; and, needless to say, they do not recognize civil authority. The power structure of the island in turn regards Mother Earth's extended family at best as mentally defective degenerates and at worst as dangerous subversives. The real "Mother Earth", Jeanette Baptiste, was incarcerated at St Ann's asylum in Port of Spain,[97] as was her fictional counterpart. The psychiatric diagnosis was schizophrenia, and perhaps this is the only "scientific" way to come to terms with an apocalyptic vision of nature's being redeemed through the total destruction of science and technology. In a sense the mas is another, more benign attempt to enclose her in a comprehensible conceptual framework, with the ritualized reality of the mas called River itself encoded within the ritualized reality of Antoni's novel.

For William, Laurence and Rachel, their energies spent by playing Earth People in Minshall's mas, the long-planned visit to the actual Earth People looms as a potentially cathartic experience. The lure of the real forest and of Mother Earth's philosophy are closely joined. On the most superficial level, a camping trip in the pristine wilderness spilling down to Madamas Beach is just the thing to decompress after the urban frenzy of Carnival. But the northern range and coast, a part of Trinidad often called "Behind God's Back" by locals,[98] appears to be a prelapsarian world profoundly in tune with Mother Earth's vision.[99] In his characters' minds Antoni has associated her with a "landscape . . . unmarred by society, history – that is some sort of refuge".[100] As Littlewood explains of the essence of the Earth People's religion, "The Way of The Mother is the Way of Nature – a return to the simplicity of the Beginning, a simplicity of nakedness, cultivation of the land by hand and with respect, and of gentle and non-exploiting human relationships."[101]

Antoni's description of the three making their way from the top of the cliffs, through the rainforest, down to the beach and finally, half a mile farther on, to the mouth of the river is reverential, as if they were entering a holy place. What they do not realize at first is that their conception of where they are is just as much an illusion as the Carnival masquerade version. The Edenic "Way of Nature" was not something Mother Earth felt she had achieved but a goal towards which she was working. The consummation of her vision would not occur until fatally tainted technological society, with all its unspeakable exploitation and dehumanization, was utterly destroyed. When Antoni's characters put down their backpacks beside the River Madamas, they have arrived in a fool's paradise.

The first hint of this occurs when they meet the three police officers, or "warriors of Rome", as Mother Earth calls them.[102] As representatives of the kind of authority that Mother Earth rejects, they are almost self-parodies. One of them warns, "All-you stay-way from them bush-niggers, is what I come to inform. Unnastand? Them niggers is nasty. They ain't civil – ain't got no education, no manners!" When Laurence shoots back, "Only three niggers round here . . . lacking civility",[103] they respond with a torrent of racist abuse and roar off in their Jeep. Despite William's apprehension, the next day passes with no further sign of the police. Eddoes, who has showed up the previous night, appears again, this time to take Rachel fishing and up to Hell Valley for a meeting with Mother Earth. Laurence and William go on a crayfishing expedition of their own.

In this part of the novel, roughly parallel to the male-bonding fishing trip in *The Sun Also Rises,* William's sexual desire for Laurence flares up and precipitates a small crisis. Although the two men are both embarrassed and angered by the incident, their friendship seems to survive. The moment is intense, but it passes like a tropical squall. Antoni leaves the underlying emotions tactfully (perhaps too tactfully) unelaborated, and Saturday ends on an improbably conciliatory note, with Eddoes leading the three of them down to the beach to watch the turtle – "the old lady of the sea" – lay her eggs.[104] What they witness is starkly poetic, with the great leatherback struggling to drag herself up onto the sand, dig her hole and give birth, as her kind have done for millions of years. It is not incidental that the leatherback is a sojourner who travels from the sea to the "foreign" world of dry land to bear her young.

The richly restorative connotations of the turtle's ancient ritual –

nature replenishing herself before their very eyes – quickly unravel the next morning. William, who the night before brought Eddoes to Rachel at her insistence, finds her alone on the beach. Eddoes is gone. All the turtle's eggs have been smashed: "a hundred of them, all torn, ripped open, their shiny contents spilled out in faintly yellow-red, star-shaped splotches – as though they'd been thrown down hard. . . . Splattered." Nearby the words "FOCK NIGA" and "WITE CUNT" have been scraped into the sand, a violent and racist counter-text to Mother Earth's message of love and respect.[105] The desecration is apparently the work of two teenaged boys who earlier had ogled Rachel and came back to spy on her and Eddoes, but when William goes looking for them, he finds the police Jeep parked on a ridge with a clear view of the whole scene.

In rapid sequence they learn that Eddoes has been shorn of his dreadlocks by the police, dragged behind their Jeep, and finally beaten and castrated by the villagers – all for an offence that is both racial and sexual. As one of the policemen later says, "[A]in't nobody round these parts accustomed to no white women bulling none a them bush-niggers . . . ! Not out in the open, front everybody."[106] The act of miscegenation in its broadest sense – not just genetic cross-dressing but mixing and swapping in various ways – is intrinsic *and* essential to Caribbean culture, but in the eyes of "Rome" it is simply "'gainst jurisdiction",[107] a challenge to an established order that itself is mimetic of colonialist power structures. "Jurisdiction" finds its voice in the local newspaper, the *Guardian*,[108] which William picks up at the airport on his way back to New York. The paper's coverage of the events at Madamas is filled with error and distortion, from the headline's double lie ("Carnival King Rapes British Tourist") to the last paragraph's sanctimonious and false assertion that the Earth People are "known for their violent history".[109] This is the official version of reality, as inside out as the Desperadoes T-shirt William wore at the beginning of the novel.

By the time the paper's account is published, William, Rachel and Laurence are all on their way out of the country, flowing back into the Gulf Stream of expatriation. Upon his return to New York, William learns that his novel, which Laurence had pushed onto his own publisher the summer before, has been cut from the press's publication list because of a slump in business. "The whole thing" – his dream of becoming a writer, a storyteller – was, he tells us, "a scam".[110] Not long afterwards Rachel arrives, but, like Brett Ashley in her last visit with Jake Barnes in Madrid, she brings scant consolation. They spend the next few days playing a kind of mas of being together, walking around New York, talking and, on their last day before Rachel goes back to Europe, getting "into one of those horse-drawn carriages for the tourists, lined up in front of Grand Army Plaza, in the southeast corner of the park. One of those carriages where you sit in the back, riding backwards."[111] *Voyageurs* to the last, they exchange their final words in the novel looking backwards at where they have been. Marcel comments in *Du côté de chez Swann* that "the countries for which we long occupy, at any given moment, a far larger place in our actual life than the country in which we happen to be".[112] For Rachel and William, that country is a state of mind as much as an actual place. Neither their voyage home nor their return to "foreign" has brought them a sense of resolution or a happy ending – only a chance that they might one day be able to incorporate those unfulfilled yearning and absent centres, confusions and hurts, psychic and physical diasporas, into the identities they may try to construct for themselves.

A comical (and typically estuarial) instance of identity construction through narrative occurs much earlier, when William first arrives at his island's *entrepôt*, the international airport, and meets the irrepressible immigration officer.[113] Ganish, who has literary pretensions of his own, tells William he has heard "this story" about how he got into Columbia's MFA programme: "Boy, the story going round here was how you did paint youself black! With shoepolish. And people say how you put on a heavy Caribbean accent for them Yankees." William attributes the incident to "confusion", but Ganish wants to hear more. The palaver continues, with Ganish eager to tell William about the novel *he* is planning – "a genuine Herness Hemingway" he calls it. There are at least fifty people in line behind William, but "instead of getting upset" several of them join in, "Elaborating Ganish's tale of Fyzabad". The scene is a paradigmatic Caribbean tableau, with the threat of tension subsumed by a good-natured orgy of collaborative storytelling, its subtext "All o' we is one". And Ganish, far from being upset at William's dubious method of getting into Columbia, happily includes him in a little meta-narrative of Caribbean ingenuity and comradeship: "Only a island boy could tink up a scheme good as that, eh? Only a scoundrel like we!"

From the beginning of the novel William repeatedly uses that same "we" to tie himself, through his own narrative, to the same cultural matrix. And he also reaches out to his audience directly, as "you", emphasizing its inclusion in the world he makes as well as his own complicated identity within it. From this perspective, William's insistence in the last chapter that he is not a novelist can be seen as a bit of *trompe l'oeil.* Is that a pose he strikes, a costume he dons (beneath the Hemingway one), his ultimate masquerade? And is *Carnival,* this story of himself, the novel that William Fletcher finally writes? If so, with his traumas unresolved, his sexuality unsettled and his memories tainted by hatred and violence, the telling of the story may well be only another stage in a lifelong struggle to embrace all the tribes that have made him, and to swim in all the tributaries of his own river.

6

NOT YET FINISHED

A Postscript and a Look Forward

I met History once, but he ain't recognize me,
A parchment Creole, with warts
Like an old sea-bottle, crawling like a crab
Through the holes of shadow cast by the net
Of a grille balcony; cream linen, cream hat.
I confront him and shout, "Sir, is Shabine!
They say I'se your grandson. You remember Grandma,
Your black cook, at all?" The bitch hawk and spat.
A spit like that worth any number of words.
But that's all them bastards have left us: words.

– Derek Walcott, "The Schooner *Flight*"[1]

The persistent estuarial current/counter-current that runs through contemporary Caribbean literature is particularly powerful in Robert Antoni's work, where the multinational reality of diaspora so directly engages the multi-tribal reality of origins. His imagined world is informed by a dialectic of exile and return, consummations and sources, the global sea and an infinitude of tributaries. In the final section of *Carnival*, William and his friends pitch their camp on the banks of the Madamas, just above the point at which its own estuary flows into the Caribbean:

> A little way downstream were the thick clumps of mangrove on both sides of the bocus. But our kitchen jutted out partially into the river, so you could look straight down it and out to sea. The color of the water changing slowly from the greenish brown of the river higher up, to blue-green, to bright aquamarine over the white rocks and sand – where the sweet water mixes with salt, welling up, appearing to become physically thicker, heavier – then the sparkling blue-black of the deep water farther out. On our other side we looked across the beach to the wide open sea.[2]

The landscape tells the people their story here. It is a tale of change and flux, shallows and depths, rushing rapids and abrupt irruptions of islands in the stream, mixing and mingling of river and ocean, the world of tributaries and the world of destinations. It is also very near the spot where the great leatherback turtle crawls out of the surf to lay her eggs, a ritual of belonging that unites her species' ancient past with an uncertain present and future. For William, Rachel and Laurence, the lesson of this landscape is not to be apprehended in a rational way or quickly, like a calculus lesson, but to be absorbed intuitively and really internalized only years later, as they work their way through their lives.

Antoni has explained elsewhere that the genesis of *Carnival* arose out of his reflecting on the differences between his aesthetic and Hemingway's. He had gone to speak to a Caribbean literature class at Yale, and afterwards he and the instructor went to a bar and talked.

> She had just written an essay on *The Sun Also Rises*, and in it she focused on a phrase taken from the book, which was "purity of line". She meant language, but also race, coupled with the idea of a "search for truth" that she

> felt Hemingway had embarked upon – the familiar modernist notion of getting back to the essence of things. And I immediately thought that my project as a writer, from the very beginning, has been exactly the opposite: that what I am interested in is "impurity", in terms of both language and race. From the beginning I have been interested in the "slipperiness" of language, the places where language becomes inventive and ambiguous, and in crossing-over *between* languages. Race is also always ambiguous for my characters.[3]

Antoni's fiction, in fact, depicts nearly everything – race, language, history, all of experience – as mixed or "impure", like the mouth of the Madamas or the manifold mutations of Carnival. The estuarial idea – of mixing and mingling but also of an "impure" stream flowing outwards from numberless tributaries into the boundless ocean – animates every one of his books.

In *Blessed Is the Fruit* the novel's central dream, blending the narratives of Vel and Lil within Bolom's fluid, prenatal consciousness, is the novel's deep structure: the story of two mothers, two races, two histories intertwined and finally joined at the novel's transparent window page: a still point of *métissage* generating the future that Antoni envisions. Bolom – who will be born, like Antoni himself, in 1958 – is inscribed into the space of African and European pasts as well as an estuarial Caribbean future. The dream foretells both "*a family for / the Caribbean in this room*" [Vel] and "*a family / for the New World in this room*" [Lil][4] – the equivalence of the two terms implying perhaps a world that will be increasingly marked by the Caribbean's estuarial spirit.

Less obvious but just as important is a subplot embedded almost at the dead centre of *My Grandmother's Erotic Folktales*: "The Story of How Gregoria la Rosa Got She Name". Gregoria came from a village inhabited by "the last people of Carib blood", who "were mixed with African blood too".[5] When her last surviving family members die, the Domingos adopt her and Granny Myna nurses her back to health, naming her after the flowers she saw on her pilgrimage to Lourdes. Eventually Granny Myna and the girl become like "mother and daughter in truth",[6] and as we have seen, when Gregoria's eventual marriage to the American Tyrone Davis foretells her destiny as the Caribbean's emissary to the United States, she takes as her viaticum the waters of the Madamas, and much, much more.

The multivocal maelstrom of *Divina Trace* is an early indicator of Antoni's appreciation of the essential plurality of Caribbean culture, as well as of the vigorous current increasingly connecting that culture to the wider world. The novel's middle thirteen pages trace a prelinguistic matrix for storytelling and identity construction that includes many tongues, peoples and myths. Those are the book's ultimate sources, both psychic and cultural. But *Divina Trace* is also about flowing out, moving past semiotic matrix to articulate expression. Johnny Domingo recalls Mother Superior Maurina's giving him her "suicide letter that is the complete entire history of Magdalena and she child and they birth and they death and you and me and all of this island of Corpus Christi", simultaneously instructing him to "carry it as far as America cross the sea".[7] And Hanuman frets in Magdalena's poem, "How might he story be publish abroad? / Where are dere monkeys enough to read it?"[8] Johnny finally locates his "imagining I" – and therefore his ability to send his story "abroad" – through the "deceptations, and combructions, and confufflations"[9] of a decidedly impure and unstable oral history. Moreover, the mirror at the centre of the book functions in part as a device to keep the confufflations going, by seducing each reader into the tale's telling in a process of revision that can never end.[10] All readers dissolve into Johnny Domingo's dreams in the mirror page; all readers adopt his perspective at the deepest level and become part of what Benítez-Rojo calls the "ethnologically promiscuous text" of the Caribbean.[11] This sublimely positive impulse to surrender oneself voluntarily (if only temporarily) to that Other, to step outside the borders of a rational, linear and exclusive concept of identity, is a feature of Caribbean being that few have captured with greater nuance or emotional force than Robert Antoni.

The "impure", estuarial nature of Caribbean identity continues to preoccupy Antoni. His first three books draw heavily from myth, folktale and dream (although they all contain important realistic touchstones as well, such as his vivid evocation of the decline of the sugar plantocracy in *Blessed Is the Fruit*). *Carnival* shines a solar beam of realism on the Caribbean present, letting the region's tormented history and its rich folk tradition percolate up from beneath the novel's main plot. After *Carnival*, however, Antoni has found himself turning back again to the past, but this time much more directly to his family history. While it is true that the earlier works (*Divina Trace* in particular) were inspired by Antoni's imaginative grasp of his paternal lineage in the West Indies, he always regarded that tributary of his family as the more colourful. In his current project, tentatively entitled *As Flies to Whatless Boys*,[12] he finds inspiration in the story of his mother's English ancestors who came to Trinidad in the nineteenth century, as part of a utopian colonization scheme to escape the social and economic oppression of Victorian Britain. The result promises once again to be a novel rich in technical innovation: a story told from the perspectives of both past and present and boldly incorporating into its fabric the undiluted autobiographical voice of the author himself.

To discuss even briefly a novel that is not yet fully realized, much less published, might seem somewhat unorthodox. But it is unthinkable to ignore a fresh direction in Antoni's fiction, particularly in view of the fact that one chapter of the new book has already appeared in *Conjunctions*.[13] This "look forward", therefore, should be taken for exactly what it is: a preview of a work in progress that will probably have changed considerably by the time it is completed. My hope is that readers will profit from, or at least excuse, a glimpse into what may be part of Antoni's final text. As it stands now, *Whatless Boys* focuses on a working-class English family in the 1840s and their involvement with

J.A. Etzler, a German-born utopianist of the day.[14] The family is a fictionalized version of Antoni's maternal ancestors, the Tuckers, and the chief centre of consciousness is their fourteen-year-old son Willy. The excerpt published in *Conjunctions* takes the family to Oxfordshire, where Etzler is to unveil a contraption he calls the "satellite" or "iron slave", which he claims is capable of ploughing fields, ripping out trees by their roots, digging trenches and levelling hills, among other unbelievable feats.[15] The satellite is the key component in his scheme to plant a colony in Trinidad, a society emancipated from the corruption of old Europe:

> What Etzler offered to every English man and woman was Free Entrance to the Lost Garden. Not the flawed Biblical Garden of our first ancestors. But a Perfect Paradise transformed by the powers of Nature – ordered, subdued, stripped of all wildness and danger. A return to innocence *and* knowledge, where Science alone – not privilege or birthright, want or fear of want – dictated the destiny of human beings. But only to those who chose to follow in his lead. Only for those who sought to save themselves. It was all so easy, simple, clear. Let them *believe!*[16]

This excerpt alone displays a clear family relationship with Antoni's previous work, from the interplay between science and faith in *Divina Trace*[17] to Mother Earth's own utopian efforts in *Carnival.*

But "Trial of the Satellite" hints of much more to come. On the day chronicled in this early chapter (May 7, 1845), two storylines are interwoven: Etzler's ludicrous efforts to demonstrate his device to a large and increasingly intoxicated crowd, and Willy's sexual awakening, abetted by Juliette, the randy niece of one of Etzler's followers. By the end of the chapter, both efforts have ended in failure. Like another Antoni protagonist, William Fletcher in *Carnival,* Willy is afflicted by sexual difficulties. He enjoys dressing in his sisters' clothes while masturbating, and when Juliette unbuttons his pants to caress him, she finds no Romeo – his "toetee" has "shrunk to the size of a stumpy fried potato". As for the satellite, the elder Tucker confesses to his son, "It'll never work . . . I've known it from the beginning. And after today I am more certain than ever."[18] The Tucker family's growing involvement with Eztler and his cohorts[19] is set against a densely detailed backdrop of the early years of Victoria's reign. Antoni richly evokes the England of public meetings and pamphleteers, of eccentrics and drunks, of rail travel in its infancy, and of a ruthlessly exploited working class. Even this brief section makes clear, however, that in the arc of the novel's greater plot, England will be left behind forever. The chapter opens with the words "Willy's mind traveled back across the sea to England, to the day of his fifteenth birthday" and it ends with a forecast from his father: "Imagine, son, a year from now, all of us together, we'll celebrate your birthday in the tropics!"[20]

Edward Said has observed that "[e]very novel is at the same time a form of discovery and also a way of accommodating discovery, . . . an enabling condition and a restraint upon . . . inventiveness".[21] In *Whatless Boys,* Antoni appears to have found yet another way of overcoming those restraints and making generic conventions participate in the process of discovery. The most obvious technical feature of this new work is its multi-textual quality. Antoni, of course, has exploited the possibilities of polyphonic narrative earlier in his career, particularly in *Divina Trace* and *Blessed Is the Fruit.* But in *Whatless Boys* the diversity of discourse extends much further than multiple points of view existing on roughly the same ontological plane. Here he is combining factual discourse with fictional, and shading the two into each other.

The fictional story of Willy Tucker is based on historical events, and the historicity of the main plot is underscored by treatises, reports and newspaper accounts relating to the actual Tropical Emigration Society. Yet at the same time the story of the story's excavation[22] – Antoni's personal quest to seek out this particular tributarial source of his family's place in Trinidad – is fictionalized. Like the narrator of *Chronicle of a Death Foretold,* Antoni is in the text, actively trying to reassemble the mirror of memory from many broken fragments,[23] but his visibility is even more pronounced. In the typescript the author appears in periodic "insertions", speaking in his own voice about the reasons he undertook the project and the difficulties involved in seeing it through. Additionally, he appears vicariously (and comically) in e-mails addressed to him, in dialect, by a Miss Ramsol, the director of the Trinidad and Tobago National Archive.

Miss Ramsol's narratives are difficult to describe. She alternately berates Antoni, implies that they have a sexual relationship ("dis tuti aint get a good airing-out like dat in many a long day"),[24] and fills in parts of island history that relate to her own East Indian family background. She also increasingly portrays this fictional Antoni as a scheming and manipulative con artist (somewhat like a latter-day King of Chacachacari) who uses trickery and even sexual blackmail to persuade her to let him photocopy documents relating to research on his family history. Miss Ramsol sees herself (rather like Granny Myna in *Erotic Folktales*) as defending the territorial integrity of the archive from a meddlesome usurper. "[U] best haul u fockin ass," she e-mails him, "& go back home to new york or whereverdefock is de shit place in amerika you comes from."[25] In a book exploring the ambiguities and impurities of cultural identity, the irony of Antoni's casting a version of himself as an exploitative outsider in Trinidad is sharp indeed.[26] And again like Granny Myna, Miss Ramsol subjectifies "Robot" Antoni (as she calls him), colonizing the colonizer, making him a character within his own work and reaffirming once again "the impossibility", as Benítez-Rojo says, "of assuming a stable identity".[27] Or, to put it another way, Antoni the author uses Antoni the character to acknowledge that his own narrative, like that of the Caribbean, is fluid and unfinished.

The looping together of the story of the Tuckers' emigration to Trinidad and the story of "Robot" Antoni's effort to cobble it together brings to vivid life a great paradox of history: it is somehow pre-existent, independent of us and our narrative constructions, yet simultaneously knowable only through the impurity of its telling. The teller trespasses on history, mixes and interferes with it, becomes part of it and finally repossesses it – all through what "them bastards have left us: words". The islanders in *Divina Trace* enact such a process when they storm Saint Mary's Cathedral, renaming it as well as the town St Maggy's, according to the impurity of Papee Vince's own telling: "[W]e even wrote over the ancient navigators' maps. We ceremoniously smashed open the glass case in the museum, and we wrote over the first official map of Corpus Christi." The action, which Papee Vince later likens to "naming weself fa the world",[28] constitutes a rewriting of history – a repossession of the past and reconstruction of the present through words.

Glissant's meditations on the dynamic between history and storytelling are relevant here:

> A reality that was long concealed from itself and that took shape in some way along with the consciousness that the people had of it, has as much to do with the problematics of investigation as with a historical organization of things. It is this "literary" implication that orients the thrust of historical thought, from which none of us can claim to be exempt.[29]

Something like this appears to be emerging in Antoni's latest work. The "problematics of investigation" not only confronts the "historical organization of things" but joins with it. No less than in *Divina Trace,* Antoni is playing with the ways in which the human imagination is both a product and producer of the collective past. The relationship of Antoni as author to his protagonist, Willy Tucker, can be seen as the embodiment of that idea. Willy is a fictional character in a novel Antoni is writing, but he is also the author's great-great-great-grandfather. The fact that the events taking place in England are remembered by Willy after he has arrived in Trinidad accounts in part for the many Caribbean words and phrases that pepper the text, even in the English scenes, but it is also true that the narrative voice is Antoni's, channelled through Willy. It is Antoni's consciousness, not Willy's, that produces the oblique references to other Caribbean writers, such as the first sentence of chapter 1, which echoes the first sentence of *One Hundred Years of Solitude.*[30] Willy's identity becomes ineluctably mingled with that of Antoni, a fact emphasized by one of Antoni's inserted commentaries on the writing of the book, when he remarks that he and Willy "were born not only in the same month, but on the same day – May 7th – 128 years apart".[31] And in another insertion he confesses, "The truth, which I have only begun to discover and to appreciate lately – in my dreams and in my everyday, waking life – is that I am, indeed, William. These days I am more William than anybody else."[32]

The identities of William John Sanger Tucker, Jr (Willy), William Fletcher and Robert William Antoni (whose mother's maiden name was Tucker) spill over each other like waves of mutual recognition and acceptance. The acceptance is not always easy, as *Carnival* clearly demonstrates. The muddy estuarial heart of that novel (later lyrically revisited in the description of the Madamas River flowing into the sea) is William's final and most explicit recollection of his and Rachel's rape. Nothing is more important in that skein of memories than this: "In my mind, in that moment, the twins merged, they became one, and I became them."[33] "I became them" – the *sine qua non* of relational, estuarial identity, of "impurity" – when William, in his most profound instant of intuition, becomes both exploiter and exploited, white and black, male and female. As Glissant understands, in the post-colonial, estuarial world epitomized by the Caribbean, "Identity is no longer just permanence; it is a capacity for variation, yes a variable – either under control or wildly fluctuating."[34] What he calls "root identity" – characterized by a violent filiation (in the sense of inherited privilege extending itself through both time and space) – must yield to "relation identity", which is produced through "contradictory experience of contacts among cultures".[35] This new concept of identity, fully imagined in the fiction of Robert Antoni, is more chaotic, less fixed and markedly less possessive, allowing "each person to be there and elsewhere, rooted and open, lost in the mountains and free beneath the sea, in harmony and in errantry".[36] Antoni's work (including, I believe, his forthcoming novel) liberates identity, culture *and* history by disaffiliating them, allowing them to mix, quite impurely, into the estuarial reality of today's Caribbean and today's world.

NOTES

CHAPTER 1: FRONTIERS OF THE WORD

1. Patrick Chamoiseau, *Texaco*, trans. Rose-Myriam Réjouis and Val Vinokurov (New York: Vintage, 1998), 327.
2. Robert Antoni, "Two-head Fred and Tree-foot Frieda", *Missouri Review* 8, no. 1 (1984–85): 87.
3. Ibid., 87–88. Conch jooking (basically gouging the flesh out of the shell) is a fine art in the Bahamas. The term also has, obviously, a slang connotation of a sexual nature. Antoni's use of it in the context of this story, however, is early evidence of his very Caribbean tendency to borrow and combine. Bahamians actually say "crack" a conch. The word *jook* is Trinidadian in origin. Antoni takes a term commonly used in his ancestral country and transplants it into the lexicon of the country in which he grew up.
4. Ibid., 87.
5. Ibid., 91.
6. Ibid., 99.
7. Édouard Glissant, *Caribbean Discourse: Selected Essays*, trans. J. Michael Dash (Charlottesville: University Press of Virginia, 1989), 139. Unlike Kamau Brathwaite, Glissant does not reject the idea of the dialectic. The estuary is a continuous metamorphosis, with no final result but a synthesis always in the process of transforming itself into a new thesis. Brathwaite posits what he calls "tide-alectic", or "the ripple and the two tide movement", as a more useful way of thinking about the place of Caribbean literature (or at the very least, his own work) within the wider world. As Paul Naylor describes it, "This image allows us to see these works in terms of a going out and a return without imposing a 'resolution' on that movement." See Naylor, *Poetic Investigations: Singing the Holes in History* (Evanston, IL: Northwestern University Press, 1999), 144–45, and Brathwaite, *Barabajan Poems 1492–1992* (New York: Savacou North, 1994).

8. Roland Littlewood, *Pathology and Identity: The Work of Mother Earth in Trinidad* (Cambridge: Cambridge University Press, 1993), 234. Littlewood is paraphrasing James Clifford in this passage. See also Clifford, *The Predicament of Culture: Twentieth-Century Ethnography, Literature and Art* (Cambridge, MA: Harvard University Press, 1988), 173. It is also worth noting that the Yoruba goddess Emanjah, "mother of the rivers", negotiated the Middle Passage along with many other African deities. Although mainly associated with fresh water in West Africa, she became linked with the sea in the Caribbean and Brazil, so her two primary fields of signification mingled like the waters of an estuary. See Littlewood, 136ff.
9. Eva Hoffman, "The New Nomads", in *Letters of Transit: Reflections on Exile, Identity, Language and Loss*, ed. André Aciman (New York: New Press, 1999), 56.
10. The term "Caribbean" normally designates a cultural as well as a geographical area – a region surrounding and including the Caribbean Sea. "West Indies" usually refers to the English-speaking areas (current or former British colonies), but the two terms have frequently been used interchangeably.
11. In this book I use the terms creolization and *métissage* (virtually interchangeably) in the broader sense of an estuarial mingling of cultures. I do not limit myself to African and European cultural currents, or to more specific usages of these terms such as Benítez-Rojo's post-plantation conception of creolization. See Antonio Benítez-Rojo, "Three Words Toward Creolization", in *Caribbean Creolization: Reflections on the Cultural Dynamics of Language, Literature and Identity*, eds. Kathleen Balutansky and Marie-Agnes Sourieau (Gainesville: University Press of Florida, 1998), 53–61.
12. Antoni and his brother Brian have been granted Bahamian passports but have not claimed them because that would necessitate renunciation of their American ones. Their sister Janine, a well-known conceptual artist (and recipient of a MacArthur Fellowship) was born in the Bahamas.
13. Antonio Benítez-Rojo, *The Repeating Island: The Caribbean and the Postmodern Perspective*, 2nd ed., trans. James Maraniss (Durham, NC: Duke University Press, 1996), 25. This book is a landmark in the study of Caribbean poetics, although its general approach has not been universally endorsed. In a review of J. Michael Dash's *The Other America*, for example, Gene Jarrett complains of "overgeneralising postmodern theory" and "ventriloquised European thought". Dash has addressed these issues, concluding however that Benítez-Rojo escapes such traps by using "his reading of the deconstructive impulse in postmodern theory to elaborate on the Caribbean as being always in motion, forever in a state of flux, not a fixed ground but an open field of signifiers". Benítez-Rojo has also been criticized for grounding too many of

his ideas in an expertise on Cuba alone, but as Edna Aizenberg points out, his "contrapuntal methodology checks his impulse to immobilise the Caribbean" in narrow nationalism. In any case, in terms of this book, the point is how much light Benítez-Rojo (and, for that matter, Glissant) sheds on the work of Robert Antoni. It is not irrelevant that Antoni has called *The Repeating Island* "one of the most important and radically innovative texts of literary criticism of the Caribbean region". See Gene Jarrett, review of *The Other America*, by Michael Dash, *Callaloo* 22, no. 4 (Fall 1999): 1096; Dash, *The Other America: Caribbean Literature in a New World Context* (Charlottesville: University Press of Virginia, 1998), 8; Edna Aizenberg, review of *The Repeating Island*, by Antonio Benítez-Rojo, *Research in African Literatures* 25, no. 2 (Summer 1994): 187; and Benítez-Rojo, interview with Robert Antoni, *Bomb* 82 (Winter 2002–2003): 33.

14. Édouard Glissant, "Beyond Babel", *World Literature Today* 63, no. 4 (1989): 561.
15. The list is long, including not only anglophone West Indian writers such as Antoni, Olive Senior, Caryl Phillips, Jamaica Kincaid, Pauline Melville and Lawrence Scott, but also those from the Hispanic and French parts of the Caribbean – figures such as Cristina Garcia and the late Reinaldo Arenas (Cuba), Julia Alvarez and Junot Diaz (Dominican Republic), Edwidge Danticat (Haiti) and Patrick Chamoiseau (Martinique).
16. J. Michael Dash, introduction to Glissant, *Caribbean Discourse*, xi.
17. This makes her, in Gérard Genette's awkward but often-cited terminology, extradiegetic, intradiegetic, homodiegetic and heterodiegetic all rolled into one. See *Narrative Discourse: An Essay in Method*, trans. Jane E. Lewin (Ithaca, NY: Cornell University Press, 1980).
18. García Márquez, who was raised partly by his maternal grandparents, has repeatedly and emphatically spoken of his indebtedness to the stories told by his grandmother, Tranquilina Iguarán Cotes. Among other things, her storytelling taught him that "[i]t's possible to get away with anything as long as you make it believable". See Stephen Minta, *Gabriel García Márquez: Writer of Colombia* (London: Jonathan Cape, 1987), 37.
19. Peter Josyph, "Walking Down the Trace: A Conversation with Robert Antoni", 1994. The interview took place in Miami in the spring of 1994 and can be found on Robert Antoni's homepage, www.robertantoni.com.html. Robert Antoni provided me with a hard copy of it (amounting to twenty-six pages in typescript) and vouches for its accuracy.
20. Her full name was María Rosario de Medina Antoni, and she was so influential that she also appears (briefly) as Granny Maria in Brian Antoni's novel, *Paradise Overdose* (New York: Grove Press, 1994).

21. All of Antoni's books take place (wholly or in part) on Corpus Christi, a thinly disguised version of Trinidad, although the island is not named in *Carnival*. Antoni reshapes Trinidad to suit his purposes, changing some names and relocating some landmarks, but the island – and particularly its history as recounted by Papee Vince in *Divina Trace* – is still recognizably Trinidad. In the Josyph interview Antoni says, with reference to two of the writers who have influenced him most, "I like the idea of my own Yoknapatawpha or Macondo."
22. And there have already been many. In addition to its publication in the United Kingdom and in North America, *My Grandmother's Erotic Folktales* has been translated into French, Finnish and Spanish.
23. Benítez-Rojo, *Repeating Island*, 23.
24. Like so much else in the history of the novel, this device has its origin in Cervantes. Ten years elapsed between the publication of Part One of *Don Quixote* and Part Two. During this period a "sequel" appeared, penned by one Alonso Fernández de Avellaneda. In Part Two Cervantes fictionalizes the other writer; he even lets a copy of Avellaneda's book fall into the hands of the "real" Quixote, who says it is badly written and "deviates from the truth". See *Don Quixote*, trans. Edith Grossman (New York: HarperCollins, 2003), 846.
25. Robert Antoni, *My Grandmother's Erotic Folktales* (London: Faber, 2000), 35.
26. The section of the book in which "Ernesto" appears, "The Tale of How Crab-o Lost His Head", is partly based on an "old West Indian folktale", according to Antoni. Needless to say, he invented the part about Hemingway. Robert Antoni, e-mail to the author, 18 November 2000.
27. The pope in question is either Pius XI, according to Johnny's reasonably sane father, or Pius IX, according to his unbalanced great-aunt, Mother Superior Maurina.
28. Or, to return to Benítez-Rojo, the mirror forces the reader to grasp that *pretext* becomes *text* only when the participatory act of reading occurs (*Repeating Island*, 23).
29. Ibid., 276.
30. Ibid., 275.
31. Dash, introduction, xxix.
32. Robert Antoni, *Carnival* (New York: Grove/Atlantic, 2005), 142.
33. Antoni told me that years after the publication of *Divina Trace* he learned of an affair his grandfather Barto had had with a mixed-race woman named Magdalena, and of an "outside child" – Antoni's uncle Arthur – by that liaison.
34. The statue is thought to have been brought to the New World from Spain

by Capuchin monks in the eighteenth century. For more on the importance of this little statue in Trinidad, and the artistic use Antoni makes of it, see the following chapter.

35. Hoffman, 51.
36. Edward Brathwaite, introduction to *Brother Man*, by Roger Mais (Oxford: Heinemann, 1974), xix.
37. Robert Antoni, *Divina Trace* (Woodstock, NY: Overlook, 1992), 132 and 157.
38. Ibid., 264.
39. Antoni, e-mail to author, 14 October 2002.
40. Josyph interview.
41. Antoni was once struck by a footnote (in a book about *Finnegans Wake*) that cited REM (rapid eye movement) as evidence that a baby dreams in the womb. Interest in dreams seems to run in the Antoni family. In 1994 I visited an exhibition by Janine Antoni at the Reina Sofia Museum in Madrid which involved Janine's sleeping in the museum while hooked up to an electronic device that recorded her REM patterns on a kind of graph. During the day, when the museum was open, she sat and wove those patterns into a bolt of fabric. Janine and Robert discussed the idea of REM in fetuses years before either work of art was conceived. See John Bishop, *Joyce's Book of the Dark: Finnegans Wake* (Madison: University of Wisconsin Press, 1986).
42. Benítez-Rojo, interview with Antoni, 35.
43. Josyph interview.
44. Littlewood, 164.
45. Antoni visited the Earth People before Mother Earth's death, which occurred in 1984 (Littlewood, xix). The earliest appearance in print of Granny Myna occurred in 1988, well after that.
46. Josyph interview.
47. Antoni, *Erotic Folktales*, 66–67.
48. Josyph interview.
49. This seemingly strange combination of literary influences is not without precedent in the region; Gabriel García Márquez has often spoken of his debt to Faulkner and Hemingway, at least once acknowledging the irony: "My great masters were the two North American novelists who seemed to have the least in common." Faulkner, he explained, "has had much to do with my soul, but Hemingway is the one who had the most to do with my craft". See García Márquez, "Gabriel García Márquez Meets Ernest Hemingway", trans. Randolph Hogan, *New York Times*, 1999. Accessed online at http://vesselka.freeservers.com/Gabriel.htm#Hemingway.
50. The island is unnamed in *Carnival*, but the currency is "CC dollars" (151).

51. Benítez-Rojo, *Repeating Island*, 187.
52. Josyph interview.
53. *Carnival* took more than four years to complete and went through numerous rewritings. Antoni has said that in the past, voices closer to his own, such as Johnny's in *Divina Trace* and Lil's in *Blessed Is the Fruit*, were harder for him to realize than those patterned after the old storytellers of his childhood. As he said in the Josyph interview, "In the dialect I can sing and I'm not worried about it, everything is right, but in Lila's voice, and in Johnny's voice, I have to be a writer." This proved to be even more of a problem in *Carnival*, in which the voice and the character grow so directly out of those of Antoni himself.
54. Josyph interview.
55. See Reinhard W. Sander, *The Trinidad Awakening: West Indian Literature of the Nineteen-Thirties* (New York: Greenwood Press, 1988) for a full discussion of this literary phenomenon. A relatively minor figure during the same period was Seepersad Naipaul, the father of V.S. and Shiva Naipaul. See also Kenneth Ramchand, *The West Indian Novel and Its Background* (London: Heinemann, 1983) and Michael Gilkes, *The West Indian Novel* (Boston: Twayne, 1981) for useful information about this early period.
56. Jamaica and Trinidad achieved independence from Great Britain in 1962 and Barbados and Guyana in 1966. By the early 1980s all the British territories that sought independent status had gained it. The generational difference between the postwar and post-independence writers can be readily seen in the Naipaul family. V.S. Naipaul went to Oxford carrying a British passport (which he retains to this day); his brother Shiva, thirteen years his junior, followed in his footsteps to Oxford but arrived there as a citizen of Trinidad. For a brief overview of the post-independence "third wave", see Richard F. Patteson, *Caribbean Passages: A Critical Perspective on New Fiction from the West Indies* (Boulder: Three Continents/Lynne Rienner, 1998), 1–13.
57. This part of Colombia, as any reader of García Márquez knows, is strongly Caribbean in culture, as are the coastal areas of Venezuela and several Central American nations.
58. As well as in their innumerable interviews with each other, blurbs on one another's books, reviews of those books and appearances together at conferences and readings.
59. Antoni, *Divina Trace*, 342.
60. See Said, *The World, the Text and the Critic* (Cambridge, MA: Harvard University Press, 1983), 174–75.

61. Nerval spelled backwards, after the schizophrenic bilingual romantic poet who incorporated fragments of dreams into his memoirs.
62. Lawrence Scott, *Witchbroom* (London: Heinemann, 1992), 151. Scott has also published a short story collection, *Ballad for the New World* (London: Heinemann, 1994) and two more novels, *Aelred's Sin* (London: Allison and Busby, 1998) and *Night Calypso* (London: Allison and Busby, 2004).
63. Ibid., 184.
64. Ibid., 2.
65. Ibid., 95–96.
66. They subsequently met, and Scott interviewed Antoni for the Spring 2005 issue of *Bomb*.
67. In both novels the Monagas family originates on the South American mainland. According to Antoni, it is an actual family from whom both he and Lawrence Scott may be descended.
68. Scott, *Witchbroom*, 59.
69. Both *Aelred's Sin* and *Night Calypso* feature multiple narrative perspectives and settings alternating between Europe and the West Indies. These later novels are also, as much as *Witchbroom*, collages of various historical periods; *Aelred's Sin* features six separate time frames ranging from the twelfth century to 1984.
70. Scott, *Witchbroom*, 270.
71. Josyph interview.
72. Édouard Glissant, *Poetics of Relation*, trans. Betsy Wing (Ann Arbor: University of Michigan Press, 2000), 33.
73. Antoni, "Two-head Fred", 100.
74. Benítez-Rojo, *Repeating Island*, 35.
75. Students such as Bill Ashcroft, Gareth Griffiths and Helen Tiffin in *Postcolonial Studies: The Key Concepts* (London: Routledge, 2003), 108.
76. Brian McHale, *Postmodernist Fiction* (London: Routledge, 1996), 90.
77. I am borrowing Glissant's construction of both *relation* and *filiation* here. See Glissant, *Poetics*, 47–48, 71, 141–46. Antoni's refiliation with writers such as Joyce and Faulkner in his earlier work is obviously continued with Hemingway in *Carnival*.
78. Benítez-Rojo, *Repeating Island*, 12.
79. Ibid., 25.

CHAPTER 2: *DIVINA TRACE*

1. Robert Antoni, *Divina Trace* (Woodstock, NY: Overlook, 1992), 384.
2. Chinua Achebe, *Things Fall Apart* (New York: Anchor Books, 1994), 141.
3. Antonio Benítez-Rojo, *The Repeating Island: The Caribbean and the Postmodern Perspective,* 2nd ed., trans. James Maraniss (Durham, NC: Duke University Press, 1996), 189.
4. Derek Walcott, "The Antilles: Fragments of Epic Memory", *New Republic* 26 (December 1992): 26–32.
5. Benítez-Rojo, *Repeating Island,* 3.
6. Edward W. Said, *Culture and Imperialism* (New York: Knopf, 1993), 216. Said calls this process "the voyage in" – a "conscious effort to enter into the discourse of Europe and the West, to mix with it, transform it, to make it acknowledge marginalised or suppressed or forgotten histories". For a brief but lucid view of *Divina Trace* as "an exemplary postcolonial novel", see Alfred J. López, *Posts and Pasts: A Theory of Postcolonialism* (Albany, NY: SUNY Press, 2001), 30–35.
7. Karl Popper, *The Open Society and Its Enemies* (Princeton, NJ: Princeton University Press, 1966), 2:369. See also Popper's *Conjectures and Refutations* and *The Logic of Scientific Discovery*. Popper's approach is not one of epistemological relativism. Unlike Rorty and other anti-foundationalists (to simplify somewhat grossly), Popper stresses the importance of the process of pursuing truth while at the same time conceding that there can never be an absolute truth accessible through a certain methodology.
8. Benítez-Rojo, *Repeating Island,* 4.
9. Antoni, *Divina Trace,* 157.
10. Édouard Glissant, *Faulkner, Mississippi,* trans. Barbara Lewis and Thomas C. Spear (New York: Farrar, Straus, 1999), 197.
11. Benítez-Rojo, *Repeating Island,* 4.
12. Antoni, *Divina Trace,* 381–82.
13. Odillo (Robert) Antoni, "A Piece of Pommerac", *Paris Review* 111 (1989): 170.
14. Jack Jordan, "I, We and Historical Memory in Patrick Chamoiseau's *Texaco*", SORAC *Journal of African Studies* 2 (November 2002): 56.
15. Antoni, *Divina Trace,* 215–16.
16. Ibid., 310. Several cognate passages in the novel point in the same general direction, including "As though the story were forming itself now not out of the dregs of human time and memory, but out of the incense-filled air

itself" (140) and "All this confusion begins before we open we eyes, before the first stories begin to tell" (102).

17. John C. Hawley, in a useful introduction to *Divina Trace,* describes this process as "the central narrator's ritualistic entry into the layers of his own consciousness, his own identity and personal mystery, and his re-emergence not only as an individual but as a Caribbean". See Hawley, "Robert Antoni's 'Divina Trace' and the Womb of Place", *Ariel: A Review of International English Literature* 24, no. 1 (1993): 93. Another substantive treatment of the novel is Rhonda Cobham's "Of Boloms, Mirrors and Monekeymen: What's Real and What's Not in Robert Antoni's *Divina Trace*", *Annals of Scholarship* 12, no. 3 (1997): 49–75.
18. Philip Lutgendorf, introduction to "A Piece of Pommerac", by Odillo (Robert) Antoni, *Paris Review* 111 (1989): 168.
19. Aamer Hussein, "The Voices of Myth", review of *Divina Trace,* by Robert Antoni, *Times Literary Supplement,* 22 November 1991, 21.
20. Antoni, *Divina Trace,* 7.
21. Ibid., 33.
22. His search bears more than a passing resemblance to Quentin Compson's in *Absalom, Absalom!* The two novels also share, in addition to multiple narrators, a preoccupation with the relationship of history to myth and an inquiry into the devices of storytelling and the links between narration and knowledge. Like *Divina Trace,* Faulkner's masterpiece poses "problems in the epistemology of narrative and the cognitive uses of plotting in a context of radical doubt about the validity of plot". See Peter Brooks, "Incredulous Narration: 'Absalom, Absalom!' " in *Modern Critical Views: William Faulkner,* ed. Harold Bloom (New York: Chelsea House, 1986), 247. Antoni himself tips his hat to his distinguished predecessor: while away at medical school, Johnny Domingo's father had a Canadian roommate named Shreve (118).
23. Antoni, *Divina Trace,* 212.
24. The "krick-krack" formula (variously spelled) occurs frequently in Caribbean literature. Providing titles for both Merle Hodge's *Crick Crack Monkey* and Edwidge Danticat's *Krik? Krak!,* it also features prominently in Lawrence Scott's *Witchbroom,* perhaps the closest cousin to *Divina Trace* in contemporary Caribbean fiction. In *Divina Trace,* Robert Antoni has said, the jingle is placed where it is partly to signal that a new story cycle (the book's second half) is about to begin. The pommerac, he goes on to say, "is a fruit that I believe nobody but Caribbeans would eat. It is small and hard and has to be soaked in salted water – to soften it up." Even then it leaves "juggers" – soft needle-like pieces – between the teeth. Antoni's own take on the

"krick-krack" tradition is that "the monkey, breaking his back for a useless pommerac, is like the monkey-narrator who will do anything to tell his tale". Antoni, e-mail to author, 14 October 2002.

25. Antoni, *Divina Trace,* 82.
26. Ibid., 157–58.
27. The novel contains what appears to be a page from an actual medical text describing (and depicting) an anencephalic fetus; the photograph is reproduced at the same point in the second half of the book, in the form of a negative, representing an X-ray of the child. Antoni has explained that because the photograph was of such poor quality (owing to its age), he created a sculpture based on the picture and had a friend photograph that object, which he says was "slightly more froglike" than the original. The mystery of conception and childbirth, obviously a subject that fascinates Antoni, also plays a central role in his second novel, *Blessed Is the Fruit.* See Josyph interview.
28. The real Warahuns, like the ones in *Divina Trace,* were indigenous to Venezuela, and some of them did come to Trinidad, though not as many as in the novel. See Melville J. Herskovits and Frances H. Herskovits, *Trinidad Village* (New York: Knopf, 1947), 224.
29. From the French *crapaud* (frog). The tale repeatedly told in *Divina Trace* is often referred to as a "crapostoy", and indeed it is both a *crapaud*-story – a tale of a frog – and a story full of crap, or a bit of a tall tale, like *Tristram Shandy* and *Finnegans Wake.*
30. Antoni, *Divina Trace,* 116.
31. Ibid., 39.
32. The road from which the novel takes its name stretches about ten miles, from the town of St Maggy (specifically from the Domingo family cemetery) to the chapel of Magdalena Divina at the edge of the Maraval Swamp. The name assumes many significations as the novel progresses. Divina Trace is literally a track cut across an island called Corpus Christi (Body of Christ), but it is also a path back into history and down into the subconscious, as well as the mark, or trace, that Johnny leaves on the world through his (divinely engendered?) narrative.
33. Antoni, *Divina Trace,* 342.
34. Ibid., 3.
35. Ibid., 114. This phrase, or something very like it, was repeated to Robert Antoni by his own "Granny Myna" – María Rosario de Medina Antoni – who said it was the only Warrahoon she could remember.
36. Ibid., 346. This occurs at another point in the novel, when Johnny remembers

"Evelina sheself" referring to "de problem you mummy and daddy was ga have burying me in Domingo Cemetery" (325).

37. Ibid., 234.
38. Ibid., 397.
39. Ibid., 335.
40. Ibid., 126.
41. Ibid., 28 and 67.
42. Ibid., 348.
43. Ibid., 342.
44. Ibid., 380.
45. R.K. Narayan, *Gods, Demons and Others* (New York: Viking, 1967), 126.
46. Benítez-Rojo, *Repeating Island,* 11.
47. Antoni, *Divina Trace,* 102.
48. Mark Kurlansky, *A Continent of Islands: Searching for the Caribbean Destiny* (New York: Addison-Wesley, 1992), ix–x.
49. Édouard Glissant, "Beyond Babel", *World Literature Today* 63, no. 4 (1989): 561.
50. Raphael Dalleo explores the connections between Antoni's work and García Márquez's in " 'Tink is you dawson dis yana?' Imitation and Creation in Robert Antoni's *Divina Trace*", *Ariel: A Review of International English Literature* 32, no. 4 (October 2001): 21–45. Dalleo correctly observes that *Divina Trace* interacts specifically with the Rabassa translation of *One Hundred Years of Solitude.* Although Antoni speaks Spanish, he does not consider his command of the language sufficient to appreciate García Márquez in the original. He has read all of García Márquez's novels in English translations.
51. Robert Antoni, "The Myth-making Process in *Absalom, Absalom!* and *One Hundred Years of Solitude*" (unpublished essay).
52. Robert Antoni, "Fifty Years after Freud and Joyce, Moses and Finnegan: Rewriting the Primal History Scene for the Absent Mother" (unpublished essay).
53. Although Amerindians appear more numerous on Corpus Christi than they have been during the past century on the real Trinidad, the fact of their virtual extinction in the Caribbean is vividly marked by the relative absence of an Amerindian belief system in *Divina Trace* that corresponds to those of Europe, India and west Africa. Their most visible artifact is the Warrahoon-made "Windsor" chair in which Johnny sits on the eve of his ninetieth birthday. As Derek Walcott puts it, "there is too much nothing here". *Collected Poems, 1948–1984* (New York: Farrar, Straus, 1986), 114.
54. C.L.R. James, "La Divina Pastora", in *Stories from the Caribbean,* ed. Andrew Salkey (London: Elek Books, 1965), 150–51.

55. Elizabeth Saft, ed., *Trinidad and Tobago* (Singapore: APA Productions, 1987), 173–74.
56. Although this particular deity appears to be Antoni's invention, many Amerindian religions included devotion to a mother goddess. The mainland Caribs of the Surinamese coast, for example, believed that the "universe has its source in Amana, a virgin mother and water goddess who has no navel (i.e. was never born)" and who "is the essence of time, has borne all things, can adopt any shape". See Walter Krickeberg et al., *Pre-Columbian American Religions*, trans. Stanley Davis (London: Weidenfeld and Nicolson, 1968), 246.
57. Antoni, *Divina Trace*, 377.
58. The real Divina Pastora in Trinidad has sometimes been as much a divisive figure as an integrative one. Peter van Koningsbruggen notes that "there are disputes every year on who the image belongs to, or rather, which community – the Christians or the Hindus – is entitled to the money that the faithful give to the image during the procession". See *Trinidad Carnival: A Quest for National Identity* (London: Macmillan Education Caribbean Publishing, 1997), 26.
59. Corpus Christi is the feast that honours the Blessed Sacrament (the Body of Christ as transformed by the Mass). For centuries the Church has placed this important holiday on the Thursday after Trinity Sunday – many weeks after Easter. However, the "natural" day for Corpus Christi is the Thursday before Easter. It was apparently observed on this day by early Christians, and Antoni chooses to restore the original day to the feast in *Divina Trace*. But his reason for doing so is that the actual festival of La Divina Pastora in Siparia, Trinidad, takes place on that day. It seems that when the Divina Pastora cult was taken up by the Hindus, many of whom were sugar cane workers, that holiday weekend was the only period during the year when there was enough time for them to travel from different parts of the island to take part in the celebration. See *New Catholic Encyclopedia*, vol. 4 (New York: McGraw-Hill, 1967), 345.
60. Although Easter is actually a moveable feast in the Christian calendar, Antoni fixes the end of Holy Week at April 16 (Holy Thursday and Corpus Christi Day) through April 19 (Easter Sunday) so that Johnny Domingo's birthday (as well as that of the Frogchild) can occur during that period.
61. Antoni, *Divina Trace*, 138.
62. Ibid., 383.
63. Ibid., 132.
64. A West Indian stew, especially popular in the southern Caribbean, made of dasheen leaves, seafood and other ingredients. "Any and everything goes into a good callaloo." Ibid., 318.

65. Ibid., 144.
66. Ibid., 15. Antoni has remarked to me that he also thought of the oldman in foil as evoking the Tin Man in *The Wizard of Oz*, with *Divina Trace*, of course, as the yellow brick road. I will leave the implications of that analogy to future commentators.
67. Ibid., 413.
68. This is the lead story in Antoni's *My Grandmother's Erotic Folktales* (London: Faber, 2000), but according to him, its genesis precedes that of *Divina Trace*.
69. Antoni, *Divina Trace*, 87.
70. Ibid., 96.
71. Ibid., 109.
72. Ibid., 141. A similar insight takes place two years earlier, on the night Johnny chooses science over religion. When he comes across a photograph of an anencephalic fetus in one of his father's medical books, his belief in the separation between science and faith (or superstition) is undermined for the first time, because the specimen resembles his mental image of the frogchild: "The very same face which had already haunted me for three years without ever having seen it – as though *my* imagination had conceived him, and carried him, and borne him into the world and given him life" (99).
73. Ibid., 241.
74. Ibid., 259.
75. Ibid., 273 and 306 respectively.
76. Ibid., 274.
77. As throughout the novel, Antoni seasons this segment with plenty of wordplay. The "*famous Irish priest Fr John Joyce*" (255) points both to John Stanislaus Joyce, James's father, and to the John Joyce who wrote a book about the real Saint Bernadette.
78. Antoni, *Divina Trace*, 154–55.
79. Antoni, "Fifty Years", 3, 22, 25 and 28. For the sake of space I have greatly condensed his argument.
80. Antoni, *Divina Trace*, 49.
81. R.K. Narayan, *The Ramayana: A Shortened Modern Prose Version of the Indian Epic* (London: Penguin, 1972), vii.
82. Antoni, *Divina Trace*, 175. In keeping with his recuperation of the "absent mother", Antoni substitutes, in his own version of *homoousios*, "body of we mummy" for Holy Spirit.
83. Ibid., 184.
84. Ibid., 215.
85. Benítez-Rojo, *Repeating Island*, 21.

86. Antoni, *Divina Trace*, 81.
87. Ibid., 322.
88. Herskovits and Herskovits (321–39) discuss Shango worship in great detail.
89. Philip Allison, *African Stone Sculpture* (New York: Praeger, 1968), 20. Eshu's identification with Satan is widespread throughout the Caribbean. Benítez-Rojo mentions that, as far north as Cuba, "the santería cult represents him sometimes as the devil, and consequently it is said of Eshu that at times 'he speaks backwards' " (*Repeating Island*, 227).
90. Robert Gover, *Voodoo Contra* (York Beach, ME: Samuel Weiser, 1985), 116.
91. Henry Louis Gates, Jr, *The Signifying Monkey: A Theory of Afro-American Literary Criticism* (New York: Oxford University Press, 1988), 6. Philip John Neimark adds that Eshu, a "carefree" and "fun-loving" figure, will "easily . . . provoke conflict or mischief among others simply to get some action going". See Neimark, *The Way of the Orisa* (New York: HarperCollins, 1993), 80 and 78.
92. It is reasonable to assume that Evelina would have absorbed, through Corpus Christi's aboriginal Warrahoons, some elements of Amerindian lore. Some indigenous American cultures associated the frog with fertility, while others linked its croaking with death and the journey to the afterlife. Both traditions seem to have some relevance to the birth, death and meaning of Antoni's crapochild. See Julie Jones and Heidi King, "Gold of the Americas", *Metropolitan Museum of Art Bulletin* 59, no. 4 (Spring 2002), 46.
93. Antoni, *Divina Trace*, 69.
94. Gates's characterization of Eshu as a fertility god (6) and Neimark's description of him as "rampantly sexual" (76) give added texture to Evelina's identification of Manuelito with Eshu, since the frogchild is believed to have been born with the genitals of a grown man, and the circumstances surrounding his conception are hyperbolically carnal, if not precisely erotic.
95. Antoni, *Divina Trace*, 84.
96. Ibid., 322.
97. This is another indication of the elasticity of the novel's chronology. Slavery ended in the British Caribbean in the 1830s.
98. Benítez-Rojo, *Repeating Island*, 192.
99. There is a thread of popular belief that links Europe's several "black madonnas" not to the Virgin but to the Magdalen – hence their distinguishing darker colour. Whether or not this has any basis in fact, Antoni certainly links the two Marys together in *Divina Trace*, almost as if they were two halves of a divided whole.
100. Antoni, *Divina Trace*, 384.
101. Antoni takes this trope a step further in *Blessed Is the Fruit* (London: Faber,

1998), where an actual child, not yet born, is the living, still developing embodiment of Corpus Christi's – and the Caribbean's – syncretic future.

102. Antoni, *Divina Trace*, 395.
103. Ibid., 126.
104. For a subtle and detailed treatment of the role of Carnival in Trinidad's cultural life, see Earl Lovelace's novel *The Dragon Can't Dance* (Harlow, UK: Longman, 1988).
105. Mikhail Bakhtin, *Rabelais and His World*, trans. Hélène Iswolsky (Bloomington: Indiana University Press, 1984), 10.
106. Bakhtin, 9–10.
107. Antoni, *Divina Trace*, 347.
108. Benítez-Rojo, *Repeating Island*, 16.
109. Antoni, *Divina Trace*, 313.
110. Ibid., 140.
111. Ibid., 91.
112. Ibid., 156.
113. Ibid., 170.
114. Ibid., 164.
115. Ibid., 116.
116. Ibid., 289.
117. Ibid., 225 and 227.
118. Ibid., 172.
119. Ibid., 13.
120. Ibid., 172.
121. Ibid., 197 and 208.
122. Ibid., 184. One might also add the reference to the Corpus Christi celebration as "monkeybusiness" (16).
123. Ibid., 215. This word, like many other references in the poem, is a creolized composite of East Indian and West Indian material. Valmiki's verse form was the sloka; the shack-shack is a musical instrument (also known as maracas) popular in Venezuela and Trinidad.
124. Henry Louis Gates speculates on a possible link between the "signifying monkey" in west African cosmologies and the god Eshu (or Elegbara) in his role as linguist and interpeter. See Gates, 13–17. It is also true that the monkey was associated with language, writing and interpretation in the religion of the Mayans, whose territory abutted the western Caribbean. The patron deities of the powerful "caste of scribes (*ah dzib*)" who "controlled epigraphic, astronomical and historical information" were Itzamná, "the Creator God and legendary inventor of writing, and the Monkey-Man gods of

the *Popol Vuh*". See Michael Coe, Dean Snow and Elizabeth Benson, *Atlas of Ancient America* (New York: Facts on File, 1989), 119.

125. Antoni, *Divina Trace,* 58.
126. Ibid., 225–26.
127. Ibid., 227.
128. Ibid., 59.
129. Ibid., 156.
130. Ibid., 157.
131. Ibid., 198.
132. Ibid., 199.
133. Antoni "signs" this book in many other ways as well. A line in Magdalena's poem – "When stand he to he treefoot Twohead-Fred" (218) – is an allusion to his very early short story "Two-head Fred and Tree-foot Frieda", and in Mother Maurina's account of the "chupidee waterhead", Bernadetta's cousin, Sister Janine, bears the same name as the noted artist Janine Antoni, the author's sister. Clearly the ultimate "imagining I" is that of Robert Antoni.
134. Hanuman's tale is also, not surprisingly, strewn with such Caribbeanisms, including this one: "Seeing in de page you own monkeyface ee-eeing, quick out you dreamsleep walcott!" (205) – a tribute that, rumour has it, the great poet did not particularly appreciate.
135. Antoni, *Divina Trace,* 200.
136. Ibid., 209.
137. For Kristeva, following Lacan, the "mirror stage" is essential in the development of signification. Analysis of the mirrors and reflections in *Divina Trace,* drawing on both Kristeva and Lacan, is one of many approaches to the novel awaiting further exploration. Eric D. Smith moves a step in this direction, calling the mirror the repository of "the creator and the created, the signifier and the signified, 'mirroring' as it were primitive humanity's first strides toward the appropriation of language and identity". See "Johnny Domingo's Epic Nightmare of History", *Ariel: A Review of International English Literature* 31, no. 4 (October 2000): 109. Taking this line of interpretation into the cultural realm, Benítez-Rojo remarks that "every mirror is a text in which the observer reads him/herself. . . . Therefore, the mirror of *Divina Trace* reflects the many faces of Caribbean readers, but in the end it reflects an identity in a state of creolisation, a reflection that oscillates between history and myth." See "Three Words Toward Creolisation", 61.
138. A signifying system "constructed exclusively on the basis of the semiotic" would have to be non-verbal, like music. Julia Kristeva, *The Kristeva Reader,* ed.

Toril Moi (New York: Columbia University Press, 1986), 92. The Greek word from which *semiotic* is derived can have as one of its meanings "trace".

139. Ibid.
140. Édouard Glissant, *Caribbean Discourse: Selected Essays,* trans. J. Michael Dash (Charlottesville: University Press of Virginia, 1989), 139.
141. Ibid., 64.
142. Antoni's presentation of history as neither fixed nor objective is also consonant with postwar "relativist" trends in historiography. See, for example, R.G. Collingwood, *The Idea of History* (Oxford: Clarendon Press, 1946), E.H. Carr, *What Is History?* (New York: Knopf, 1962) and Timothy Paul Donovan, *Historical Thought in America* (Norman: University of Oklahoma Press, 1973).
143. Glissant, *Caribbean Discourse,* 243.
144. The confluence of the Eucharist, Corpus Christi, the Resurrection and the Incarnation occurs in myriad ways in *Divina Trace.* The mudspot tilak that Magdalena places in the middle of Johnny's forehead certainly suggests the smudge borne by Christians on Ash Wednesday (the day before Corpus Christi Day, in Antoni's formulation), and the woman Johnny ultimately marries is named "Ash".
145. Antoni, *Divina Trace,* 381–82.
146. Ibid., 396.
147. The gift of the rosary, in addition to closing the novel on a note of Christian charity, provides an iconic link to Antoni's next novel, *Blessed Is the Fruit.*
148. Dean Karpowicz, "A Postmodern Collective: Deconstruction, Identity and Faith in Robert Antoni's *Divina Trace*", *Caribbean Quarterly* 46, no. 1 (March 2000): 37–45.
149. Antoni, *Divina Trace,* 170.
150. Gates, 7. Neimark describes *ase* as "similar to, but more than, aura, soul, or spirituality. It is a living, breathing, palpable flow of energy that can either increase or diminish, depending upon our behavior" (76).
151. Antoni, *Divina Trace,* 175.
152. Traditionally it is Brahma, not Kali, who intervenes. Antoni's version of the myth obviously works better if a goddess is the source of inspiration. See Narayan, 136.
153. Bolívar is said to have encamped his army of liberation under a gigantic samaan tree (the same astonishing tree earlier described by the naturalist Humboldt) near Maracay, Venezuela. Outside the room where Bolívar died, on a ranch near Santa Marta, Colombia, stands another samaan, and beneath it, a statue of the Liberator. See *Flowering Trees of the Caribbean* (New York: Rinehart, 1951), 56–58.

154. Antoni, *Divina Trace*, 421.
155. Ibid., 171.

CHAPTER 3: *BLESSED IS THE FRUIT*

1. Mother Earth (Jeanette Baptiste), quoted in Ronald Littlewood, *Pathology and Identity: The Work of Mother Earth in Trinidad* (Cambridge: Cambridge University Press, 1993), 101.
2. Carlos Fuentes, introduction to *Don Quixote*, by Miguel de Cervantes Saavedra, trans. Tobias Smollet (New York: Random House, 2004), xix.
3. Antonio Benítez-Rojo, *The Repeating Island: The Caribbean and the Postmodern Perspective*, 2nd ed., trans. James Maraniss (Durham, NC: Duke University Press, 1996), 189.
4. Édouard Glissant, "Beyond Babel", *World Literature Today* 63, no. 4 (1989), 561.
5. In addition to Derek Walcott's play *Ti-Jean and His Brothers* (see note 39 below), a "Bolom baby" appears in Nalo Hopkinson's novel *Brown Girl in the Ring* (New York: Warner, 1998), 33.
6. The rosary, strictly speaking, refers to the exercise in which prayers are said and counted on a string of beads, although in common parlance the word usually refers to the beads themselves. The full rosary, like Antoni's novel, is composed of three chaplets, each chaplet containing five decades, or sets of ten beads. Each decade is also associated with a mystery – an event from the life of Jesus or the Virgin Mary. It remains the task of a future critic to identify the "mysteries" linked to the fifteen decades of *Blessed Is the Fruit*. Saying the entire rosary – 150 Ave Marias, not to mention the accompanying fifteen Lord's Prayers and fifteen Gloria Patris – is obviously a task for the truly devout, and in practice many "rosaries" used by ordinary Catholics are in fact chaplets. The form of *Blessed* completes a circle, in that Granny Myna, who asks Johnny Domingo to give her rosary to Magdalena at the end of *Divina Trace*, is based on Robert Antoni's paternal grandmother.
7. Michel de Certeau, *Heterologies: Discourse on the Other*, trans. Brian Massumi (Minneapolis: University of Minnesota Press, 1986), 70.
8. Mikhail Bakhtin, *Rabelais and His World*, trans. Hélène Iswolsky (Bloomington: Indiana University Press, 1984), 10.
9. Robert Antoni, *Blessed Is the Fruit* (London: Faber, 1998), 56. Pagination is identical in the original American edition (New York: Henry Holt, 1997).
10. Ibid.
11. Ibid., 79.

12. Ibid., 90.
13. Ibid., 62.
14. Ibid., 66.
15. The close connection of religious fervor and sexual desire in *Blessed Is the Fruit* is only one of many threads that tie this novel with its predecessor. Mother Superior Maurina in *Divina Trace* would have understood all too well why Lil "gets off" while saying the rosary.
16. Antoni, *Blessed*, 57.
17. Ibid., 77.
18. Ibid., 96–97.
19. Ibid., 155. This is self-evidently the statue associated with Magdalena Domingo in *Divina Trace*. As in that novel, the trace leads ten miles to the little chapel where the statue resides. But in *Blessed Is the Fruit* Antoni refers to it only as La Divina Pastora – the name of a real statue and object of veneration in Siparia, Trinidad.
20. Ibid., 225–26.
21. Ibid., 392.
22. Ibid., 23.
23. Ibid., 295.
24. Ibid., 200.
25. Most particularly with his notion of the "*métissage* without limits" mentioned in "Beyond Babel" (561). Glissant argues that this "*métissage* or cross-breeding" is associated with "a new dimension", permitting a sense of both rootedness and openness. Elsewhere he links these ideas to the trope of the estuary; see *Caribbean Discourse: Selected Essays*, trans. J. Michael Dash (Charlottesville: University Press of Virginia, 1989).
26. Though the rosary may be the main inspiration for the novel's arrangement of narrative materials, another source may be the Asian *t'ai-chi t'u* (better known as the yin and yang symbol). The halves of the *t'ai-chi t'u* – one light, one dark – are not divided by a straight line but rather bulge towards and into each other's space. The dark half also contains a small light-coloured circle and the light half a dark one – rather like the presence of Vel's letter within Lil's narration and Lil's journal within Vel's story.
27. Glissant, *Caribbean Discourse*, 64.
28. Benítez-Rojo, *Repeating Island*, 29.
29. Bakhtin, 10.
30. Ibid., 7.
31. J. Michael Dash, *The Other America: Caribbean Literature in a New World Context* (Charlottesville: University Press of Virginia, 1998), 128.

32. Richard Burton, "Cricket, Carnival and Street Culture in the Caribbean", quoted in Dash, *Other America.*
33. Antoni, *Blessed,* 16.
34. Ibid., 139.
35. Peter Mason, *Bacchanal! The Carnival Culture of Trinidad* (Philadelphia: Temple University Press, 1998), 14.
36. Such irony is characteristic of Trinidad's Carnival tradition. In Sam Selvon's *Moses Migrating,* for instance, the title character, returning to Trinidad to recapture his lost island affiliation after years of living in Britain, plans to masquerade as a black Britannia pulled by two white British "slaves", his friends Bob and Jeannie.
37. Antoni, *Blessed,* 142.
38. Ibid., 275.
39. Derek Walcott, *Dream on Monkey Mountain and Other Plays* (New York: Farrar, Straus, 1992), 94.
40. Theodore Colson, "Derek Walcott's Plays: Outrage and Compassion", *World Literature Written in English* 12, no. 1 (1973): 83.
41. Antoni, *Blessed,* 204–7.
42. Glissant, *Caribbean Discourse,* 169.
43. Wlad Godzich, foreword to Certeau, *Heterologies,* xvi. Godzich is discussing the thought of Talmudic scholar Emmanuel Lévinas, whom Tzvetan Todorov calls "the philosopher of alterity". See also Todorov, *The Conquest of America: The Question of the Other,* trans. Richard Howard (New York: Harper and Row, 1984), 258.
44. Antoni, *Blessed,* 147.
45. Ibid., 52.
46. Ibid., 374.
47. Ibid. 399.
48. Ibid., 204.
49. Ibid., 207.
50. Sidney W. Mintz and Sally Price, eds., *Caribbean Contours* (Baltimore: Johns Hopkins University Press, 1986), 129.
51. Olive Senior, "Colonial Girl's School", in *Caribbean Poetry Now,* ed. Stewart Brown (London: Edward Arnold, 1992), 32.
52. Glissant's formulation, in *Caribbean Discourse,* 62, is not unlike what Wilson Harris calls, with somewhat more florescence, "the monolithic character of conquistadorial legacies of civilization". *The Womb of Space: The Cross-Cultural Imagination* (Westport, CT: Greenwood Press, 1983), xv.
53. Certeau, 67–68.

54. Edward Said, *Culture and Imperialism* (New York: Knopf, 1993), 78.
55. Ibid., 216.
56. Ibid., 96.
57. Ibid., 96 and 59.
58. Charles Dickens, *Our Mutual Friend* (New York: Penguin, 1997), 316.
59. Gaston Bachelard, *The Poetics of Space*, trans. Maria Jolas (Boston: Beacon, 1969), xxxii.
60. Ibid., 7, and 91.
61. This is why, parenthetically, it is so important for Antoinette to set her husband's English house afire at the end of *Wide Sargasso Sea* – a purgative act that, like the birth of Bolom in Antoni's novel, will presumably occur outside the actual bounds of the text.
62. Derek Walcott, *Collected Poems, 1948–1984* (New York: Farrar, Straus, 1986), 19.
63. Bachelard, 6.
64. Ibid., 17.
65. Dash, *Other America*, 107.
66. Antoni, *Blessed*, 51.
67. Ibid., 98.
68. Ibid., 80.
69. Ibid., 366. Vel explains that this is a white man who is a vagrant or wastrel. The gulf between plantation owners in the Caribbean and those lower-class or poorer whites variously called "bacra-johnnies", "white cockroaches", "red-legs" (in Barbados) or "petits blancs" (in Haiti) was often vast.
70. Ibid., 47.
71. Ibid., 389.
72. Ibid., 207.
73. Ibid., 79.
74. Édouard Glissant, *Faulkner, Mississippi*, trans. Barbara Lewis and Thomas C. Spear (New York: Farrar, Straus, 1999), 42.
75. Ibid., 178–79.
76. Ibid., 183.
77. Ibid., 83.
78. Ibid., 84.
79. Ibid., 87.
80. Ibid., 98.
81. Elsewhere Glissant explicitly includes Faulkner in the broad tradition of writers who have flourished in the "ruins of the Plantation", and clearly Antoni, a product of Trinidad's plantocracy, lies (however uncomfortably)

within this tradition as well. See Édouard Glissant, *Poetics of Relation*, trans. Betsy Wing (Ann Arbor: University of Michigan Press, 2000), 73.

82. Antoni, *Blessed*, 86.
83. Ibid., 134.
84. Ibid., 161.
85. Ibid., 316.
86. Ibid., 329.
87. Ibid., 338.
88. Ibid., 243.
89. Ibid., 270.
90. Bachelard, 81–82.
91. Antoni, *Blessed*, 234.
92. Bachelard, 78–79.
93. Antoni, *Blessed*, 33.
94. Glissant, *Poetics*, 75.
95. Antoni, *Blessed*, 70.
96. Bachelard, 18.
97. Antoni, *Blessed*, 379.
98. Ibid., 83.
99. Ibid.
100. Ibid., 84–85.
101. Ibid., 84.
102. See Jacques Lacan, *Ecrits: A Selection*, trans. Alan Sheridan (London: Tavistock, 1977), 4–23; and Anika Lemaire, *Jacques Lacan*, trans. David Macey (London: Routledge, 1977), 78–92.
103. Antoni, *Blessed*, 142.
104. Ibid., 380.
105. Emmanuel Lévinas, *Otherwise Than Being; or Beyond Essence*, trans. Alphonso Lingis (The Hague: Martinus Nijhoff, 1981), 3 and 182.
106. Antoni, *Blessed*, 339.
107. Ibid., 375.
108. Ibid., 84.
109. Bachelard, 103.
110. Ibid., 10.
111. Derek Walcott, "The Schooner Flight", in *Collected Poems*, 361.
112. Antoni, *Blessed*, 397.
113. Ibid., 398.
114. Ibid., 207.
115. Ibid., 399.

116. Ibid., 29.
117. Ibid., 398.
118. Ibid., 52.
119. Antonio Benítez-Rojo, interview with Robert Antoni, *Bomb* 82 (Winter 2002–2003), 34.
120. Antoni, *Blessed*, 35.
121. Ibid., 370.
122. Bachelard, 61.

CHAPTER 4: *MY GRANDMOTHER'S EROTIC FOLKTALES*

1. Édouard Glissant, *Caribbean Discourse: Selected Essays*, trans. J. Michael Dash (Charlottesville: University Press of Virginia, 1989), 64.
2. Antonio Benítez-Rojo, *The Repeating Island: The Caribbean and the Postmodern Perspective*, 2nd ed., trans. James Maraniss (Durham, NC: Duke University Press, 1996), 187.
3. Ibid., 4.
4. Describing Caribbean literature in general, for instance, Benítez-Rojo calls it "a stream of texts in flight, in intense differentiation among themselves and within whose complex coexistence there are vague regularities, usually paradoxical". *Repeating Island*, 27.
5. Lawrence Scott, *Witchbroom* (London: Heinemann, 1992), 200.
6. Benítez-Rojo, *Repeating Island*, 2.
7. Robert Antoni, *Divina Trace* (Woodstock, NY: Overlook, 1992), 62.
8. Ibid., 170.
9. Literary history is filled with similar, if not precisely cognate, works, such as Elizabeth Gaskell's *Cranford*, Anderson's *Winesburg, Ohio* and Faulkner's *Go Down, Moses*.
10. Antoni, *Divina Trace*, 238.
11. Robert Antoni, *My Grandmother's Erotic Folktales* (London: Faber, 2000), 35.
12. Glissant, *Caribbean Discourse*, 84.
13. Eric D. Smith, in an interesting study of the book, addresses its "successful appropriation of exoticist codes of representation" and its "subversive counter-narrative . . . that forces us to acknowledge patterns of neo-colonial cultural consumption". See "Pandering Caribbean Spice: The Strategic Exoticism of Robert Antoni's *My Grandmother's Erotic Folktales*", *Journal of Commonwealth Literature* 39, no. 3 (2004): 6.

14. Roland Littlewood, *Pathology and Identity: The Work of Mother Earth in Trinidad* (Cambridge: Cambridge University Press, 1993), 164.
15. Antoni, *Folktales,* 3.
16. Benítez-Rojo, *Repeating Island,* 11.
17. Ibid., 187.
18. Glissant, *Caribbean Discourse,* 244.
19. J. Michael Dash, introduction to Glissant, *Caribbean Discourse,* xxix.
20. Glissant, *Caribbean Discourse,* 106.
21. Antoni, *Folktales,* 35.
22. Ibid., 135. Possibly a sly comic reference to Grenada's socialist New Jewel Movement.
23. Ibid., 7.
24. I have borrowed this word (taking it slightly out of context) from Glissant. See Édouard Glissant, *Poetics of Relation,* trans. Betsy Wing (Ann Arbor: University of Michigan Press, 2000), 71.
25. Antoni, *Divina Trace,* 163. I call her Granny Myna here because the skein of relationships with characters and situations in *Divina Trace* clearly establishes her as such, although in *Erotic Folktales* she is referred to chiefly by nicknames such as Skip and Lady Lobo. As for her full name, it is María Rosa de la Plancha Domingo in the first story in *Erotic Folktales* (18), Maria Pilar Rosa de la Plancha Domingo in an earlier version of that same tale, and María Rosario Domingo in *Divina Trace.* The name of Antoni's paternal grandmother, on whom Granny Myna is at least partly based, was María Rosario de Medina Antoni.
26. In England, not Canada, as in *Folktales,* 34.
27. Antoni, *Folktales,* 16.
28. Ibid., 176.
29. Benítez-Rojo, *Repeating Island,* 11.
30. Originally published, in a slightly different form, in *Conjunctions* 18 (1992): 281–300.
31. Antoni's characterizations of both the King of Chacachacari and his cohort in the fifth tale, the Kentucky Colonel, may draw to some degree on the tradition of the con artist figure in United States literature, and particularly on the figures of the King and the Duke in Mark Twain's *Huckleberry Finn.*
32. Antoni, *Folktales,* 9.
33. Ibid., 10.
34. Ibid., 3.
35. Ibid., 7–8. Granny's etymology is essentially correct. *Chagua* may well derive from the Spanish *chacra* (small farm). *Ramo* can mean branch but also, as *ramo*

de flores, bouquet. And *ramera* is one of many words for prostitute. The actual place in Trinidad is usually spelled Chaguaramas.

36. Peter Mason, *Bacchanal! The Carnival Culture of Trinidad* (Philadelphia: Temple University Press, 1998), 27.
37. V.S. Naipaul mentions this place too, including it in a list of "glorious Amerindian names forming an imaginary route that took in the four corners of the island and one place, Chacachacare, across the sea". In the same novel he also refers to the leper settlement on that island. See Naipaul, *A House for Mr. Biswas* (New York: Penguin, 1992), 79 and 382.
38. Antoni, *Folktales*, 11–13.
39. Ibid., 9.
40. Ibid., 15.
41. Ibid., 30.
42. Glissant, *Poetics*, 69. In the glossary of *Caribbean Discourse* Glissant defines *djobeurs* [*sic*] as "those who subsist by doing odd jobs, in particular by recycling used materials" (264).
43. Antoni, *Folktales*, 34.
44. Antoni, *Divina Trace*, 170.
45. This is another one of the book's many anachronisms. The real Kentucky Colonel's fried chicken franchise did not begin until the 1950s, well after this story takes place. Within the book's semiotic system, however, it is particularly appropriate, inasmuch as KFC – at least partly because of its identification with a food product more widely acceptable than pork or beef – has become one of America's most visible emissaries in the developing world.
46. Antoni, *Folktales*, 69–70.
47. Although Gregoria la Rosa is an autonomous character in *Erotic Folktales*, there are faint traces of links between her and figures in Antoni's other work. Like Magdalena in *Divina Trace*, she appears to be of mixed blood and comes from a remote part of Corpus Christi, and like Vel in *Blessed Is the Fruit*, she occupies a middle ground between servant and member of the family. Also, both Gregoria and Vel find themselves wearing a key and a crucifix entwined around their necks (*Blessed*, 52; *Folktales*, 113).
48. Antoni, *Folktales*, 76.
49. Ibid., 109.
50. Ibid., 78.
51. Olive Senior, interview with Charles H. Rowell, *Callaloo* 11, no. 3 (1988): 487.
52. Caryl Phillips, *A State of Independence* (London: Faber and Faber, 1986), 131.
53. The Mighty Sparrow, "The Yankees Back", in *The Penguin Book of Caribbean Verse in English*, ed. Paula Burnett (New York: Penguin, 1986), 43.

54. Antoni, *Folktales*, 106.
55. Ibid., 179.
56. Benítez-Rojo, *Repeating Island*, 189.
57. Antoni, *Folktales*, 150–51. The Elizabethan reference is more than casual. This invective tournament is only one of numerous suggestions of Shakespearean comedy in *Erotic Folktales*. The book is arranged in five parts with a wedding at the end, for example, and it is filled with disguises and instances of mistaken identity.
58. Ibid., 156.
59. Ibid., 93.
60. Ibid., 20.
61. Ibid., 175.
62. Ibid., 180. Peter Mason points out that kalinda singing (the precursor of calypso) "gradually seems to have become a male preserve", until by the turn of the twentieth century, when calypso had evolved into a form recognizable today, women had "faded into the background" (22).
63. Antoni, *Folktales*, 196.
64. Ibid., 194.
65. Ibid., 177–78.
66. Ibid., 188.
67. Between the two world wars, the British, alarmed by the subversive potential of calypso, censored and harrassed leading calypsonians, and after the Second World War calypso became increasingly associated with the nationalist movement. The irony here, of course, is that Granny's calypso, like her commercials, never extends beyond her own house. See Mason, 25–26.
68. Antoni, *Folktales*, 90.
69. Ibid., 199.
70. Antoni has told me that the germ of this story comes from an actual Trinidad folktale. The original, however, explains only how Crab-o lost his head as a result of divulging the woman's name. Antoni added the rest, including Blanchisseuse's lovers and their dismemberments.
71. Antoni, *Folktales*, 36.
72. Blanchisseuse is also the name of a real village on the north coast of Trinidad.
73. Antoni, *Folktales*, 30. Here too is a slight echo of *Blessed Is the Fruit*. At one point Lil recalls bathing naked, like Blanchisseuse, in a river and being spied on by interested local residents: "Till one afternoon I opened my eyes to discover half-a-dozen boys and a couple grown men too . . . all hiding behind a clump of bamboo on the other side of the river, all staring at me cokeeeyed, their

tongues dripping-down red and obscene from out their mouths" (108). *Cokeeeyed* is *crosseyed* in the earlier American edition (1997).

74. Ibid., 40–41.
75. Ibid., 44–45.
76. Ibid., 65.
77. Benítez-Rojo, *Repeating Island*,293.
78. Antoni, *Folktales*, 58.
79. Mariposa (butterfly) is a common term for homosexual in many Spanish-speaking countries.
80. Antoni, *Folktales*, 66–67. As Granny Myna points out, this title is "exactly the opposite of what he tale was telling in truth" (67). Blanchisseuse cuts off the heads, not the foreskins, of the men's penises. Undoubtedly both the decapitations and Ernesto's perspective on them owe something to Antoni's interest in Freud's inability (or disinclination) to assign a role "to the mother-goddess in his genesis of religious illusion." Antoni hypothesizes in an unpublished essay that "the ancient and bizarre practice of circumcision" may have been "instituted by the mother . . . as a visible sign" of the sons' exogamy. If circumcision was "a symbolic castration", he asks, "what better sign of the sons' promise to their mother, or their covenant with her?" "Fifty Years after Freud and Joyce, Moses and Finnegan: Re-writing the Primal History Scene for the Absent Mother", unpublished essay, n.d.
81. Antoni, *Folktales*, 37.
82. Ibid., 59.
83. Ibid., 66–67.
84. Glissant, *Caribbean Discourse*, 74.
85. Ibid., 243.
86. Antoni, *Divina Trace*, 342.
87. Antoni's historical rearrangements in this tale are complicated. At the time the tale opens (1595), the "real" Fernando de Barrío was only a teenage boy, although his father, Antonio, had long been searching for El Dorado, and Antonio Sedeño's involvement in Trinidad occurred a full half-century earlier. For a lively but "factual" account of some of these events, see V.S. Naipaul, *The Loss of El Dorado* (New York: Vintage, 1984). Subtle reshaping of Trinidad's historical dimension occurs in the other tales also, as when Granny calls 1776 (rather than 1797) "the year the English took Corpus Christi" (10).
88. Antoni, *Folktales*, 126.
89. Ibid., 127.
90. Ibid., 130–31.

91. Ibid., 135.
92. Ibid., 138–39.
93. Glissant, *Caribbean Discourse,* 85.
94. Antoni, *Folktales,* 140.
95. Ibid., 142–43.
96. Ibid., 144–45.
97. Glissant, *Caribbean Discourse,* 142.
98. Antoni, *Folktales,* 145.
99. Wlad Godzich, foreword to Certeau, *Heterologies,* xvi. I quoted this passage in chapter 3, but its core meaning – desire for the Other as a need to "leave the realms of the known" and "settle in a land that is under its [the Other's] rule" – is equally applicable to the tale of Iguana.
100. Antoni, *Divina Trace,* 43.
101. Jeffrey Knapp, *An Empire Nowhere: England, America and Literature from Utopia to The Tempest* (Berkeley and Los Angeles: University of California Presss, 1992), 329.
102. Knapp, 330.
103. Naipaul, *Loss,* 18 and 38.
104. Antoni, *Folktales,* 143.
105. Ibid., 122.
106. Ibid., 121–22.
107. Benítez-Rojo, *Repeating Island,* 187.

CHAPTER 5: *CARNIVAL*

1. Henry Beissel, "Pans at Carnival", in *The Penguin Book of Caribbean Verse in English,* ed. Paula Burnett (London: Penguin, 1986), 241.
2. Robert Antoni, *My Grandmother's Erotic Folktales* (London: Faber, 2000), 201.
3. Decca Aikenhead, "Irates of the Caribbean", *Guardian Unlimited,* 2 July 2005, http://books.guardian.co.uk/review/story/O,,1518452,00.html.
4. Robert Antoni, *Divina Trace* (Woodstock, NY: Overlook, 1992), 303.
5. Ibid., 248.
6. Ibid., 303.
7. The name change acknowledges the character's closeness to the "real" Antoni, since William is his actual middle name, as well as the name of William John Sanger Tucker, his earliest maternal ancestor on the island of Trinidad and the subject of his current novel in progress.
8. Robert Antoni, *Blessed Is the Fruit* (London: Faber, 1998), 385.

9. Ibid., 351–52.
10. Antoni, *Folktales,* 35–36.
11. There are numerous other works on this subject, including Wilson Harris's *Carnival Trilogy,* Lawrence Scott's brief but memorable "King Sailor One J'Ouvert Morning" (see note 33) and Elma Napier's "Carnival in Martinique".
12. Antoni, *Divina Trace,* 395.
13. Even within Carnival the "life-affirming and life-enhancing 'spirit' . . . shares the stage with a lurking, less than benevolent, even demonic twin, which, in a sometimes flirtatious manner that can have disastrous results, will smile upon and favor death rather than life". David K. Danow, *The Spirit of Carnival: Magical Realism and the Grotesque* (Lexington: University Press of Kentucky, 1995), 1. This darker spirit manifests itself in carnival as "dirty mas", played out on jouvert morning.
14. This designation is later somewhat qualified.
15. Robert Antoni, *Carnival* (New York: Grove/Atlantic, 2005), 5.
16. Antoni would certainly agree with Edward Said's characterization of the city: "New York is in so many ways the exilic city *par excellence.*" See *Culture and Imperialism* (New York: Knofp, 1993), xxvii.
17. Antoni, *Carnival,* 39.
18. Roland Littlewood, *Pathology and Identity: The Work of Mother Earth in Trinidad* (Cambridge: Cambridge University Press, 1993), 204.
19. Even the most casual reader must readily perceive, moreover, that *The Sun Also Rises* has nothing to with the Caribbean. But Hemingway was one of the first truly transnational novelists, and he did spend many years in the northern reaches of the Caribbean basin – a region he knew better than any other American writer up to that time. See Bill Ashcroft, Gareth Griffiths and Helen Tiffin, *The Empire Writes Back: Theory and Practice in Post-colonial Literatures* (London: Routledge, 1989).
20. Antoni, *Divina Trace,* 158.
21. Robert Antoni, interview with Lawrence Scott, *Bomb* 91 (Spring 2005): 56. There is even a ghostly affinity in the evolution of the two books' titles. Earlier working titles for *The Sun Also Rises* included *The Lost Generation, River to the Sea* and *Fiesta,* which lived on in the British edition; the book is still available under that title. Antoni, on the other hand, began with *All the Rivers Run into the Sea,* later shortened to *River,* then switched to *Behind God's Back* before finally settling on *Carnival.*
22. Ernest Hemingway, *The Sun Also Rises* (New York: Scribner's, 1970), 20.
23. Antoni, *Carnival,* 167.

24. Ibid., 135.
25. Ibid., 202. Compare Jake Barnes's description of Botin's in Madrid: "It is one of the best restaurants in the world" (Hemingway, 246), and Brett Ashley's remark in the little Spanish chapel, " 'Come on,' she whispered throatily. 'Let's get out of here. Makes me damned nervous' " (208).
26. Antoni, *Carnival*, 3.
27. Ibid., 294.
28. Ibid., 30 and 220.
29. Ibid., 47.
30. Ibid., 64.
31. Ibid., 12.
32. Ibid., 8.
33. Lawrence Scott, "King Sailor One J'Ouvert Morning", in *Ballad for the New World* (Oxford: Heinemann, 1994), 16.
34. Minshall is both an inspiration for *Carnival* and a character in it. He is one of a number of real people mentioned in the book, including Paul Bowles (whom Laurence interviews in Morocco), the calypsonian David Rudder and, most amusingly, "Herness Hemingway" (78).
35. Peter Mason, *Bacchanal! The Carnival Culture of Trinidad* (Philadelphia: Temple University Press, 1998), 88. About his own relationship with Minshall, Antoni has said, "I admire Minshall enormously, and I wanted to capture a moment when his genius really flourished. Under his hand Carnival just exploded and became wonderful and extraordinary, a theatrical and profoundly revolutionary thing, actually. I play mas in Minshall's band practically every year, and he's a close friend." Interview with Scott, 60.
36. Dylan Kerrigan and Nicholas Laughlin, "The Dramatist", *Caribbean Beat* 65 (January/February 2004), http://www.meppublishers.com/online/caribbean-beat/archive/article.php?issue=65&id=cb65-1-62 (accessed 7 November 2005). Antoni may have also incorporated some ideas from Minshall's 1996 mas, The Song of the Earth, which was described as "a tribal mas, of everyone, the tribe of mankind, the tribe of ourselves, of the Trinidadian and the Tobagonian, . . . the Callaloo of cultures". Callaloo Company, "Minshall Mas Callaloo 96", http://www.callaloo.co.tt/masbands/sote1996/SONG.HTML (accessed 8 November 2005).
37. Callaloo Company, "The Lost Tribe: Mas1999 – by Minshall", http://www.callaloo.co.tt/masbands/lost_tribe1999/about1.html (accessed 7 November 2005).
38. Antoni, *Carnival*, 37.
39. L'Ouverture died in 1803, a prisoner at Fort de Joux, in the French Alps.

40. Antoni, *Carnival,* 3 and 8.
41. Ibid., 66 and 75.
42. Ibid., 55.
43. Ibid., 65.
44. Ibid., 222.
45. Ibid., 230 and 282.
46. Ibid., 57.
47. Michel de Certeau, *Heterologies: Discourse on the Other,* trans. Brian Massumi (Minneapolis: University of Minnesota Press, 1986), 70.
48. Antoni, interview with Scott, 56.
49. Antoni, *Carnival,* 73.
50. Ibid., 28.
51. Ibid., 128. William says that the two "disappeared . . . for several months, down the islands" (43), providing one of many minute links between the novel's main locale and the actual Trinidad. "Down the islands" is the way Trinidadians refer to the small archipelago reaching across the Dragon's Mouth between their country and Venezuela.
52. Ibid., 67. Peter Mason writes that as far back as the nineteenth century, after emancipation (1834–38), Carnival became so Africanized that the "white elite . . . largely withdrew to their exclusive house parties in fear and disgust", though in recent years "it has gained general acceptance among all strands of society in what is a country of great racial diversity" (14). The reaction of William's parents suggests that there remain some holdouts.
53. Antoni, interview with Scott, 60.
54. Derek Walcott, "A Far Cry from Africa", in *The Penguin Book of Caribbean Verse in English* (London: Penguin, 1986), 243.
55. Antoni, *Carnival,* 27.
56. Ibid., 77.
57. Ibid., 125.
58. Ibid., 54.
59. Ibid., 40.
60. Ibid., 40 and 231.
61. Antoni, interview with Scott, 57.
62. Antoni, *Carnival,* 12.
63. Ibid., 20.
64. Ibid., 47.
65. Ibid., 102.
66. Ibid., 157.
67. Ibid., 195.

68. Ibid., 102.
69. Ibid., 45.
70. Ibid., 103.
71. Ibid., 169.
72. Ibid., 88.
73. Ibid., 89.
74. Ibid., 92 and 91.
75. Ibid., 215.
76. Ibid., 49. A buller is a homosexual.
77. Ibid., 21.
78. Mason, 7.
79. Earl Lovelace, *The Dragon Can't Dance* (Harlow, UK: Longman, 1988), 224. The ephemeral nature of the Carnival experience is beautifully embodied in Lovelace's novel.
80. The men of Mother Earth's group wear dreadlocks but they are not Rastafarians. Their belief system is quite different, as Littlewood explains: "For the Rastas, as for Muslims, their religion is the final revelation of which Christianity was a necessary precursor, but for the Earth People Christian monotheism is altogether a snare and a delusion, a view pithily expressed in one of their favourite aphorisms, 'Fuck God!' " (109).
81. Gordon Rohlehr, introduction to *The Hummingbird Tree*, by Ian McDonald (London: Heinemann, 1974), xxi; also quoted in Mason, 110. This Bakhtinian conception of Carnival is endorsed by Mario Vargas Llosa, who calls Carnival in Rio de Janeiro a "brazen, irreverent, fiercely sarcastic response to established patterns of morality and beauty, that vociferous negation of the social categories and borders that so often divide and stratify races, classes, and individuals, in a celebration that equalises and mixes everyone, rich and poor, white and black, employee and employer, master and servant". See *The Language of Passion: Selected Commentary*, trans. Natasha Wimmer (New York: Farrar, Straus, 2003), 233.
82. Antoni, *Carnival*, 183.
83. Antoni, interview with Scott, 55.
84. Antoni, *Carnival*, 123.
85. Ibid., 139.
86. Ibid., 86.
87. Mason, 50.
88. Antoni, *Carnival*, 197.
89. Antoni, interview with Scott, 60.
90. Antoni, *Carnival*, 112. This is only one of many figures of fecundity in

Antoni's work. Others include Vel in *Blessed Is the Fruit,* Granny Myna and even Magdalena Domingo in *Divina Trace,* who, whether her actual child lives or not, becomes the mother of an entire island.

91. Ibid., 110.
92. Ibid., 112. In this section of the novel Antoni is being utterly faithful to the real Peter Minshall, who according to Mason "has tried to bring messages to his mas, pursuing complicated themes with many different sections and giving teams of designers free range" (88).
93. This is another echo from Peter Minshall's actual career. Mason records that in Minshall's 1982 band a famous carnival king named Peter Samuel, playing "the Sacred and the Profane", wore "a bodystocking" in which "he appeared to be naked and was mobbed by female fans eager to determine the real state of his undress" (88).
94. Antoni, *Carnival,* 140–42.
95. See especially Littlewood, 79–85. Antoni also recasts a few details relating to the Earth People. For example, in the novel Mother Earth's husband is named Breadfruit (70), while according to Littlewood it is Cyprian, later changed to Jakatan – although there was a Breadfruit in the community. There was also an Eddoes, though at twenty-eight years of age or thereabouts in 1981, he would have been too old to be the novel's teenage Carnival king. The name recalls V.S. Naipaul's Eddoes in *Miguel Street* as well (New York: Vintage, 1984). See Littlewood, 158, 238 and 282 n. 35.
96. Littlewood, 6.
97. Ibid., 60.
98. Ibid., 4.
99. Antoni's debt to the oral tradition and the Caribbean folktale in his previous work is evident. His exploration of the Earth People in *Carnival* is certainly linked to his more general interest in Caribbean belief systems (especially non-Western ones), but it should be pointed out that Mother Earth's religion was (to whatever degree based on earlier tradition) a relatively recent phenomenon. Mother Earth's upbringing included "some contact with the 'African' understandings of shango" and she later practised Shouter Baptism, "an accommodation of shango within respectable Christianity". Only in the mid-1970s did she experience the revelations that led to the founding of the Earth People: "She came to understand that the Christian teaching of God the Father as creator was false and that the world was the work of a primordial Mother, whom she identified with Nature and with the Earth." See Littlewood, 4–6 and 226. For information on the Spiritual Baptists (Shouters) see also Melville J. Herskovits and Frances H. Herskovits, *Trinidad*

Village (New York: Knopf, 1947); for a brilliant fictional treatment of the Spiritual Baptists, see Earl Lovelace, *The Wine of Astonishment* (Oxford: Heinemann, 1989).

100. Antoni, interview with Scott, 59.
101. Littlewood, 5.
102. Antoni, *Carnival*, 241.
103. Ibid., 230.
104. Ibid., 258. Although this particular Hemingway reference is obvious and unmistakable, it bears mentioning as a witty sign of the extent to which Antoni has "cross-dressed" *The Sun Also Rises*. Scott even suggests that Antoni has "challenged or undermined" Hemingway's conception of machismo through the "use of the homoerotic, the way sexuality unravels . . . in *Carnival*." Interview with Scott, 57.
105. Antoni, *Carnival*, 267–68.
106. Ibid., 281.
107. Ibid., 230.
108. The Trinidad *Guardian* is that country's best-known newspaper. Long established, it is the journal for which Seepersad Naipaul, V.S. Naipaul's father, was a correspondent. The *Guardian* is masked as the *Sentinel* in *A House for Mr Biswas* (New York: Penguin, 1992).
109. Antoni, *Carnival*, 287, 289.
110. Ibid., 290.
111. Ibid., 294.
112. Marcel Proust, *Swann's Way*, trans. C.K. Scott Moncrieff and Terence Kilmartin (New York: Vintage, 1989), 423. In the original this passage reads: "les pays que nous désirons tiennent à chaque moment beaucoup plus de place dans notre vie veritable, que le pays où nous nous trouvons effectivement". *Du côté de chez Swann* (Paris: Editions Gallimard, 1954), 465.
113. Antoni, *Carnival*, 77–78.

CHAPTER 6: NOT YET FINISHED

1. Derek Walcott, *Collected Poems, 1948–1984* (New York: Farrar, Straus, 1986), 350.
2. Robert Antoni, *Carnival* (New York: Grove/Atlantic, 2005), 227–28.
3. Robert Antoni, interview with Lawrence Scott, *Bomb* 91 (Spring 2005): 57.
4. Robert Antoni, *Blessed Is the Fruit* (London: Faber, 1998), 207.
5. Robert Antoni, *My Grandmother's Erotic Folktales* (London: Faber, 2000), 90.

6. Ibid., 93.
7. Robert Antoni, *Divina Trace* (Woodstock, NY: Overlook, 1992), 162.
8. Ibid., 215.
9. Ibid., 342.
10. As Eric Smith puts it, the reader encounters "his own subjective presence in the novel as both a receiver of the message and a contributor to its creation"; see "Johnny Domingo's Epic Nightmare of History", *Ariel: A Review of International English Literature* 31, no. 4 (October 2000): 109–10. Antoni amusingly glosses his mirror-page device in the poem: "Only when Hanuman inform dem each, / With he mirror-form simple enough, / Clear as you face you recalling from de sacred book, / Red as de roukou red in you palmhand palm, / Did Hanuman begin to dress he story in Valmiki shacksloka" (*Divina Trace,* 215).
11. Antonio Benítez-Rojo, *The Repeating Island: The Caribbean and the Postmodern Perspective,* 2nd ed., trans. James Maraniss (Durham, NC: Duke University Press, 1996), 189.
12. The full title is now *As Flies to Whatless Boys: The Story of the Tropical Emmigration Society in Britain and Trinidad, West Indies, 1845–46*. An earlier working title was *TES,* for Tropical Emigration Society.
13. Robert Antoni, "Trial of the Satellite or How My Great-great-great-grandfather Almost Lost His Virginity on His Fifteenth Birthday", *Conjunctions* 47 (2006): 85–106. Robert Antoni also generously allowed me to read 150 pages of the new novel in typescript in 2006. Since then he has been in the process of reworking it, making changes such as shifting the bulk of the narration from omniscient to first-person point of view.
14. Etzler immigrated to the United States in 1831 but by the 1840s was back in Europe. Whether he was a visionary humanitarian or simply a con man – a matter of debate among historians – is a fact perhaps best left to fiction to determine.
15. Antoni, "Trial", 92.
16. Ibid., 86.
17. Repeatedly in Antoni's work, faith is subjected to the scrutiny of reason or empirical evidence. In *Divina Trace,* Johnny recalls his father amusingly commenting that "when it comes to matters of faith, the Church don't believe nothing without hard scientific proof" (295). And in *Erotic Folktales,* after hearing the King describe an angel's penis as "a celestial silver sausage", Granny, who has "seen plenty" of angels, knows he is lying, because "they all are *smooth*" (15). In *As Flies to Whatless Boys* Etzler seems to want to use science to transform and reify one of the underlying myths of Western civilization.

18. Antoni, "Trial", 103 and 106.
19. Both Etzler and his associate, C.F. Stollmeyer, were real people (as were, of course, the Tucker family). The Tropical Emigration Society project actually took place, although the results were disastrous.
20. Antoni, "Trial", 85 and 106. In the 2006 typescript that first sentence of "Trial of the Satellite" reads like this: "Eight months later, already suffocating beneath the early morning tropical sun, as he dropped his drawers and sat his skinny, jaundice-yellow bamsee down on moldering air among the musty sad disheveled figs-o'-heaven stumps in yet another frustrated B.M., Willy's mind traveled back across the sea to England, to the day of his 15th birthday, the day of his family's excursion to Oxfordshire for the first trial of the Satellite."
21. Edward Said, *Beginnings: Intention and Method* (Baltimore: Johns Hopkins University Press, 1978): 82–83.
22. The effort to reconstruct a past through fiction in *Whatless Boys* recalls again Glissant's observation that the Caribbean writer must "dig deep" to salvage remnants of the collective consciousness. See Édouard Glissant, *Caribbean Discourse: Selected Essays,* trans. J. Michael Dash (Charlottesville: University Press of Virginia, 1989), 64.
23. ". . . tratando de recomponer con tantas astillas dispersas el espejo roto de la memoria". Gabriel García Márquez, *Crónica de una muerte annunciada* (Barcelona: Plaza and Janés, 1993), 10–11.
24. Robert Antoni, *As Flies to Whatless Boys* (unpublished manuscript, 2009), 5.
25. Antoni, *As Flies to Whatless Boys* (unpublished manuscript, 2006), 184. In the most recent draft, Miss Ramsol's frequent use of "fockin" has been toned down to "effin".
26. That irony is considerably foregrounded in another excerpt from the novel to be published soon. Antoni has carefully selected, shaped and stitched together Miss Ramsol's messages into an autonomous short story that focuses on the outsider's struggles to gain possession of the documents he needs. "How to Make Photocopies in the Trinidad & Tobago National Archive" – as over the top as anything in *My Grandmother's Erotic Folktales* – is included in the collection *Trinidad Noir,* edited by Lisa Allen-Agostini and Jeanne Mason (New York: Akashic Books, 2008).
27. Benítez-Rojo, *Repeating Island,* 27.
28. Antoni, *Divina Trace,* 387.
29. Glissant, *Caribbean Discourse,* 65.
30. In an earlier version of Antoni's manuscript one chapter begins with: "A year later, already suffocating beneath the tropical early morning sun, as he

dropped his drawers and sat his skinny yellowed bamsee down on moldering air among the dusty sad disheveled *figs-o'-heaven* stumps in yet another frustrated BM, William John Sanger Tucker, Jr, my great-great-great-grandfather, recalled that first day when his father took him to discover bananas" (*Whatless Boys*, 15). García Márquez's famous first sentence reads: "Many years later, as he faced the firing squad, Colonel Aureliano Buendía was to remember that distant afternoon when his father took him to discover ice." *One Hundred Years of Solitude*, trans. Gregory Rabassa (New York: HarperCollins, 1998), 1.

31. Antoni, an earlier draft of *Whatless Boys*, 137.
32. In this excerpt from a 2006 draft, Antoni is referring to the fact that his own middle name is William. It is also no coincidence in this context that he changed the name of his previous novel's protagonist from Johnny to William.
33. Antoni, *Carnival*, 169.
34. Édouard Glissant, *Poetics of Relation*, trans. Betsy Wing (Ann Arbor: University of Michigan Press, 2000), 141.
35. Ibid., 143–44.
36. Ibid., 34.

SELECT BIBLIOGRAPHY

Achebe, Chinua. *Things Fall Apart.* New York: Random House/Anchor Books, 1994.

Aikenhead, Decca. "Irates of the Caribbean". *Guardian Unlimited,* 2 July 2005. http://www.guardian.co.uk/books/2005/jul/02/featuresreviews.guardian review36

Aizenberg, Edna. Review of *The Repeating Island,* by Antonio Benítez-Rojo. *Research in African Literatures* 25, no. 2 (Summer 1994): 185–88.

Allison, Philip. *African Stone Sculpture.* New York: Praeger, 1968.

Allsopp, Richard, ed. *Dictionary of Caribbean English Usage.* New York: Oxford University Press, 1996.

Anderson, Benedict. *Imagined Communities: Reflections on the Origin and Spread of Nationalism.* Rev. ed. New York: Verso, 2006.

Antoni, Brian. *Paradise Overdose.* New York: Grove, 1994.

———. *South Beach: The Novel.* New York: Grove Atlantic, 2008.

Antoni, Robert. "Another Day under the Black Volcano". *Outside* (May 1998): 118–28, 192–93.

———. *As Flies to Whatless Boys.* Unpublished novel, 2007.

———. *Blessed Is the Fruit.* London: Faber, 1998.

———. *Carnival.* New York: Grove/Atlantic, 2005.

———. *Divina Trace.* Woodstock, NY: Overlook, 1992.

———. "Fifty Years after Freud and Joyce, Moses and Finnegan: Re-writing the Primal History Scene for the Absent Mother". Unpublished essay, n.d.

———. "How to Make Photocopies in the Trinidad & Tobago National Archives". In *Trinidad Noir,* edited by Jeanne Mason and Lisa Allen-Agostini. New York: Akashic Books, 2008.

———. Interview with Lawrence Scott. *Bomb* 91 (Spring 2005): 55–60.

———. *My Grandmother's Erotic Folktales.* London: Faber, 2000.

———. "My Grandmother's Tale of the Buried Treasure and How She Defeated the King of Chacachacari and the Entire American Army with Her Venus-Flytraps". *Conjunctions* 18 (1992): 281–300.

———. "The Myth-making Process in *Absalom, Absalom!* and *One Hundred Years of Solitude*". Unpublished essay, n.d.

———. "A Piece of Pommerac". *Paris Review* 111 (1989): 168–83, 271.

———. "Trial of the Satellite or How My Great-great-great-grandfather Almost Lost His Virginity on His Fifteenth Birthday". *Conjunctions* 47 (2006): 85–106.

———. "Two-head Fred and Tree-foot Frieda". *Missouri Review* 8, no. 1 (1984–85): 87–100.

———. "Walking Down the Trace: A Conversation with Robert Antoni". Unpublished interview with Peter Josyph, 1994.

Ashcroft, Bill, Gareth Griffiths and Helen Tiffin. *The Empire Writes Back: Theory and Practice in Post-colonial Literatures.* London: Routledge, 1989.

———. *Post-colonial Studies: The Key Concepts.* London: Routledge, 2003.

Babin, Maria Teresa. "Trends in Caribbean English Fiction". *Caribbean Studies* 20, no. 1 (March 1980): 69–74.

Bachelard, Gaston. *The Poetics of Space.* Translated by Maria Jolas. Boston: Beacon, 1969.

Bakhtin, Mikhail. *The Dialogic Imagination.* Translated by Michael Holquist and Caryl Emerson. Austin: University of Texas Press, 1981.

———. *Rabelais and His World.* Translated by Hélène Iswolsky. Bloomington: Indiana University Press, 1984.

Barthold, Bonnie. *Black Time: Fictions of Africa, the Caribbean and the United States.* New Haven: Yale University Press, 1981.

Benítez-Rojo, Antonio. Interview with Robert Antoni. *Bomb* 82 (Winter 2002–2003).

———. *The Repeating Island: The Caribbean and the Postmodern Perspective.* 2nd ed. Translated by James Maraniss. Durham, NC: Duke University Press, 1996.

———. "Three Words Toward Creolization". In *Caribbean Creolization: Reflections on the Cultural Dynamics of Language, Literature, and Identity,* edited by Kathleen Balutansky and Marie-Agnes Sourieau, 53–61. Gainesville: University Press of Florida, 1998.

Bhabha, Homi K. *The Location of Culture.* London: Routledge, 1994.

Bishop, John. *Joyce's Book of the Dark: Finnegans Wake.* Madison: University of Wisconsin Press, 1986.

Brathwaite, Edward. *Barabajan Poems 1492–1992.* New York: Savacou North, 1994.

———. Introduction to *Brother Man,* by Roger Mais, v–xxi. Oxford: Heinemann, 1974.

Bristol, Michael D. *Carnival and Theater: Plebeian Culture and the Structure of Authority in Renaissance England.* New York: Methuen, 1985.

Brooks, Peter. "Incredulous Narration: 'Absalom, Absalom!' " In *Modern Critical*

Views: William Faulkner, edited by Harold Bloom, 247–68. New York: Chelsea House, 1986.

Brown, Stewart, ed. *Caribbean Poetry Now*. London: Edward Arnold, 1992.

Burnett, Paula, ed. *The Penguin Book of Caribbean Verse in English*. New York: Penguin, 1986.

Callaloo Company. "The Lost Tribe: Mas 1999 – by Minshall". http://www.callaloo.co.tt/masbands/lost tribe 1999/about1.html (accessed 7 November 2005).

———. "Minshall Mas Callaloo 96". http://www.callaloo.co.tt/masbands/sote1996/SONG. html (accessed 8 November 2005).

Carew, Jan. "The Caribbean Writer and Exile". *Caribbean Studies* 19, nos. 1 and 2 (1979): 111–32.

Carr, E.H. *What Is History?* New York: Knopf, 1962.

Cassidy, F.G., and R.B. LePage, eds. *Dictionary of Jamaican English*. London: Cambridge University Press, 1967.

Certeau, Michel de. *Heterologies: Discourse on the Other*. Translated by Brian Massumi. Minneapolis: University of Minnesota Press, 1986.

Cervantes Saavedra, Miguel de. *Don Quixote*. Translated by Edith Grossman. New York: HarperCollins, 2003.

Chamoiseau, Patrick. *Texaco*. Translated by Rose-Myriam Réjouis and Val Vinokurov. New York: Vintage, 1998.

Clifford, James. *The Predicament of Culture: Twentieth-Century Ethnography, Literature and Art*. Cambridge, MA: Harvard University Press, 1988.

Cobham, Rhonda. "Of Boloms, Mirror and Monkeymen: What's Real and What's Not in Robert Antoni's *Divina Trace*". *Annals of Scholarship* 12, no. 3 (1997): 49–75.

Coe, Michael, Dean Snow and Elizabeth Benson. *Atlas of Ancient America*. New York: Facts on File, 1989.

Collingwood, R.G. *The Idea of History*. Oxford: Clarendon Press, 1946.

Dalleo, Raphael. "'Tink is you dawson dis yana?' Imitation and Creation in Robert Antoni's *Divina Trace*". *Ariel: A Review of International English Literature* 32, no. 4 (October 2001): 21–45.

Dance, Daryl Cumber. "Matriarchs, Doves and Nymphos: Prevalent Images of Black, Indian and White Women in Caribbean Literature". *Studies in the Literary Imagination* 26, no. 2 (1993): 21–31.

Danow, David K. *The Spirit of Carnival: Magical Realism and the Grotesque*. Lexington: University Press of Kentucky, 1995.

Dash, J. Michael. Introduction to *Caribbean Discourse: Selected Essays*, by Édouard Glissant, xi–xlv. Charlottesville: University Press of Virginia, 1989.

———. *The Other America: Caribbean Literature in a New World Context*. Charlottesville: University Press of Virginia, 1998.

Dathorne, O.R. "Africa in the Literature of the West Indies". *Journal of Commonwealth Literature* 1 (September 1965): 95–116.

Dickens, Charles. *Our Mutual Friend*. New York: Penguin, 1997.

Donovan, Timothy Paul. *Historical Thought in America*. Norman: University of Oklahoma Press, 1973.

Flowering Trees of the Caribbean. New York: Rinehart, 1951.

Fuentes, Carlos. Introduction to *Don Quixote*, by Miguel de Cervantes. Translated by Tobias Smollet, vii–xxix. New York: Random House, 2004.

García Márquez, Gabriel. *Crónica de una muerte annunciada*. Barcelona: Plaza and Janès, 1993.

———. "Gabriel García Márquez Meets Ernest Hemingway". Translated by Randolph Hogan. New York: *New York Times*, 1999. http://vesselka.freeservers.com/Gabriel.htm#Hemingway.

———. *One Hundred Years of Solitude*. Translated by Gregory Rabassa. New York: HarperCollins, 1998.

Gates, Henry Louis, Jr. *The Signifying Monkey: A Theory of Afro-American Literary Criticism*. New York: Oxford University Press, 1988.

Genette, Gérard. *Narrative Discourse: An Essay in Method*. Translated by Jane E. Lewin. Ithaca, NY: Cornell University Press, 1980.

Gikandi, Simon. *Writing in Limbo: Modernism and Caribbean Literature*. Ithaca, NY: Cornell University Press, 1980.

Gilkes, Michael. *The West Indian Novel*. Boston: Twayne, 1981.

Glissant, Édouard. "Beyond Babel". *World Literature Today* 63, no. 4 (1989): 561–63.

———. *Caribbean Discourse: Selected Essays*. Translated by J. Michael Dash. Charlottesville: University Press of Virginia, 1989.

———. *Faulkner, Mississippi*. Translated by Barbara Lewis and Thomas C. Spear. New York: Farrar, Straus, 1999.

Godzich, Wlad. Foreword to *Heterologies: Discourse on the Other*, by Michel de Certeau. Translated by Brian Massumi, vii–xxii. Minneapolis: University of Minnesota Press, 1986.

Gover, Robert. *Voodoo Contra*. York Beach, ME: Samuel Weiser, 1985.

Harris, Wilson. "History, Fable and Myth in the Caribbean and Guianas". *Caribbean Quarterly* 16 (1970): 1–32.

———. *Tradition and the West Indian Novel*. London: London West Indian Students' Union, 1964.

———. "The Unresolved Constitution". *Caribbean Quarterly* 14, nos. 1 and 2 (1968): 43–47.

———. *The Womb of Space: The Cross-Cultural Imagination.* Westport, CT: Greenwood Press, 1983.

Hawley, John C. "Robert Antoni's 'Divina Trace' and the Womb of Place". *Ariel: A Review of International English Literature* 24, no. 1 (1993): 91–104.

Hemingway, Ernest. *The Sun Also Rises.* New York: Scribner's, 1970.

Herskovits, Melville J., and Frances H. Herskovits. *Trinidad Village.* New York: Knopf, 1947.

Hoffman, Eva. "The New Nomads". In *Letters of Transit: Reflections on Exile, Identity, Language, and Loss,* edited by André Aciman. New York: New Press, 1999.

Hussein, Aamer. "The Voices of Myth". *Times Literary Supplement,* 22 November 1991, 21.

James, C.L.R. "La Divina Pastora". In *Stories from the Caribbean,* edited by Andrew Salkey, 150–51. London: Elek Books, 1965.

Jarrett, Gene. Review of *The Other America,* by Michael Dash. *Callaloo* 22, no. 4 (Fall 1999): 1094–97.

Jones, Julie, and Heidi King. "Gold of the Americas". *Metropolitan Museum of Art Bulletin* 59, no. 4 (Spring 2002): 46.

Jordan, Jack. "I, We and Historical Memory in Patrick Chamoiseau's *Texaco*". *SORAC Journal of African Studies* 2 (November 2002): 55–62.

Karpowicz, Dean. "A Postmodern Collective: Deconstruction, Identity and Faith in Robert Antoni's *Divina Trace*". *Caribbean Quarterly* 46, no. 1 (March 2000): 37–45.

Kempadoo, Oonya. *Buxton Spice.* New York: Penguin/Plume, 2000.

———. Interview with Lisa Gee. http://www.orangeprize.co.uk/projects/futures/kempadoo1.html (accessed 26 October 2004).

———. *Tide Running.* New York: Farrar, Straus, 2003.

Kerrigan, Dylan, and Nicholas Laughlin. "The Dramatist". *Caribbean Beat* 65 (January/February 2004). http://www.meppublishers.com/online/caribbean-beat/archive//index.php?pid=6001&id=cb65-1-62 (accessed 7 November 2005).

Knapp, Jeffrey. *An Empire Nowhere: England, America, and Literature from* Utopia *to* The Tempest. Berkeley and Los Angeles: University of California Press, 1992.

Knight, Franklin W. *The Caribbean: The Genesis of a Fragmented Nationalism.* 2nd ed. New York: Oxford University Press, 1990.

Koningsbruggen, Peter van. *Trinidad Carnival: A Quest for National Identity.* London: Macmillan Education Caribbean Publishing, 1997.

Krickeberg, Walter, et al. *Pre-Columbian American Religions.* Translated by Stanley Davis. London: Weidenfeld and Nicolson, 1968.

Kristeva, Julia. *The Kristeva Reader.* Edited by Toril Moi. New York: Columbia University Press, 1986.

Kurlansky, Mark. *A Continent of Islands: Searching for the Caribbean Destiny*. Reading, MA: Addison-Wesley, 1993.

Lacan, Jacques. *Ecrits: A Selection*. Translated by Alan Sheridan. London: Tavistock, 1977.

Lemaire, Anika. *Jacques Lacan*. Translated by David Macey. London: Routledge, 1977.

LePage, R.B. "Dialect in West Indian Literature". *Journal of Commonwealth Literature* 7 (July 1969): 1–7.

Lévinas, Emmanuel. *Otherwise Than Being: Or Beyond Essence*. Translated by Alphonso Lingis. The Hague: Martinus Nijhoff, 1981.

Lionnet, Françoise. *Postcolonial Representations: Women, Literature, Identity*. Ithaca, NY: Cornell University Press, 1995.

Littlewood, Roland. *Pathology and Identity: The Work of Mother Earth in Trinidad*. Cambridge: Cambridge University Press, 1993.

Livingston, James T. *Caribbean Rhythms: The Emerging English Literature of the West Indies*. New York: Pocket Books, 1974.

López, Alfred J. *Posts and Pasts: A Theory of Postcolonialism*. Albany, NY: SUNY Press, 2001.

Lovelace, Earl. *The Dragon Can't Dance*. Harlow, UK: Longman, 1988.

———. *The Wine of Astonishment*. Oxford: Heinemann, 1989.

Lutgendorf, Philip. Introduction to "A Piece of Pommerac", by Odillo (Robert) Antoni. *Paris Review* 111 (1989): 168–69.

Mason, Peter. *Bacchanal! The Carnival Culture of Trinidad*. Philadephia: Temple University Press, 1998.

McHale, Brian. *Postmodernist Fiction*. London: Routledge, 1996.

McWatt, Mark. "The Preoccupation with the Past in West Indian Literature". *Caribbean Quarterly* 28, nos. 1 and 2 (1982): 12–19.

Minta, Stephen. *Gabriel García Márquez: Writer of Colombia*. London: Jonathan Cape, 1987.

Mintz, Sidney W., and Sally Price, eds. *Caribbean Contours*. Baltimore: Johns Hopkins University Press, 1986.

Naipaul, V.S. *A House for Mr. Biswas*. New York: Penguin, 1992.

———. *The Loss of El Dorado*. New York: Vintage, 1984.

———. *Miguel Street*. New York: Vintage, 1984.

Narayan, R.K. *Gods, Demons and Others*. New York: Viking, 1967.

———. *The Ramayana: A Shortened Modern Prose Version of the Indian Epic*. London: Penguin, 1972.

Naylor, Paul. *Poetic Investigations: Singing the Holes in History*. Evanston, IL: Northwestern University Press, 1999.

Neimark, Philip John. *The Way of the Orisa*. New York: HarperCollins, 1993.

The New Catholic Encyclopedia. New York: McGraw-Hill, 1967.

Patteson, Richard F. *Caribbean Passages: A Critical Perspective on New Fiction from the West Indies*. Boulder: Lynne Rienner/Three Continents, 1998.

Phillips, Caryl. *A State of Independence*. London: Faber and Faber, 1986.

Popper, Karl. *The Open Society and Its Enemies*. Princeton, NJ: Princeton University Press, 1966.

Proust, Marcel. *Swann's Way*. Translated by C.K. Scott Moncrieff and Terence Kilmartin. New York: Vintage, 1989.

Ramchand, Kenneth. *The West Indian Novel and Its Background*. London: Heinemann, 1983.

Saft, Elizabeth, ed. *Trinidad and Tobago*. Singapore: APA Productions, 1987.

Said, Edward. *Beginnings: Intention and Method*. Baltimore: Johns Hopkins University Press, 1978.

——. *Culture and Imperialism*. New York: Knopf, 1993.

———. *The World, the Text and the Critic*. Cambridge, MA: Harvard University Press, 1983.

Sander, Reinhard W. *The Trinidad Awakening: West Indian Literature of the Nineteen-Thirties*. New York: Greenwood Press, 1988.

Scott, Lawrence. *Aelred's Sin*. London: Allison and Busby, 1998.

———. *Ballad for the New World*. London: Heinemann, 1994.

———. *Night Calypso*. London: Allison and Busby, 2004.

———. *Witchbroom*. London: Heinemann, 1992.

Senior, Olive. Interview with Charles H. Rowell. *Callaloo* 11, no. 3 (1988): 480–89.

Simpson, George Eaton. *Black Religions in the New World*. New York: Columbia University Press, 1978.

Slemon, Stephen. "Post-colonial Allegory and the Transformation of History". *Journal of Commonwealth Literature* 23, no. 1 (1988): 157–68.

Smith, Barbara Herrnstein. "Narrative Versions, Narrative Theories". *Critical Inquiry* 7, no. 1 (1980): 213–36.

Smith, Eric D. "Johnny Domingo's Epic Nightmare of History". *Ariel: A Review of International English Literature* 31, no. 4 (October 2000): 103–15.

———. "Pandering Caribbean Spice: The Strategic Exoticism of Robert Antoni's *My Grandmother's Erotic Folktales*". *Journal of Commonwealth Literature* 39, no. 3 (2004): 5–24.

Taylor, Patrick. *The Narrative of Liberation: Perspectives on Afro-Caribbean Literature, Popular Culture and Politics*. Ithaca, NY: Cornell University Press, 1989.

Todorov, Tzvetan. *The Conquest of America: The Question of the Other*. Translated by Richard Howard. New York: Harper and Row, 1984.

Vargas Llosa, Mario. *The Language of Passion: Selected Commentary*. Translated by Natasha Wimmer. New York: Farrar, Straus, 2003.

Walcott, Derek. *Collected Poems, 1948–1984*. New York: Farrar, Straus, 1986.

———. *Dream on Monkey Mountain and Other Plays*. New York: Farrar, Straus, 1992.

Walker, Benjamin. *The Hindu World: An Encyclopedic Survey of Hinduism*. Vol. 2. New York: Praeger, 1968.

Williams, Eric. *From Columbus to Castro: The History of the Caribbean, 1492–1969*. New York: Harper and Row, 1970.

Wolf, Manfred. "The Two Cultures in West Indian Literature". *World Literature Today* 65, no. 1 (Winter 1991): 25–29.

INDEX

www.ingramcontent.com/pod-product-compliance
Lightning Source LLC
Chambersburg PA
CBHW020655030726
47498CB00002B/517